428 AD

428 AD

An Ordinary Year at the End of the Roman Empire

GIUSTO TRAINA

Translated by Allan Cameron

PRINCETON UNIVERSITY PRESS

PRINCETON AND OXFORD

English translation copyright © 2009 by Princeton University Press
Italian edition copyright © 2007 by Gius. Laterza & Figli
This translation of *428 dopo Cristo. Storia di un anno* is published by arrangement
with Gius. Laterza & Figli SpA, Roma-Bari.
Requests for permission to reproduce material from this work should be sent to
Permissions, Princeton University Press

Published by Princeton University Press, 41 William Street,
Princeton, New Jersey 08540
In the United Kingdom: Princeton University Press, 6 Oxford Street,
Woodstock, Oxfordshire OX20 1TW

Fourth printing, and first paperback printing, 2011
Paperback ISBN: 978-0-691-15025-3

The Library of Congress has cataloged the cloth edition of this book as follows

Traina, Giusto, 1959-
[428 dopo Cristo. English]
428 AD : an ordinary year at the end of the Roman Empire /
Giusto Traina ; translated by Allan Cameron.
p.   cm.
Includes bibliographical references and index.
ISBN 978-0-691-13669-1 (hardcover : alk. paper)   1. Rome—History—Empire,
284-476.   2. Europe—History—To 476.   3. History, Ancient.
I. Cameron, Allan.   II. Title.   III. Title: 428 A.D.
DG338.T7313 2009
937'.09—dc22   2008053724

British Library Cataloging-in-Publication Data is available

This book has been composed in Adobe Caslon
Printed on acid-free paper. ∞
press.princeton.edu

Printed in the United States of America

5   7   9   10   8   6   4

There is no true history without chronology.

MOSES KHORENATS'I
History of the Armenians, 2, 82

· CONTENTS ·

· PREFACE ·

IT IS A MARK of the best history writing that it makes us rethink what we
thought we knew. Giusto Traina's book is no exception. His idea was
both simple and brilliant—to approach the period we now call "Late
Antiquity" by taking just one year and presenting its events and its regional contexts in a panoramic perspective round the Mediterranean
world and its appendages, from Iran in the east to Britain in the west.
The year is 428 AD. We might have expected a more traditional date,
such as 476 AD, the traditional date for the "end of the Roman Empire,"
when the last Roman emperor in the West was deposed, or perhaps
410 AD, when Rome was sacked by Alaric and the Visigoths, an event
which prompted the heartfelt questionings that are reflected in St. Augustine's great work *The City of God.* Traina's choice of 428, the year that
marks the end of the Kingdom of Armenia, occurred naturally enough
to a historian who is the author of many studies of Armenia in the
Roman and early Christian period, but, as he tells us in his Introduction,
it was only as he sought to understand the context of that event that he
had the felicitous idea of making the year 428 the focus of an essay which
surveys the state of the entire Roman Empire and its near neighbors.

It was an intriguing and highly successful choice. In the first place
the choice of a single year subverts the otherwise often sterile debate
about the "fall of the Roman Empire" (which, after all, was a historical
process rather than an event, and not one that can be reduced to a single set of occurrences). Secondly, by taking a geographical and panoramic view, starting with the Kingdom of Armenia on the eastern
edges of the Roman Empire, and ending with Iran, a point even further
east, after a circular tour which has reached Britain, the farthest extent
of the empire in the west, he encourages us to rethink our ideas about
overall historical causation. How does what happens in North Africa in
428 relate to the situation in Gaul, or does it? How do the regions relate
to the center, and what are the cultural interactions between imperial

territories and neighboring areas? But with his emphasis on a single year Traina also encourages us to focus again on chronology. One of the characteristics of the rather recent discipline of "Late Antiquity" or "late antique studies" is its broad chronological sweep, from the third century to the seventh, or even continuing as late as 800 AD.[1] Some have felt that this sweep has been achieved at the expense of the dia-chronic perspective which is the essence of historical writing; Traina's choice of bringing a single year into sharp focus reminds us in a salu-tary manner not only of the unexpected juxtapositions of history, but also of the crucial role of events, expected or not. It is all the more salu-tary that 428 is not the obvious choice of date, except perhaps for histo-rians of Armenia like Traina himself. This is a device which in a single stroke cuts through and turns upside down the huge mass of current writing about periodization which often seems in danger of engulfing the very subject it is designed to elucidate.[2] Historical change proceeds at different speeds in different regions, but events matter and so do spe-cific contexts. The emphasis of Traina's book is on simultaneity rather than on a chronological sweep, but he gives us a perspective on a whole world, not a discussion of the Roman Empire of late antiquity.

The effect is exhilarating. We tend to think of history in terms of narrative—the chronological story of events. Yet when the canvas is so large as to encompass the entire Mediterranean world and beyond, it is as hard when contemplating the past as it is in the modern world to grasp the differing situations in places and regions so vastly far apart. Rather than telling a story, Traina provides some vivid and imaginative sketches of particular places, especially Ravenna, since 402 AD the "young capital" of the Roman court in the West and destined to be the seat of the Ostrogothic kings. In the early fifth century the bishop who presided over this marshy city was Peter Chrysologus ("golden orator"), and the mosaics in its churches paraded a harmonious orthodoxy person-ified by the figure of the emperor. Rome, the eternal city, had recovered from the sack of 410 AD, but traces of paganism, and certainly nostalgia for the past, remained among the grand senatorial elite. Traina's chapter on North Africa has the striking title "Waiting for the Vandals." In 428 St. Augustine was writing to his correspondents, in letters that were rediscovered only in 1975, about the evils of slave trading and compil-ing a book detailing the long list of heresies that constituted threats to orthodoxy. He put them in chronological order, ending in Traina's "ordinary year" of 428, and it is one of the most poignant and human of details that the aged Augustine died just as the Arian, i.e., heretical, Vandals imposed their rule on Roman Africa. Another chapter is entitled "Easter in Jerusalem." It enables Traina to evoke a further powerful bishop, as well as to describe the monasteries of the Judaean desert and the vineyards of the Negev. High Roman aristocrats were among those who went on pilgrimage and settled in Palestine, and the Empress Eudocia bestowed her patronage on it. At about the same time there also ceased to be a Jewish patriarch or *nāsī*, not in itself a mark of Christian superiority but a pointer nevertheless to the heightened Christian consciousness of Jews in Palestine in the next centuries.

And yet this panoramic "tour" does indeed tell a story. Traina's "choice" of 428 AD turns out to be significant in different ways all over the empire. In Britain, the Roman military presence had been largely withdrawn less than twenty years earlier and the province was attempting to adjust to a local leadership faced with incursions by Picts, Scots, Angles, and Saxons. In 428 one chronicle claims that Vortigern called in Saxon mercenaries to his aid, while Bishop Germanus of Auxerre was preparing a mission to the island. In Constantinople, the home of the eastern court, a new bishop had been elected; this was Nestorius, a monk from Antioch in Syria. In the next few years, the run-up to the Council held at Ephesus in Asia Minor in 431, at which Nestorius was condemned, involved dramatic clashes of personalities. The Christians of Sassanian Persia had recently gained the support of the shah and claimed ecclesiastical independence from Constantinople, and the deposed Nestorius was destined to give his name, wrongly, to a body of belief with a centuries-long future. "Nestorian" remains can still be seen in parts of Asia and in China to this day. And 428 was the year that marked the end of the ecclesiastical history written in Greek by another bishop, Theodoret of Cyrrhus in northern Syria, himself a controversial churchman, and also the author of a detailed account of the colorful ascetics of contemporary Syria, the most famous of whom was Symeon, the "Stylite," who had taken up residence on top of a pillar. On the eastern fringes of the empire at this time one can also see local bishops engaging in attempts to convert and civilize the "Saracens," the Arab tribes visible in Syria in the historical records long before the arrival of Arab armies in the seventh century. Looking back with hindsight, it is clear that Traina's seemingly artless claim that 428 was just an ordinary year conceals a much more complex reality. Change was happening all around, not in the same way and not at the same pace, but change for all that. It is a salutary lesson in how history happens.

Of course we must not actually write history from hindsight. The Epilogue swiftly wraps up some of what would happen next in some of the areas and to some of the people Traina has so vividly described. It is rather like the end of a novel where one is told the fates of the main characters after the narrative itself has ended. But for all his deliberately subversive approach, Traina ends with an unequivocal statement of historical confidence: in 428 the Roman Empire still mattered. It was not "a mere concept" but the central reference point for all the voices heard in his text. This is an important, and perhaps surprising, result, and all the more so in that it emerges from such a disarming, unusual, and graceful way of approaching old problems.

AVERIL CAMERON

· ACKNOWLEDGMENTS ·

I wish to thank the publisher Laterza for coming up with this annalistic format and encouraging me to follow an unusual approach to the study of ancient history.

Jean-Michel Carrié, Andrea Giardina, and Michel-Yves Perrin have read the manuscript, and their invaluable suggestions have helped to improve the structure of the work and to correct numerous inaccuracies and imperfections.

Various other suggestions concerning research and reading came from friends, colleagues, and students, of whom I would particularly like to thank Garnik Asatrian, Alessandro Barbero, Béatrice Caseau, Carlo Cereti, Riccardo Contini, Bernard Coulie, Lietta De Salvo, Alessio De Siena, Carlo Franco, the late Augusto Fraschetti, Nina Garsoian, Dagmar Gottschall, Anne-Marie Helvétius, Sylvain Janniard, David Konstan, Fabrizio Lelli, Gianfranco Lepore, Patrick Le Roux, Michael Maas, Federico Marazzi, Valerio Marotta, Fergus Millar, Claudia Moatti, the late Yves Modéran, Paolo Ognibene, Antonio Panaino, Arietta Papaconstantinou, Bernardo Santalucia, Alain Segonds, Jean-Pierre Vallat, Kostja Zuckerman, and Harriet T. Zurndorfer.

My thanks to Allan Cameron for helping me to make improvements in this English edition through our correspondence and conversations.

Gérard Marino, the translator of the forthcoming French edition (Les Belles Lettres: Paris), was of great help, detecting several misprints in the bibliography.

Michael Alram, of the Numismatic Commission of the Austrian Academy of Science, assisted me in finding some illustrations. My student Federico Montinaro produced the maps (with the exception of the one for Constantinople, for which I am indebted to Adriana Anzelmo).

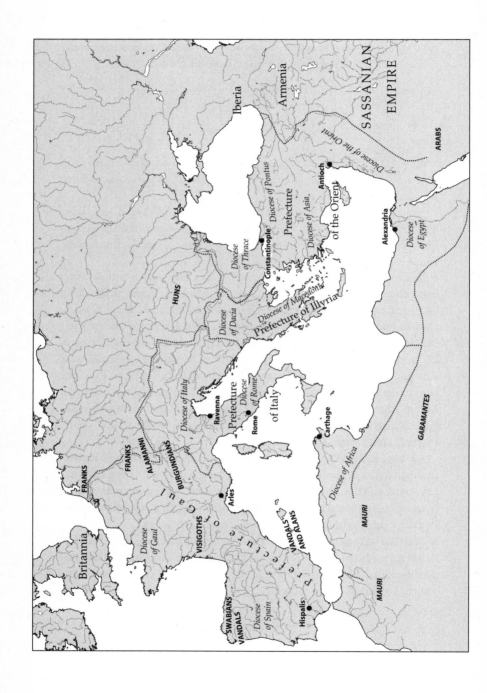

· INTRODUCTION ·

THIS BOOK will examine the events and microevents of a single year on a scale that will be as global as is possible. The chosen year is 428 AD.[1] This historiographical approach is not unheard of, but is unusual for ancient history. There have been individual or collective works devoted to epoch-making dates such as 1000 AD or 1492, or of national importance such as 1688 for England or 1947 for France.[2] However, there is a substantial difference between such works and this one, at least in terms of the great sweep of history: the year 428 is undoubtedly less significant. One could with good reason ask, why choose such an apparently unexceptional year, when we could have chosen a much more evocative one, like 410 when Alaric and his Visigoths sacked Rome, or the fateful 476, when Odoacer deposed Romulus Augustus and brought about the end of the Western Roman Empire?[3]

The year 428 AD was in fact chosen on the basis of fairly "marginal" factors, in which serendipity played its role. We started by researching the year's most politically significant event: the end of the Kingdom of Armenia.[4] The initial intent was to determine the reasons for and the effects of the deposition of Artashes IV, the last Armenian king, and above all to understand why this event is only discussed in the local tradition, in spite of its international significance. As the research progressed, I became aware of a concatenation of events involving persons and realities that were considered to be separate in traditional studies, but which actually constituted elements of a complex and delicately balanced geopolitical reality.

I then decided to investigate the situation in the Western Roman Empire, and this revealed something quite surprising: even when the empire had entered a period of terminal decline, its structures continued to guarantee a degree of cohesion between East and West, and to interact with the Church's almost parallel campaign against pagans, Jews, and heretics. Distant events, such as Flavius Aetius's campaign against the Franks, or Gaiseric's accession to the Vandal throne, can be better explained if you also take into account the situation in the East.

Besides, it was around 428 that the question of imperial unity was once again on the agenda in both its parts. The "empire without end" was now just a distant memory, and some important political and religious decisions had to be taken. Of course, the separation of the East and the West was not up for discussion. Theodosius II, emperor of the East, could be considered the first "Byzantine" emperor.[5] However, the Roman Empire was still presented as a unitary structure in the language of propaganda and official documents,[6] and most importantly, there was a momentary halt to the process by which the two parts of the empire had been drifting apart—a process that had been exacerbated by political disagreement during the thirty-year period between 395 and 425.[7] In the second quarter of the fifth century, a return to the degree of unity that existed long before was not simply a utopian idea fed by propaganda and wishful thinking on the part of legislators.

The empire was no longer simply restricting itself to the struggle for survival, but was also developing new forms of power. As Santo Mazzarino observed over sixty years ago, it was following the death of Theodosius I that "the foundations were laid for a new world, which some four centuries later would prove to be highly efficient in its new organization and in meeting new cultural and economic needs."[8] Although the documentation is limited, it is clear that a transition was taking place, and that it was closely connected to the process of Christianization, which radically altered the prerogatives of power.[9] The unity of the Mediterranean world was indeed more precarious than during the high pomp of the imperial age, but it had not entirely faded away. Nevertheless the changes were considerable and often traumatic. In many areas, there was a fall in population accompanied by centrifugal forces of various kinds, such as the emergence of local differences, which became typical of the culture of Late Antiquity. In spite of everything, then, the machinery of empire continued to work, and the perception of a "broken history," however appealing, cannot be applied to the many features and facets of a complex reality.[10]

As is well known, historians are not in agreement on the manner in which the transformation took place: some have taken the revisionism so far that they question the very fall of Rome, while at the opposite extreme, others have theorized a radical break between the period of the Roman Empire and the history of the modern west. In reality, both positions constitute two sides of the same coin: both those who believe in continuity and those who believe in discontinuity use the sources in an impressionistic manner with the intent of demonstrating their own theories.[11]

There is little purpose in adopting dogmatic and formulaic templates to define a complex period of transition, whose ambiguity has been nicely summarized by Evelyne Patlagean: "The Empire of the fifth century was still a stable unit in its cultural diversity, [and] still formed an intricate totality.... This complex fifth century was perhaps the real turning point between the ancient past and the medieval future."[12] Anthea Harris's recent historical overview shows that, at least in the period from the fifth century to the seventh, cultural ties between the East and the West were not suspended.[13] In Chris Wickham's masterly work on the early Middle Ages, he gives appropriate weight to the political disintegration of the empire during the social and economic transformation of Europe and the Mediterranean, but at the same time he demonstrates that the process of transformation was slow and less dramatic than we like to imagine.[14] In 428, the empire was already aware of this risk and was attempting to react with appropriate strategies.

Besides, time was not equal for all people during Late Antiquity, nor did it have the same importance for everyone. The circumstances surrounding events were indeed crucial for rulers and generals, but for the majority of citizens (particularly slaves and those living on the margins of society), time was primarily interpreted as a repetition of events. In spite of the enormous political changes that were occurring, the life of a typical community was governed by liturgical and civil calendars and, of course, the ubiquitous seasonal rhythms of the rural economy. For many intellectuals of the time, the calculation of time almost seemed an inappropriate concern, whose elimination was prompted by the anxieties of the times or the "pain of living" as portrayed by Bianchi Bandinelli.[15] Thus the man who was buried in Apamea of Syria in a Christian sepulcher dated to the early fifth century must have requested the ancient pagan motto that appears on its threshold and no doubt expresses his fatalism: "Are you rushing?—I am. And where are you rushing?—To this place."[16] At a higher level of intellectual debate, everything revolved around the present, a view shared by Saint Augustine, who died in 430. Out of force of habit, people continued to talk about the past and the future, but in reality "the future no longer exists, nor does the past" (*Confessions*, 11, 26). History became something secondary to time experienced by memory.[17]

However, these slow rhythms governed by nature and human activities, which have been emphasized in recent studies, represented only one of the many aspects of late-Roman society.[18] This debunking of Late Antiquity has a weakness: it has neglected and almost expunged the history of events.[19] This book's principal ambition is to investigate historical events in order to recover their most "dynamic" features, which can then be linked to various geographical scenarios and placed within a social and cultural context.

Ours will be a journey through the late-Roman world, a snapshot of a particular moment in history and, above all, of an important year in that world's political evolution. We shall follow the circular routes that were so dear to the compilers of "gazetteers" of Late Antiquity, such as the anonymous *Expositio totius mundi et gentium*, written in the mid-fourth century, or that "frontier book" written two centuries later by Procopius, *De aedificiis*.[20] It may seem a desperate undertaking to apply this model to such a shadowy area as the fifth century, but in fact the written documentation has proved to be extensive, occasionally surprisingly so, even without a key historian who provided a clear overview of the period, as in the case of Ammianus's work on the fourth century or Procopius's on the sixth.

Starting with the politically most important event—the fall of the Kingdom of Armenia—we will cross the Mediterranean and Europe, and then return to the East as far as the first section of the Silk Road and the borders with other worlds. During our travels we will encounter cities and deserts, palaces and monasteries, pagan schools and Christian sanctuaries. Above all, we will live with the *dramatis personae* of this long year: the emperors Theodosius II and Valentinian III, and King Bahrām V; Roman generals like Flavius Dionysius, Flavius Aetius, and Bonifacius, barbarian leaders like Gaiseric and Chlodio, and warlords such as the Saracen al-Mundhir; clerics such as Nestorius, Simeon Stylites, Paulinus of Nola and of course Augustine; powerful women such as Aelia Galla Placidia and Pulcheria; pagan intellectuals such as Macrobius and Plutarch of Athens; and energetic bishops such as the Syrian Rabbula and the Copt Shenute. This was a disparate group of personalities, whose lives and destinies differed, but who are gathered together here in a choral narrative. The backstory is the decline of the Roman Empire, or if you prefer, the dawn of the Middle Ages.

428 AD

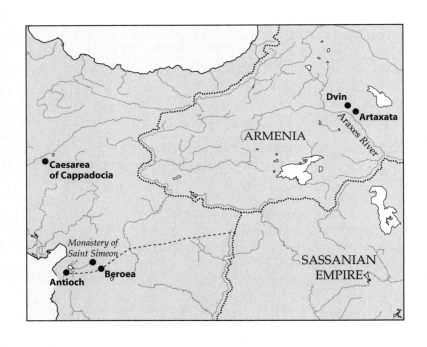

· I ·

The Travels of Flavius Dionysius
and the End of Armenia

To START our journey, we go back to Antioch, the capital of Syria and the headquarters of the Roman army in the East. An imperial diplomatic delegation, escorted by an elite military unit, left the eastern gate of the city and moved towards the Persian Empire. At the same time, a group of Iranic plenipotentiaries left from Ctesiphon, the main residence of the Sassanian rulers. The two diplomatic missions were to meet at the border in a part of Mesopotamia. The Romans were led by Flavius Dionysius, a military man and native of Thrace, who at the time held the rank of supreme commander of the army for the entire sector of the eastern border (*magister utriusque militiae per Orientem*).[1]

Before leaving, Dionysius had started to suffer from facial paralysis. There was a great deal at stake for the general: any delay to his departure would have effectively been an insubordination, given that it could have compromised the mission. In order to get well quickly, he turned to one of the most revered clerics in Syria, a monk called Simeon but also known as the "Stylite" because of his particular form of asceticism: he lived day and night at the top of a high column (*stȳlos* in Greek).[2] The pious official had therefore gone to Telanissos (Tell Neshin, today Qala'at Sema'ān), which was Simeon's village. From the height of his column, the saint prayed for the general's health, and the general was immediately cured (*Syriac Life of Saint Simeon Stylites*, 71).[3] Dionysius could then set off on his march without fearing the wrath of Theodosius II, the ruler of the eastern part of the Empire.

In the fifth century, there was no diplomatic corps in the modern sense, nor indeed was there any codified protocol. Given this lack of fixed rules, we cannot be sure of the composition of the Roman delegation.[4] Diplomatic missions were organized on an ad hoc basis in accordance with instructions from above. They were usually made up of various imperial dignitaries, interpreters, a military escort (which transported not only the baggage but also the emperor's gifts),[5] often emissaries from the Church, and a few merchants who took advantage of the expedition to reach a destination which was normally forbidden.[6] The outcome of the mission was entirely in the hands of its leader, who could be a high-ranking soldier, a nonmilitary official, or a churchman. The emperor chose his ambassadors on the basis of specific requirements: apart from the requisite diplomatic skills, they had to have demonstrated their honesty and incorruptibility, and they had to possess the necessary physical constitution to undertake such a journey, which was itself no mean task. An embassy to the Sassanians required even greater professional experience, because of the enormous importance attributed to pacts and agreement within the Persian religious system.[7]

The *Syriac Life of Simeon Stylites* is the only source for Dionysius's mission, but does not specifically mention its date or purpose. However, other texts tell us that the general was on active duty in the East from 428 to 431. There is further evidence that allows us to date the mission to the year 428: according to Callinicus (*Life of Saint Hypatius*, 32, 1), Dionysius was instructed to escort Nestorius from Antioch to Constantinople when the latter was appointed the capital's bishop. Now, it is well known that Nestorius's investiture on the episcopal throne of Constantinople took place on 10 April 428, and that he arrived in the city three months after the death of his predecessor, Sisinnius, which happened on 24 December 427 (Socrates, *Ecclesiastic History*, 7, 28). The road from Antioch to Constantinople crossed Anatolia and the journey would have taken at least a month. If the situation on the frontier was not peaceful, the supreme commander of the eastern sector would not have been able to leave his theater of operations for such a long period. Dionysius must therefore have concluded his agreement with the Persians immediately before his journey to Constantinople, during the winter of 427/8, and winter is the best time to travel across Mesopotamia.

Negotiations entrusted to such a very high official could only have been of the greatest importance. In fact, this was to be the first meeting between Romans and Persians since the war of 421/2.[8] The key item for discussion can be inferred from the historical context: we know from two historians writing in Armenian, Moses of Khoren and Lazarus of Pharpi, that in 428 the Persians deposed Artashes IV, the unworthy and dissolute descendant of the prestigious dynasty of the Arsacids and the last king of Armenia.[9]

The Armenian sources provide a detailed narration of the event. He ascended to the throne in 422, as the result of a compromise between Theodosius II and the Great King Bahrām V, and he lacked the charisma he needed to govern and to gain the respect of others. He quickly incurred the hostility of the local potentates (*nakharark'*), who organized what can only be called a Fronde with the support of the Persian Empire. A crisis became inevitable. After years of trying, the Persians finally succeeded in overturning the balance that kept the king of Armenia in a position above the other noble families.[10] As a result, the *katholikós* Sahak, the noble and authoritative leader of the Armenian Church, was unable to impose his will.[11] Moses of Khoren tells the story:

> But Artashir [a Persian variant of Artashes, used here to show contempt], the king of Armenia, began to plunge without restraint into licentious pleasures to the extent that all the princes became disgusted with him. Coming to Sahak the Great they raised a complaint and invited him to help them in denouncing him to the Persian king, in deposing their own king, and in bringing a Persian as lord of this country. But he said: "I do not consider you to be liars; I too have heard of this shameful disgrace. Often have I reprimanded him, but he denied it. So we must endure for a while the man's faults until we are able to arrange a solution with the Greek emperor Theodosius, and not hand him over to the lawless to be derided and mocked." (Moses Khorenats'i, *History of the Armenians*, 3, 63; R.W. Thomson's English translation, which was published in 1978 by Harvard University Press, has been used here and will be used throughout—*translator's note*)

The patriarch Sahak challenged the *nakharark'* with a powerful argument: although a dissolute fornicator, Artashes was still a Christian king. Moreover, it was to be hoped that Theodosius II, an extremely devout Christian, would again concern himself with Armenian affairs once he had sorted out his own domestic problems. But the nobles, who were united and implacable, contacted the Great King directly and castigated both their king and the *katholikós* for their favoring the "Greeks," by which they meant the Roman Empire.

Now that Armenia was controlled by the Sassanids, any association with the rival power would have been considered high treason. A few Armenian clergymen, it is true, had recently been able to cross the border on a few occasions to carry out important diplomatic missions. In such cases, the most educated members of the clergy were sent, and they were typified by the anonymous one who, everywhere he stopped on his journey, captivated the bishops who gave him hospitality with his knowledge of Greek, his noble birth, and his good manners (Firmus of Caesarea, *Epistle* 22). But the recent war had increased tensions between the two rival empires, which further limited contacts between Armenia and Constantinople. Besides, even before the treaty of 422, Roman presence on Armenian territory was barely tolerated, and every citizen of the empire was seen as a potential spy. Consequently, restrictions were imposed on travel through the kingdom, first through a regulation laid down in the previous treaty, and then reaffirmed in a law during the time of Honorius that prohibited merchants from traveling past the former capital of Artaxata. The transgressors were condemned to perpetual exile and the payment of a large fine (*Code of Justinian*, 4, 53, 4, year 408 or 409).[12]

At Ctesiphon, court officials attempted to persuade Sahak to abandon the cause of the king, who was now in disgrace, but the patriarch rejected these Persian overtures. At this stage, the Great King decided to start trial proceedings, in which the principal prosecutor would be the Armenian priest Surmak, who had been promised the post of *katholikós* by the nobles. Artashes was deposed and imprisoned, and the property of the Arsacid dynasty was confiscated. Armenia lost its ancient independence and became a frontier province of the Persian Empire, administered by a frontier governor (*marzban*). The appointed dignitary left for Armenia in the company of the treacherous *nakharark'*, whom Bahrām V handsomely rewarded.

At least as far as appearances were concerned, the fall of the kingdom did not bring about domestic change or international repercussions.

According to another Armenian historian, Elysaeus (*Ełishē*), Armenia without its king became not a Persian possession, but rather a kind of satrapy administered by the nobles (*The History of Saint Vardan and the Armenian War* I, p. 6, 5–7). By eliminating their king, the Armenian lords increased their power over their own territories, and by paying tributes and providing troops to the invader they were guaranteed autonomy and religious freedom. This system, which has sometimes been incorrectly defined as "feudal," would survive the fall of the Sassanian Empire by many centuries, as various powers took turns to control the Armenian lands.[13] Although the country's internal balance of power had shifted, the end of the Arsacid dynasty is not supposed to have changed the traditional social order. This was at least what the *nakharark* had hoped would happen, but as Moses of Khoren acutely observed, they had committed nothing less than political suicide (*History of the Armenians*, 3, 64). The Fronde of contemptible and shortsighted *nakharark* had been manipulated by the shrewd and masterly policy of the Sassanian emperor, Bahrām V, who was very keen to eliminate the independence of Armenia (Lazarus of Pharpi, *History of the Armenians*, 1, 14).

If Artashes was the straw man he is portrayed as in the Armenian sources, why was the Great King so interested in eliminating him? The fact is that Bahrām's clever move had deep historical roots. The Armenian branch of the Arsacids had controlled the country more or less without interruption since 63 AD, and the Roman Empire had every interest in maintaining this balance of power.[14] In spite of forceful interference by the Persians, the presence of an Arsacid on the Armenian throne guaranteed the maintenance of tradition, and above all confirmed the authority of the Christian religion, which had been introduced more than a century earlier and guaranteed Armenian autonomy in relation to the Sassanids' imperialist aims.[15] By removing the Armenian dynasty, the Persians hoped to draw the country back to the Zoroastrian faith and protect it forever from the pernicious influences of the West.

The fate of the kingdom could not be decided unilaterally. It was therefore necessary to enter into further negotiations to update the treaty of 422 and annul the clauses about Armenia's independence and the sovereignty of Artashes. This clearly was the real reason for Flavius Dionysius's mission: it was to save face by officially abandoning Armenia without allowing this to appear a passive acceptance of a fait accompli.

In spite of its complex geopolitical implications, the fall of Armenia was recorded exclusively by local sources, which presented the affair as a domestic one without significant international ramifications. No other text, whether Greek or oriental, appears to have shown interest in this event: Greek and Syriac historians, chroniclers and ecclesiastical writers appear to have suppressed it.[16] Evidently Roman imperial propaganda made every effort to gloss over such a dishonorable outcome. The absence of "Western" sources is probably not due to any gaps in the tradition, but rather reflects the embarrassed silence of official historiography on the fate of Armenia, a Christian land that was now at the mercy of intolerant and hostile persecutors. This explains why an important diplomatic mission led by Flavius Dionysius was only worthy of a brief mention in the *Syriac Life of Saint Simeon*. Any reference to the fall of Armenia would have pointed to the complicity of the Roman Empire, and it was best to pass over the whole argument.

Besides, Theodosius II had little choice. The political and military context did not allow for other solutions. The centuries-long Armenian question, which had so often led to conflict between Rome and Persia, appeared to end with a serious blow to the prestige of the Roman Empire, in spite of its military superiority over the Persians. The imperial delegation would attempt some damage limitation by obtaining the appropriate guarantees for the Christian community.[17] Flavius Dionysius must have been fully aware of the disastrous nature of this turn of events, and it is not impossible that his facial paralysis, which was to be healed by the spiritual solace of Saint Simeon, was the psychosomatic effect of his frustrated military pride.[18]

· II ·

The World of Nestorius

BISHOPS, MONKS, AND SARACENS

HAVING concluded his sensitive diplomatic mission, Flavius Dionysius returned to Antioch, but he did not stay there long. The general soon had to set off on his travels to carry out another important mission: to escort the Syrian cleric Nestorius from the monastery close to Antioch's city gates, where he was the prior, to the capital Constantinople where he had just been elected bishop. The election of Nestorius was part of Theodosius II's carefully worked-out plan: the emperor chose a prelate unconnected with the scheming that went on in Constantinople, because he wanted to bring a halt to the endless bickering that went on there and appeared to take up most of the clergy's time.

This was not the first time that a brilliant churchman from Syria had been elected bishop of the capital. For Christians, Antioch was an ancient city of considerable prestige, and it enjoyed special privileges not shared by the rest of the community. Its bishop had a degree of authority over the other eastern prelates, and he administered a wealth of assets. The emperor was counting on Nestorius's talents as a brilliant and charismatic preacher to bring the community of believers and the increasingly influential monks under control.

Moreover, the new bishop appeared to satisfy the political requirements of the time. It is true that the supremacy of Christianity was no longer in question—the Roman Empire was now also a Christian empire—but the "Catholic" Church was unable to control believers who lived outside its borders. Following the abandonment of Armenia and the subsequent weakening of the local Church, Constantinople risked losing contact with the Christians living in the Persian Empire, who belonged to a Church which had been founded in 410 under the auspices of the Great King and, following the Council of Ctesiphon in 424, had become fully independent (or "autocephalous," to use the correct term).[1] The Church of Persia used Syriac for its liturgy and official documents (this language was the variant of Aramaic spoken in Edessa, and Aramaic was the traditional lingua franca of the Persian Empire).[2] This threatened the supremacy of Greek as the ecumenical language of the Christian East, which was harmful to Constantinople's political aims.

To strengthen relations between the Christian communities, the empire needed to use Syrian clerics as intermediaries, as most of them were bilingual.[3] Hence the choice of Nestorius, who, according to some sources, had distant Persian origins.[4] With an oriental on the bishop's throne in Constantinople, the rivalry between Antioch and the capital was much reduced, and this favored the authority of the imperial court. The citizens of Antioch, who were often in a state of unrest, would willingly submit to the authority of one of their own. At the same time, Nestorius maintained control over the Syrian city: he exploited the death of Bishop Theodotus, which occurred in the same year, to have one of his own placemen elected, the like-minded John.

By playing the Nestorian card, Theodosius made a specific political and doctrinal decision. Antioch was an important center of Christian theological thought, where Greek rhetoric and the spiritual experiences of the East coexisted and occasionally clashed. Although Antioch did not have an actual theological "school" like Alexandria (where the "archbishop" supervised the organization of studies and, in a sense, "handed down the doctrinal line"), the city's monasteries were particularly lively, with a propensity for polemics, not without a touch of local pride.

Officially, the bishop of Constantinople did not have the same privileges as the bishops of Alexandria and Antioch. However, they were in practice all on the same level, and the eastern capital could even compete with Rome. The election of Nestorius in 428 therefore constituted an important moment for the Syriac tradition, and this continued to be true even after 431, when Nestorius was deposed and repudiated by the Council of Ephesus. It was not chance that Theodoret, the Bishop of

Cyrrhus (about a hundred kilometers to the north of Antioch), ended his ecclesiastical history in 428.[5] Theodoret, who lived until 466, could not have openly declared that this was the real reason for the chronological period he chose, but he had little difficulty in using this year as the end of an era, given that it marked the death of the patriarch Theodotus and, more especially, the eighty-year-old Theodore of Mopsuestia, an eminent theologian and exegete, who had a powerful influence on Nestorius.[6]

It is, in fact, very difficult to recognize the Antioch of Nestorius in the one so closely tied to the traditions of the Greek *polis*, that is evoked in the works of Libanius, the great pagan rhetorician who died around 393 (the year of Theodoret's birth).[7] But Libanius's world was only one of this great city's many faces. With more than two hundred thousand inhabitants, the city, which had once been the capital of the mighty Seleucid Empire, was made up of a composite and multilingual population in which Hellenic and also Aramaic pagan traditions coexisted with fervent Christianity that often bordered on heresy. On the other hand, both pagans and Christians agreed in depicting the city as a breeding ground for vices and temptations, the "inevitable defects" of the great cities of all times.[8] In his evocative writings, Peter Brown has defined Antioch as "a world of its own."[9] Both center and periphery, this metropolis clearly reflected the tensions in the area—the military frictions that troubled the eastern sector, and the development of the caravan trade to Central Asia and the Far East.[10]

The election of Nestorius marked a reversal in the imperial policy on Syria. Constantinople had been gradually asserting itself to the detriment of Antioch's prestige, and no emperor had set foot in the Syrian metropolis for fifty years. Now, however, the political and military situation meant that the city was once more at the center of imperial concerns. Besides, Antioch had always been the most important city in the Roman East and seat of the highest-ranking officials. With the progressive decline in the city's political autonomy, the new protagonists on its political scene were the governor of Syria and the powerful *comes Orientis*, who had more than six hundred officials in his employ (*Code of Theodosius*, 1, 13, 1). Around 428, the essential heart of the city was no longer the *agorá* (principal space for markets and assemblies), but rather the fearful complex of the *praetorium*, with its sinister prisons.[11]

Antioch's recovery was accompanied by spectacular demographic growth throughout the region. Archeological surveys of cities, villages, and monasteries reveal an exponential growth of human activity in the Syria of Late Antiquity.[12] The spread of Christianity and the increasing presence of monasticism helped to consolidate and strengthen this sector of the Roman frontier, which safeguarded the rich cities of the Mediterranean coastal band. Above all, the imperial policy aimed to strengthen the districts and villages in mountainous areas through a careful and exhaustive civil and religious reorganization, because this prevented these small settlements from becoming incorporated into the large estates of the wealthy, and thus ensured a civic dimension to these semirural sites. Of course, they did not correspond to the traditional concept of cities and towns of the time, but they did play a part in consolidating the empire's defenses.[13]

There are many literary texts in both Greek and Syriac that throw light in various ways on this composite and intriguing world. Because of the new religious and spiritual climate, there was a greater awareness of humbler landscapes and social contexts, which the classical tradition had obscured or neglected altogether. The real world not only of villages, but also of desert nomads and foreigners, now came out of the shadows to which it had been relegated by the rigid norms of literature up to that time.[14] This phenomenon was part of a wider process that was changing classical values and led to a veritable "democratization of culture" in Late Antiquity.[15]

Of course, the ideology of the classical Hellenic *polis* had roots in the culture that ran too deep for the countryside to prevail over the city. For instance, the writings of Theodoret, who was elected bishop of Cyrrhus in 423, reveal that he was working hard to adapt classical terminology, which was traditionally somewhat vague, to the disparate reality of the frontier landscapes.[16] The rhythm of Christian life continued to follow an urban logic, while the empire embarked on a fairly utopian plan to bring the city even to those territories that displayed the least urban vocation. To achieve this, the empire often used its bishops as the "vanguard" in a process of Romanization that the army would have been unable to implement on its own. In a letter written around 428, the young and dynamic Theodoret, who was committed to maintaining the urban decorum of his see of Cyrrhus, criticized the

noble Maranas for remaining at his country estate and not participat-
ing in the city's religious festivals and its life in general (Theodoret,
Epistle 34).[17]

The thing that outside observers found most striking about Syriac
Christianity was the more radical and bizarre features of its monasticism. Syrian ascetics indulged in every kind of excess, much to the disapproval of Egyptian monks who behaved very differently (see John
Cassian, *The Conferences*, 21, 11).[18] These "athletes of Christ" subjected
themselves to extreme privations, such as shutting themselves up in
dark cells or covering themselves with heavy chains. Such practices
were used to imitate the martyrs during the persecutions or, more simply, the wretches who ran up against the imperial justice.[19] The *xeniteía*,
"estrangement," of the Syrian monks allowed them to develop a de-
tached and disinterested viewpoint on the world.

The most famous figure in this movement was Saint Simeon Stylites,
the revered monk who healed Flavius Dionysius. In 428, the ascetic,
who was not yet forty years old, had lived for ten years at the top of a
tall column, close to the village of Telanissos. While experiencing the
hardships caused by the sun and the discomfort of having to stand constantly, Simeon prayed or preached to the crowd from the moment the
sun came up. This extreme lifestyle earned authority and respect, in
spite of the fears of the Church authorities and the protests of Egyptian monks, who were shocked at such an eccentric form of asceticism.[20]
Simeon's success was mainly due to the unconventionality and dramatic
effect of his austerity. Many would follow the saint's example and, during the decades that followed, a stylite movement would evolve and become famous throughout the Christian world.[21]

Because of Simeon, Telanissos became an important destination for
pilgrims, who rushed to see Simeon and his column not only from all
the provinces of the empire, but also from its neighboring kingdoms
and barbarian lands: "All the subjects of the Roman Empire know him,
but he is no less famous among the Persians, the Indians and the Ethiopians, and his fame has even reached the Scythian nomads [by which
he meant the Goths and the Huns]" (Theodoret, *Ecclesiastical History*,
26, 1).[22] The height of the column (nine meters at the time of Flavius
Dionysius's visit) instilled the faithful with a sense of the imposing and
the spectacular.

As the worship of saints spread to every locality, Christianized Syria thus established its own sacred sites, which were of course less prestigious than the nearby Holy Places of Palestine, but nevertheless of fundamental importance in consolidating the new identity of these frontier areas. A typical example was the tomb of Saint Sergius, the quintessential Syriac martyr, who was particularly venerated in Resafa. By the end of the fifth century, a considerable township would build up around the site and would take the name of Sergioupolis, the see of a bishopric. But during our period, the saint's tomb was the object of particular solicitude and rivalries between prelates. Thus Alexander, the bishop of nearby Hierapolis, got himself into debt by building a church in honor of Saint Sergius, but this first shrine was "stolen" from him by his rival John, the patriarch who was a friend of Nestorius (*Collectio Casiniensis*, in *Acts of the Councils*, I, ɪᴠ, p. 185, 32).[23]

Urha (now Şanlıurfa) was another city of crucial importance to the region and a bulwark of Syriac culture. It was called the "blessed city" and was known to the Greeks by its Macedonian name of Edessa. It rose to prominence after 363, when Julian's ill-fated expedition forced the empire to give up the important city of Nisibis and transfer the provincial government to Edessa (Moses Khorenatsʻi, *History of the Armenians*, 2, 10).[24] Paganism and Christianity became intertwined in this cosmopolitan city, causing considerable concern among the Church authorities.[25] Heresies were particularly widespread in border country: Urha/Edessa was home to a great number of Arians and Manichaeans, and in its territory there were increasing numbers of followers of the doctrine of Marcion, a second-century theologian who did not accept that the Old Testament was a sacred text. Some "Marcionite" communities had survived in the peripheral Syriac-speaking areas and even in Armenia, as was recorded in Eznik Kołbatsʻi's *Refutation of the Sects*.[26]

The theologians of Antioch protested strongly against this development, which they perceived as a dangerous threat to orthodoxy and therefore to the stability of the Church and to the empire itself. One of the leading figures who reacted with hostility was Rabbula, the bishop of Urha/Edessa until 412, whom contemporaries described as a model of spiritual authority, but the reality was that the traditional models of Syriac spirituality were entirely foreign to him.[27] Unlike most of the other Syrian bishops, who were products of a closed monastic environment, Rabbula had been a rich landowner and had received an aristocratic education. His surviving writings are testament to a substantial literary output relating to his pastoral activities: homilies, epistles, and hymns. Following his conversion to Christianity, he renounced his worldly goods but not his old habits: the bishop was well known for his violent bouts of anger against arrogant or recalcitrant clerics, whom he beat unashamedly just as he had once done with the slaves on his properties.[28]

Rabbula undertook the repression of paganism with ruthless thoroughness: one of the hospices he had built, in this case for women, was funded by plundering four pagan temples. Moreover, he zealously set about improving the morals of his diocese by severely repressing the local clergy's propensity for a dissolute life. According to Rabbula's regulations, the clergy of Edessa were required to fast, dress simply, abstain from contact with women, and avoid washing unless instructed to by a doctor. Monks had to minimize contact with civil society as far as was possible, and to stay away from all places where the public used to meet. They even had to avoid legal proceedings.

This harsh discipline was not just the product of a violent and fanatical temperament. Rabbula wanted to create a suitably humble and saintly image for his own clerics, something that would be essential if he were to succeed in repressing heresies and convincing the people to follow him into orthodoxy. Ultimately, Rabbula was a typical product of his time. Although he chose an austere way of life, he never forgot that he belonged to the ruling class of the empire. According to Theodosius II's plans, Christian values were indissolubly linked to the empire's need for unity; the principal aim of this twin policy was a merciless campaign against adversaries of every kind, no matter whether they were military or religious.[29]

The example of Rabbula demonstrates that the ostentation of a monastic style of austerity had now established itself as one of the most effective ways of communicating with the outside world and was practiced by all members of the clergy, including Nestorius (see Theodoret, *Compendium of Heretical Accounts*, in *Patrologia Graeca*, 83, col. 433). Radical and nonconformist ascetics had succeeded in imposing their model of Christianity, and this meant that they were now accepted by the Church authorities, but success came at the cost of having to be controlled by those authorities.[30]

This policy was being implemented in tandem with another: the Christianization of the frontier areas, which engaged all the zeal and commitment of the clergy and was favorably received by the minor aristocracy. Records dating from 426 detail the inauguration of a *martyrium* of Saint Thomas in the small diocese of Anasartha (Khanāsīr). A Greek inscription shows that the shrine was dedicated to *Maouia* (Māwiya), a woman of Arab descent.[31] The inscription on another *martyrium*, of more or less the same date as that of Māwiya, reveals some interesting aspects of this borderland society:

> To the martyrs who tunefully sing the sacred hymns,
> Silvanus, senator who always governs the *Eremboí*,
> dedicated this well-built temple with outer wall
> and wide porticoes, and full of supplicants.
> His dead young daughter inspired its construction,
> Chasidathē, famous for all her virtues,
> young wife, joined by the lords to a phylarch.
> She brought her father's pain to an end,
> and did not incite him to seek his reward in war,
> but in psalms and prayers . . .
> and the Sacred Scriptures . . .
> *(Inscriptions grecques et latines de Syrie*, II, 296)

Chasidathē, the young woman's name, is the Greek version of the Syriac *Khasīdtā*, meaning "full of grace." The epic language, which was appropriate for the hexameters of the *martyrium*'s epigraph, interpreted the reality of the desert frontier in a lofty language, starting with *Eremboí*, the Homeric name that the ancients attributed to the Arabs. The term *ánaktes*, "lords," had an equally epic flavor, and was used for Homeric heroes. Here it was used for the chiefs of the Bedouin tribes, whom the Romans called "Saracens" (from the Arab *shirkat*, "confederation").[32]

The young Chasidathē was given in marriage to the chief of a tribe by her father Silvanus, who, in spite of making a great play of his senatorial rank, was clearly another tribal chief, whose "eternal" power is emphasized in the epigraph. Silvanus's inscription demonstrates the role of Arab tribes in the Christianization of this sector of the frontier, and probably also indicates the impact of the Christian message on the warrior code: inspired by the religiosity of his dead daughter, Silvanus appears to be laying down his arms and rejecting the traditional stereotype of the Saracens, who were seen as eternal rebels and inveterate raiders.[33]

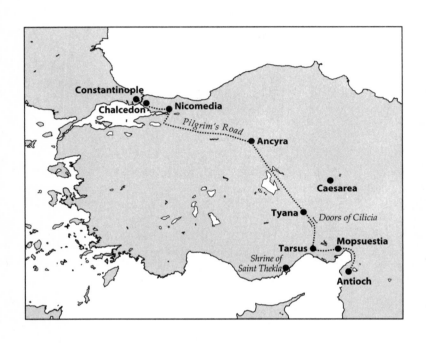

·III·

On the Pilgrim's Road

THE MILITARY UNIT required to escort Nestorius to Constantinople was organized in February and March. It was not prudent to travel by sea at this time of year, and Flavius Dionysius would have had no choice but to travel overland along a set route with post houses at regular intervals. This imperial service, which relied on carts and horses requisitioned from local communities, was only granted to senior officers and officials, but the privilege was often extended to the members of the clergy who were in the public eye.[1] The expedition would spend the night in a *mansio* (a halting place or "post house"), whose caretaker would provide fresh horses and would see to any repairs to the baggage wagons.[2]

Generally the "Pilgrim's Road" was used by travelers from Antioch to Constantinople, and this road connected the West to the Holy Places.[3] The route is described in an anonymous account by a pilgrim (possibly a woman) from Bordeaux, who completed the journey in 333. The *Itinerarium Burdigalense* specifies the stages and distances, and every now and then adds some brief comment on the more important localities. To get to Constantinople from Antioch, you had to travel through Cilicia, Cappadocia, Galatia, and Bithynia, with stops at many small settlements and the occasional large city (*Itin. Burd.*, pp. 570, 9–81, 6 Wesseling).[4] Nestorius undoubtedly took this route, partly because this meant that he would have met the bishops of Tyana, Ancyra, and Nicomedia, who were his allies: the hagiographer Callinicus records that "during that journey, he visited everyone everywhere" (*Life of Saint Hypatius*, 32). Thus the religious leader was able to consolidate his own network of friends and prepare for the imminent doctrinal clashes.

If you add up the figures provided in the *Itinerarium*, you arrive at a total of 792 Roman miles, almost 1,200 kilometers, which the pilgrim from Bordeaux had to cover while taking numerous breaks in the journey to make the experience more pleasant and comfortable. Flavius Dionysius, who had to meet his deadline, would have used a more expeditious system (*cursus velox*), which was implemented for more rapid movement, and used better horses and lighter carts pulled by mules. It was a veritable trial of endurance, but Nestorius was used to the trials of asceticism, and the final destination was well worth the hardship.[5]

On leaving Syria, the caravan entered Cilicia. According to his hagiographers, Nestorius stayed for two days in Mopsuestia, so that he could visit his old teacher Theodore. The two clergymen visited the nearby shrine of Saint Thekla on the hill to the south of Seleucia (now Ayatekla in Turkey), where the elderly bishop is supposed to have urged his disciple to moderate his zeal (Barhadbeshabba Arbaia, *Ecclesiastical History*, pp. 519ff.; *Legend of Nestorius*, pp. 5ff.).[6] The shrine was dedicated to a saint of the second century, who came from the region, but was also associated with the memory of the apostle Paul of Tarsus, the greatest glory of Christian Cilicia. It was one of the sites most visited by pilgrims, particularly at the time of the annual festivals of Saint Paul and Saint Thekla. Surrounded by an imposing wall to protect the saint's treasure from any raids, the complex constituted a veritable monastic citadel. A sacred wood and a spring, which provided water for the miraculous thermal baths, were close to the church that constituted the core of the shrine. The living quarters of the nuns were within the external wall, whereas the clergymen who led the religious services lived outside.[7]

The first important stop on the journey was Tarsus, the capital of Cilicia famous for its marble products and linen manufacture, and the glorious memory of Saint Paul (and also the theologian Diodore, who had been an inspiration to Nestorius and died at the end of the fourth century).[8] A few years later, the discovery was announced of the casket containing the apostle's sandals, and the manuscript of the *Apocalypse of Paul*, an apocryphal text in which the saint, escorted by the angels to the next world, tells of the treatment of the just and the sinners by a heavenly tribunal very similar to the judicial courts of the time.[9]

Antioch ignored Tarsus when it came to culture and religion. The rivalry between the dioceses was fueled by the "orthodox" bishop of Tarsus, the impulsive Marianus. The latter, some time after the claimed visit by Theodore and Nestorius to the shrine of Saint Thekla, fell out for unknown reasons with his neighbor and rival Dexianus, who had been the custodian of this sacred site before becoming the bishop of Seleucia. Marianus prohibited his followers from visiting the shrine for the saint's feast day, but shortly afterwards he died. Naturally the devotees of Saint Thekla loudly proclaimed a miracle (*Miracles of Saint Thekla*, 29).

The surrounding territory was not safe: the great movements of populations at the beginning of the fifth century had provoked the Isaurians, a local population who had been able to maintain a considerable degree of autonomy, even under the Romans.[10] The Isaurian warlords were favored by the nature of the territory, a rugged and infertile region immediately inland from Cilicia, and a region where an adult man had to choose between working as a herdsman or a brigand (or both, as these activities were not incompatible). In Isauria, the local pagan beliefs resisted the pressure of Christianization, but even the Christian brigands had no scruples about attacking holy sites such as the Shrine of Saint Thekla.[11] However, the saint kept a watchful and protective eye over her protégés. The imperial messenger Ambrosius prayed to Saint Thekla during a mission along those dangerous roads and, quite miraculously, the saint conjured up an entire squadron of horsemen and infantry, which made it possible for him to continue his journey to Constantinople in complete safety (*Miracles of Saint Thekla*, 16).[12]

Apart from the protection of saints, the empire could still rely on the means for keeping such situations under control. In this very period, a local governor called Achilles was particularly active in ensuring the safety of travelers in the area. Firmus, the bishop of Caesarea of Cappadocia, praised him in a letter written around 428:

You have organized the subjects according to your orders, and the terror has been removed from the lands of the borders (*eschatíai*). As people say, the road crosses the high and precipitous rocks; yet now we can travel through this region that you have pacified. Thus you have freed us from those waves of criminality by making the rocky road over the Taurus Mountains peaceful and practicable for travelers (Firmus of Caesarea, *Epistle* 1).

This does not necessarily mean that Achilles resorted to military repression. It is more likely that the empire entered into negotiations with the Isaurians, who at the time were being recruited into the higher ranks of the army, given their skills as warriors and their excellent knowledge of that difficult terrain. Very likely, Flavius Dionysius recruited Isaurian soldiers for his escort for Nestorius. Yet he certainly would not have imagined that a few years later, a particularly enterprising group of these high-ranking soldiers would take advantage of a military crisis and take over the leadership of the empire, placing one of their number, Zeno, on the imperial throne in 474.[13]

To reach Tyana, Nestorius's escort took the rocky road over the Taurus, traveled the mountain pass known as the "Doors of Cilicia," and then headed for Cappadocia, along the administrative border between the dioceses of Pontus and Asia, an area that had generally been unaffected by wars, but had not been appreciably Romanized. Unlike the Hellenized coast, these lands of the interior still reflected all the weight of tradition, and there was a marked diversity of cultures and languages, which the current changes tended to emphasize. The empire reacted by attempting to increase the urbanization of small towns, particularly those in the interior. This policy often turned out to be utopian, but in some cases it appears to have worked. The provincial organization of Late Antiquity helped to develop the towns of the interior and especially the provincial capitals, which also became important episcopal sees.

However, the development of minor towns damaged the prestige of the cities, and revived ancient rivalries or created new ones. Thus the division of the ancient province of Cappadocia ultimately damaged the prestige of Caesarea, which in the fourth century was still one of the most active centers of Christianity and even influenced the Church of Armenia. But the growth of Constantinople (and the competition of other rival cities), along with the closure of the Armenian border, diminished the grandeur of Caesarea, which was gradually demoted in the hierarchy of episcopal sees, in spite of the great efforts of its bishop, Firmus, who was a worthy successor to Saint Basil the Great.[14] This was all to the advantage of Tyana, the capital of *Cappadocia Secunda*, which was very probably the city in which Achilles was active.[15] In 428, the local bishop was Eutherius, one of the clerics closest to Nestorius, and one who continued to support him through difficult times.[16]

Halfway along the route, there was the city of Ancyra (Ankara), capital of Galatia and the see of Bishop Theodotus, who at the time was a friend of Nestorius but would betray him at Ephesus.[17] Like most of the Anatolian cities, Ancyra had been subject to a radical makeover to reflect its adoption of Christianity. It was during this period that the great temple of Augustus and Rome was transformed into a Christian building, which might possibly have been the monastery of the great ascetic Saint Nilus of Ancyra, who had been a student of Saint John Chrysostom.[18]

In this region, they still spoke Celtic, a legacy of the invaders who had settled there centuries earlier, giving it the name of Galatia (which in Greek means the "Country of the Gauls").[19] Livestock farming was the region's main resource. Large herds were also kept by the local monasteries, and this provoked the anger of Nilus who, in his last work written some time around 428, condemned this situation and preached a return to the ideal of monastic life based on abstinence and moderation (Nilus of Ancyra, *On Voluntary Poverty*, 30). According to Nilus, monks were required to avoid the dangerous allure of worldly goods and therefore had to renounce their property in order to devote themselves exclusively to prayer and hard manual labor.[20] A man like Nestorius was inevitably drawn to the elderly ascetic.[21]

The abbot of Ancyra's monastic ideals were fully shared by another Galatian monk, Palladius, the bishop of the small town of Aspuna in Phrygia. Palladius, who was the same age as Nilus, had returned to Anatolia after having lived for long periods in Palestine and Egypt, where he had known the greatest ascetics of the time. A few years before, this experience had induced him to write a collection of edifying monastic *exempla* which would become an enormous success among Greek-speaking Christians, the *Lausiac History* (so named in honor of the court official Lausus, to whom Palladius dedicated the work).

Apart from the struggles against temptations and emotional unease, the ascetics of Asia Minor were often engaged in a fierce battle against pagan demons: in Bithynia, the famous abbot Hypatius drove off a monstrous being in female form, which was terrorizing the countryside and was called Artemis by the locals. She was "as high as ten men," and devoted her time to entirely innocuous occupations, such as spinning and grazing her pigs. This divinity, which was benign for pagans, was thought by Christians to be on a par with an evil demon (*Life of Saint Hypatius*, 45).[22]

Similar stories are often found in hagiographies or other religious works, which provide a one-sided vision that deliberately exaggerates the process of Christianization. Christian texts or texts inspired by Christian beliefs constitute the majority of the sources and tend to conceal the stubborn survival of paganism, or rather, they only talk about it when exalting the intolerant campaigns waged by these "athletes of Christ" against the phantasms of the past. However, this obstinacy of the pagan cults reveals that they were not simply the intellectual affectation of an urban culture based on pagan Greek influences (*hellēnismós*). Christians in Asia Minor came up against ancient traditions and the enormous prestige of time-honored local or Iranic divinities, which had been Hellenized to some degree and assimilated to Apollo or Artemis, or of local heroes such as the mythical Sarpedon, Thekla's great "adversary," who was even venerated by Christian families (*Miracles of Saint Thekla*, 11).[23] Of course, this paganism was largely clandestine: only passive resistance was possible in the face of imperial diktats and the zealotry of clerics and monks.

By this time, the great pagan sites had lost their former shine and greatness.[24] In Ephesus, pagans had to meet in secret in the great temple of Artemis to celebrate the ancient cult of this goddess (Isidore of Pelusius, *Epistle* 1, 55). Meanwhile, the industrious Christians set about systematically destroying the pagan images of "false gods" or *daímones*. One of these zealots, called Demeas, commemorated her act with an inscription in verse on a stone base that probably held up a cross:

Having destroyed the misguided image of Artemis the false goddess,
Demeas wished to dedicate this symbol of Truth,
Thus to honor God, who is the enemy of all idols,
And the Cross, which is Christ's immortal and triumphant symbol.[25]

Such events occurred with the blessings of bishops and the consent of the civil authorities. A little later, in 435, an edict was issued that condoned the destruction of pagan temples and images, and most significantly, it was signed by the two Roman emperors of the East and West (*Code of Theodosius*, 16, 10, 25).

Even certain kinds of Christianity were considered dangerous to public order. One Christian sect that was very powerful in western Anatolia was called Novatianism and had had organized what could only be called an alternative Church (it was founded in the third century, and was also well established in Rome and Spain).[26] During his journey, Nestorius was able to verify personally the spread of heresies in Anatolia, and the great number of bishops belonging to alternative Churches. Shortly afterwards, he would unleash his crusade against heretics, particularly in the western part of Asia Minor and the provinces of Caria, Asia, and Lydia. Anthony, Bishop of Germe and a follower of Nestorius's, indulged in what can only be called pogroms against heretics and pagans, whose resistance was drowned in blood (Socrates, *Ecclesiastical History*, 7, 31).[27]

But Christianization was not only progressing through violence and repression. Although Christian sources extol the victory of faith over ignorance and barbarism, in several cases bishops preferred to operate peacefully and adapted the cult of saints and reliquaries to local beliefs, producing some notable examples of cultural hybrids. The salvation of the empire also involved the integration of indigenous elements, and not only in the remotest areas of the Anatolian interior. Even in a rather Hellenized Mediterranean province like Caria in the diocese of Asia, the indigenous element remained considerable. An inscription from Mylasa, which has been dated to 427–29, reproduces an imperial order on maritime customs duty, but also mentions a governor with the exotic name of Flavius Baralach (Grégoire, *Inscr. gr. chrétiennes d'Asie mineure*, 242).[28] Some have thought it a Semitic name, but it is improbable that our governor was called *bar 'Alaha* ("son of God"), and it is more likely to have been a local name, possibly a Carian one.[29]

The last great city on Nestorius's journey was Nicomedia, an important port on the Sea of Marmara (on the Gulf of Izmit that opens into the Sea of Marmara), a former imperial residence and a "friendly" episcopal see.[30] He was now close to the capital. When he came to Chalcedon, just before crossing from Asia to Europe, he preferred not to visit the important monastery of *Rouphinianai*, whose abbot, the revered Hypatius, had shown himself to be extremely hostile:

> Just as he was approaching the city, Saint Hypatius had a vision: some lay people were putting Nestorius on the throne in the holy church of this metropolis. Suddenly he heard a voice that said, "This weed shall be uprooted in three and a half years." ... Nestorius came to know—I do not know how or from whom—of Hypatius's vision, so when he passed the monastery, he did not go to visit the holy man during that journey in which he visited everyone everywhere. On reaching the metropolis and becoming bishop, he hurriedly sent some clergymen to Hypatius, saying, "Go and see the visionary! For all your dreams, I shall rule over the city for twenty years." (Callinicus, *Live of Hypatius*, 32)[31]

Perhaps Nestorius was not expecting such hostility from another monk. The clerics of Constantinople, who once again had been sidelined in favor of a foreigner from Syria, had good reason to hate him, but at least the monks, who practiced a similar lifestyle to his own, should have supported the new bishop. Although in charge of a communitarian institution with significant assets, Hypatius preached the abandonment of all worldly things, and subjected himself to a particularly strict form of asceticism; moreover, contacts between Syrian and Anatolian monks were nothing new. The opposition of an influential figure like Hypatius was a bad sign. This severe and purist monk, a native of Phrygia, was very popular because of his miraculous healing powers and, as we have seen, his battles against demons and false gods.

In reality, Hypatius was not alone in holding these views. Nestorius's arrival was opposed by the main exponents of monastic orthodoxy, such as the influential Dalmatius, known as the "archimandrite and father of the monasteries," who evidently perceived the arrival of a Syrian as something that would upset the delicate balance between the empire and the Christian community. Whatever the case, Flavius Dionysius had reason for being pleased with his work: Theodosius rewarded him with the nomination to be consul the following year. As for Nestorius, his moment of glory was to be short-lived. His enthronement as bishop of Constantinople would turn out to be the beginning of a long and painful fall from grace.

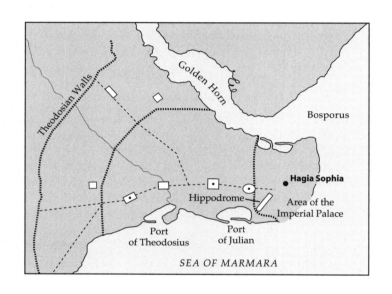

·IV·

The New Rome and Its Prince

ON 10 April 428, the Tuesday after Palm Sunday, Nestorius was officially appointed bishop of Constantinople in one of those complex ceremonies that mixed Roman tradition with Christian symbolism, for which the Byzantine Empire became famous.[1] Theoretically, he was just a bishop like any other: at the time, those in charge of the capital's diocese did not yet hold the title of "patriarch" or "archbishop." Yet everyone knew that this episcopal throne had the same importance as Saint Peter's in the West.[2] Founded by Constantine as the city that had to symbolize his radical overhaul of the empire, Constantinople was gradually transforming itself into the principal Christian city of what had become the Eastern Empire (*pars Orientis*), in which the emperor influenced the political and doctrinal developments of the Church.[3]

Places of worship and charitable foundations were being set up everywhere with the support and funding of the court. In the propaganda of the time, Constantinople was exalted as the "new Rome" with a "most saintly throne," the "most royal metropolis of the Christian world (inhabited world)," or, more simply, the "ruling city."[4] Of course, there was also a "civic" Constantinople, with ambitious public buildings that were to some extent inspired by Rome of the imperial period. But, unlike Rome, the city of Constantine did not have a Capitol or any similar places that kept alive the memory of the pagan tradition. The monuments in the new plan for the city essentially alluded to the continuity between the great conquerors of the past and the dynasty of Theodosius, while being careful not to evoke any pagan traditions.[5] During this period at least, the city might have appeared to be an uncontaminated organism, which made it easier to identify as the "Christian" capital of the Empire.

Constantinople, which now had between three and four hundred thousand inhabitants, was growing exponentially. Around 428, building work reached its peak. Back in 421, work had finished on the first of the great water-storage tanks open to the air, the one built by Aetius close to the Adrianople Gate (*Chronicle of Marcellinus*, Year 421). The following year, after ten years of work, new city walls were complete: veterans of campaigns in the East were used to man the towers, probably because an attack by the Huns was considered likely (*Code of Theodosius*, 7, 8, 14).[6] In 427, after eighty years of work, the finishing touches were made to the Constantinian Baths, later called the Theodosian Baths (*Chronicle of Marcellinus*, Year 427; *Easter Chronicle*, pp. 580ff.).[7] During the same period, a former imperial official drew up the *Notitia urbis Constantinopolitanae*, a list of the principal buildings of the capital. The *Notitia* lists four *fora* or public squares, six *horrea* (warehouses for storing goods), and four *macella* (food markets), as well as nineteen public ovens for making bread. The information contained in the *Notitia* also makes it possible to calculate the existence of at least 2,600 shops and workshops in the 52 *stoai*, porticoed streets that were used for traders and artisans.[8]

The old suburb of the fourth century was gradually incorporated into a metropolis that increasingly concentrated the economy and trade of this sector of the Mediterranean. At that time, a new port was made ready, and numerous warehouses were built along the banks of the Golden Horn. And like Rome, Constantinople had accumulated a stockpile of foodstuffs that could have fed the city for a year, and which involved enormous quantities of wheat, oil, wine, and salted pork, with the associated problems of their preservation and distribution, not to mention the risk of needless waste.[9] One factor of great importance to the capital was that its inhabitants had an abundant supply of water, which came from Thrace along a massive aqueduct built by Valens in 373 and improved upon by Theodosius I.

On 10 April 428, they were not only honoring the new bishop, but also Emperor Theodosius II, who on that date turned twenty-seven.[10] The grandson of Theodosius the Great was the most powerful man in the world, in spite of the clear setback he had suffered at the hands of his Persian rivals, who had forced him to yield on the Armenian question.

The much greater difficulties of the Empire of the West had consolidated the prestige of the Empire of the East and its religious authorities. This had also increased the political weight of the capital founded by Constantine. A skillful use of propaganda had enhanced the emperor's charisma, and raised him higher than his immediate predecessors. Besides, Theodosius II was the first porphyrogenite emperor, namely one "born in the purple."[11] To be born in the purple, a symbol of royalty, indicated a divine decision to perpetuate the dynasty founded by Theodosius the Great, and represented an important stage in the sacralization of the emperorship, which reached extreme refinements in the Byzantine Empire.[12]

For much of the year, the Porphyrogenite was confined to the imperial palace, a powerful military stronghold overlooking the Sea of Marmara. The complex was defended by a garrison of about three thousand soldiers, whose officers answered directly to their emperor. During this period, the regiments, called *scholae*, had an important role in the general organization of the army, and were made up of elite soldiers, mainly from the east. All these factors contributed towards a powerful exaltation of imperial autocracy, played out through rituals and ceremonies, and consolidated by imperial privileges. A hall was used for the meetings of the imperial council (*consistorium*) and the senate of Constantinople, in which legislative proposals were discussed, often in joint session.

However, the real heart of the palace was the *sacrum cubiculum*, the complex of residential rooms used by the imperial family, which were looked after by the *cubicularii*, eunuchs of oriental origin, which the court received as gifts from foreign nobles or purchased in the slave markets beyond the frontier (the Christian empire prohibited castration of its citizens). These eunuchs controlled and regulated access to the palace for outsiders, a duty that made them powerful, influential and, of course, rich: anyone who wanted an introduction to the court had to bribe the *cubicularii*. In spite of their servile origins, the ones who became the more important officials could rise to the rank of senator, while the head of the *cubiculum* held one of the highest posts in the empire. Some laws, which were passed between January and July of 428, assigned important privileges to the *cubicularii*, a sign of the increasing importance of these palace officials (*Code of Theodosius*, 6, 2, 26 and 27, 22; 13, 3, 19; *Code of Justinian*, 12, 5, 2).[13]

A section of the *cubiculum*, managed by a particular official and looked after by a multitude of female servants, the *cubiculariae*, was used by the influential empresses: Empress Eudocia and Pulcheria, the sister of Theodosius and his spiritual guide. In a period in which doctrinal controversies did not appear to compromise Christian unity (Nestorius would be the one to reopen hostilities), the two empresses represented the two souls of the community: Pulcheria, who had secured the support of monks, contrasted with the more tolerant Eudocia, who was the descendant of a family of pagan intellectuals and had, it appears, become a protector of heretics.[14]

The most important woman at the court, however, was Pulcheria, who had a fundamental role in court politics throughout her brother's reign.[15] Eudocia, who converted only at the time of her marriage to Theodosius, could not compete with her sister-in-law's prestige, which had been considerably enhanced by her decision never to marry. Indeed, young women like Pulcheria who took a vote of celibacy acquired an aura of holiness within Christian society. As Peter Brown has observed, "The girl who found herself among the 'brides of Christ' was spoken of by the clergy as a human *ex voto*."[16] "Consecrated" women of the Christian aristocracy who had been brought up reading sacred books and kept away from the coarse physicality of the world became the depositaries of an exclusively Christian culture. This "cultural virginity" must have set up an example for men of the Christian community, who were necessarily more exposed to the temptations of pagan culture. Pulcheria had been destined for such a role, but with the much greater responsibility of providing an example to a brother who ruled over a Christian empire, while also supervising his religious policies.

In any event, both the empresses, who at this time were not yet in dispute with each other, exercised a powerful influence over Theodosius II's religious decisions (and therefore, to some extent, also his political ones). For this reason, historians have long cultivated a distorted image of his personality, by presenting him as a gentle and weak emperor. Edward Gibbon famously depicted him as a man

> condemned to pass his perpetual infancy encompassed only by a servile train of women and eunuchs. . . . Separated from the world by an impenetrable veil, Theodosius trusted the persons he loved;

he loved those who were accustomed to amuse and flatter his indolence; and as he never read the papers that were prepared for the royal signature, the acts of injustice most repugnant to his character were frequently perpetrated in his name.[17]

This judgment needs to be moderated. Of course, Theodosius the Younger did not have the same military qualities that his grandfather Theodosius the Great had had (he was never seen on a battlefield throughout the half century of his reign), and the meddling by the ladies of the court was not solely an invention of malicious tongues. However, the decision to shut himself up in the palace was not an expedient dictated by his timid character. Quite the opposite, it was part of a specific plan developed by court officials and Theodosius himself, which was to leave its mark on Constantinople's political future. Gilbert Dagron has observed very acutely:

> This is the underlying contradiction that goes back to the beginning of Byzantine history—its "Oedipus," if you like: in Constantinople the maintenance of the Roman spirit and tradition went hand in hand with the abandonment of the Roman frontier, and ultimately the very system of provinces. In the East, you could not save Rome and the empire at the same time.[18]

The image that Theodosius II evoked around 428 was that of a profoundly religious sovereign who bordered on becoming an ascetic.[19] This was the result of court propaganda, which had created the myth of a perfect emperor whose royal charisma had existed since his birth. The Porphyrogenite represented a pure state of royalty, which had been conferred upon him by his untarnished childhood. According to Socrates, the Church historian who praised his religious policies, he is supposed to have turned his court into a monastery and Constantinople into a great religious center, by removing all temptations from courtly circles and doing so with the gentleness and purity that typified him (Socrates, *Ecclesiastical History*, 7, 22).[20] Another Church historian, Sozomen, praises his abilities to coordinate the different spheres of imperial power. His predecessors, however virtuous, were sovereigns characterized by a particular inclination: some were oriented towards politico-administrative order (*kósmos*), while others were more productive in culture (*lógos*), and still others were expert in the military arts (*pólemos*). Theodosius II, however, was the ideal emperor who was capable of excelling virtuously in everything (Sozomen, Preface to *Ecclesiastical History*).

Theodosius appears above all to have been a severe and charismatic autocrat. The education he received in the palace had modeled his character and strengthened his religious charisma. It was said that by his prayers he was capable of bringing an end to war and famine (Socrates, *Ecclesiastical History*, 7, 22). He knew how to act at the most opportune moment and to govern not just the court and the clergy, but also the army and Constantinople's urban population.[21] From the time of his baptism and the imposing public ceremony that accompanied it, the emperor had practically been adopted by the city and the army. Any attempt to break that link by a revolt or an uprising would have amounted to an act of sacrilege.[22]

Theodosius relaunched the great Roman tradition of empire as spectacle, but did so with a Christian interpretation. An excellent judge when it came to the increasingly rigid court ceremonial, the emperor managed his own image with masterly and well-timed public appearances.[23] This complex interweaving of ritual and propaganda came under a political authority that could now be rightly called "Byzantine," and was powerfully affected by the question of religious orthodoxy. The symbolic meeting place for the emperor and his people was the hippodrome, which was connected to the imperial complex by a secret passage.[24] There they ran the traditional races for four chariots, just as in Rome and the other main cities of the empire. The contestants who displayed the traditional colors—green, blue, white, and red—were supported by their respective factions. As is well known, the factions of the Hippodrome were much more than mere fan groupings, and carried out various social and religious functions in the city. The emperor was not impartial, but was required to support one of the teams. For example, Theodosius II supported the "Greens."[25]

The rituals organized by court officials and the clergy intensified Theodosius's charisma and he became comparable with his great rival, the emperor of Iran. He could rely upon a group of trusted officials, men who had gradually occupied key positions in the administration. This explains a few exceptionally rapid careers, such as that of his childhood friend Paulinus (who, it seems, assisted Pulcheria in the search for a wife for Theodosius).[26] We encounter Paulinus again in 430; he had just turned thirty and was the Master of Offices [*magister officiorum,* the most powerful civilian official after the Praetorian Prefect] (*Code of Theodosius,* 6, 27, 23). These meteoric careers were assisted by the lack of a long-established nobility, unlike Rome where the pagan component was much stronger. On the other hand, there were still pagan officials in the higher spheres of the court, who were tolerated because of their talent. They were also protected by Empress Eudocia, who clearly had not forgotten her own origins.

The authorities kept a watchful eye on the training of the new ruling group. In 425, the Auditorium was founded in Constantinople; this was a center for higher studies which, while only slightly straining the argument, could be considered the first "state university."[27] Between 427 and 428, the imperial government used it to dismiss all the public teachers who had not been integrated into its courses (*Code of Theodosius,* 13, 3, 18 and 19). From that time on, teaching in private houses was tolerated only on condition that this did not involve teachers from the Auditorium; anyone who continued that private activity would have been expelled. The regular instructors in grammar and the court doctors continued to enjoy various privileges.[28] As Alan Cameron has observed, "After 425, education in Constantinople was in effect the monopoly of a Christian government."[29]

The situation of an imperial official was an advantageous one, but it was not without professional risks. If the head of an office lost documents from the archive, it would take a miracle to avoid the death sentence, as on one occasion was supposed to have occurred thanks to the intervention of Saint Hypatius. An absentminded bureaucrat rediscovered his papers as a result of the saint's prayers, but he was prudent enough to abandon high society and join a Christian community where he devoted himself to "a saintly and pious life" and used all his savings to assist monks and the needy (Callinicus, *Life of Saint Hypatius,* 40, 27–36).

The tendency of imperial power to evolve in a "Byzantine" direction can also be detected in the administration of justice, which was now concentrated in the hands of the emperor and his officials. The new system was increasingly inquisitorial. The permanent courts of old ceased to exist, and justice was administered by officials who in practice were the emperor's own trusted men. During the fourth century, trials lost their previous public connotations, and started to be held in the *secretaria*, secluded rooms that were hidden by gates and curtains, and were open to the public only at specific stages in the trial. In such trials, the debate between the accuser and the accused was kept to a minimum, and the main role fell to the magistrate who directed the court. The defense was often a mere formality, and some trials of the time recall Kafka rather than Cicero.[30]

The empire was drifting towards increasing absolutism. The social implications of the developments are illustrated by a law passed on 21 April 428, which intended to curb the exploitation of prostitutes and made provisions for the expropriation of procurers and the loss of their powers over the young women. In the most serious cases, they could be punished with exile or forced labor in the mines (*Code of Theodosius*, 15, 8, 2). At first sight, the law would appear to be a simple measure to protect public morality against procurement in accordance with Christian values. In reality, the situation was more complex: the law was not so much directed against professional pimps as against citizens who, driven by poverty, sold their daughters' bodies.[31] The law of 428 was part of a wider project to control social order and aimed to repress all forms of "barbaric" promiscuity, often on the margins of society, with the intention of safeguarding the *kósmos*, the imperial order, against all its enemies.[32]

The new bishop Nestorius shared the imperial desire to maintain concord and unity. Above all, he feared the powerful tensions between the various factions of the Church, which threatened orthodoxy and fomented new and old heresies.[33] One of the most famous heretical doctrines was that of the priest Arius of Alexandria (*c.* 260–336), who reinterpreted the nature of Christ and did not attribute him with the substance of the Father. Arian Christology had already been condemned by Theodosius the Great, with a law that only concerned citizens of the empire, while the Gothic *foederati* (see chapter VII, note 2), who converted around 360, were free to profess Arianism. Many of these lived on the outskirts of the capital: up until 430 the presence of an Arian "anti-bishop" to all intents and purposes installed in Constantinople was tolerated. Besides, the differences between Arians and "Catholics" were essentially restricted to the liturgy.[34]

Great importance has been attributed to Nestorius's role in the repression of heretics, partly because of Theodosius II's image of a weak sovereign. In reality, it was a concerted action in which imperial conduct was already displaying the features of Byzantine caesaropapism.[35] In any event, the agreement between the emperor and the bishop was advantageous for both: Nestorius would have promised Theodosius a reward both in heaven and on earth if the emperor were to get rid of the heretics. His first act was to prohibit Arians from having a place of worship in the city. Their church was burnt down, but their problems did not end there: they were accused of having burnt it down themselves to avoid its being handed over to the orthodox clergy. As often occurred in large cities, the fire spread to an entire neighborhood (Socrates, *Ecclesiastical History*, 2, 29, 31–2). Arians and possibly other heretics called Nestorius the "arsonist."

Having settled old scores with the Arians, Theodosius took more general measures in June 428, when he passed a law removing the right of all heretics to meet together and practice their religion (*Code of Theodosius*, 16, 5, 65). This provision first mentioned the Arians and then went on to list all the heresies still being observed on imperial territory: "Macedonians [pneumatomachians], Apollinarians, Novationists and Sabbatians, Eunomians and Valentinians, Montanists or Priscillianists, Phrygians, Marcionites, Borborites, Messalians, Euchites or Enthusiasts, Donatists, Audians, Hydroparastates, Tascodrogites, Photinians, Paulians, and Marcellians."[36]

This religious diversity should come as no surprise. The increasingly populous Constantinople was receiving new citizens every day, and they mainly came from nearby Anatolia. They arrived with their own spiritual traditions, and following the war with Iran, many Eastern Christians sought refuge in the empire.[37] These refugees included many adherents of Manichaeism, a religion of Persian origin founded on a radical religious dualism, which contained some notable Gnostic elements but also shared several beliefs with Christianity, so that it could pass for a Christian heresy. Later, anti-heretical legislation would consider it the "mother of all heresies."[38] Many Christians were suspected of secretly sympathizing with the Manichaeans, and the law of 428 punished them with the same rigor.

By reopening the question of heretics, Theodosius II appeared to be following in the footsteps of Theodosius I, and there can be no doubt that in many provinces these new measures were applied with violence. The conflicts with their Iranian neighbor to the east were fomenting chauvinism, which went hand in hand with religious orthodoxy. Hence the bad reputation of the Manichaeans, especially among those who, like Nestorius, grew up in a border area, where the Persian threat was more evident. According to Peter Brown, this period was characterized by a "deceptively unruffled consensus." A "central core of Christian notables," a kind of social bloc made up of imperial and ecclesiastical officials, brought about the "closing of ranks ... against obdurate non-Christians, on the one hand, and against the radical forces that their more ruthless predecessors had unleashed, on the other." [39]

However, a comprehensive examination of the legislation on religious matters, gathered together in Book XVI of the *Code of Theodosius*, shows how the situation had changed profoundly in the intervening half century. In fact, Theodosius II's legislation appears to have been much less severe than that of Theodosius I. While the latter wanted to apply the death penalty to all heretics, the law of 428 imposed a milder treatment not only of radical ascetic sects but also of Manichaeans themselves, who were simply exiled. The assets of heretics could be legally transferred to their orthodox relations. Basically, the preferred treatment of heretics was now to marginalize them rather than persecute them with unprecedented violence. [40] The empire acknowledged the authority of the Church and accepted its interference in internal affairs, but at the same time, it tried to avoid taking action against citizens' property in the name of religious orthodoxy, given that such incriminations were often based on gossip and betrayals. [41] Moreover, Nestorius used accusations of Manichaeism to inflict damage on his enemies in the Church and claimed they belonged to a clandestine Manichaean hierarchy (see his letter to Saint Cyril in *Acts of the Councils*, I, 1, 32).

With imperial approval, the bishop also enacted some severe measures. According to his fictionalized biography, which has been handed down in the Syriac tradition, "He also suppressed games, theaters, singing, concerts, dancing, and the amusements practiced by Romans. For this reason, the city started to hate him intensely. They even went so far as to throw their furniture in the sea, saying: we do this because of Nestorius" (*Syriac Legend of Nestorius*, p. 7 Brière).[42]

Mindful of how he had been treated by Hypatius, Nestorius decided to attack the monastic circles. The ultraorthodox local monks did not represent a danger in the doctrinal sense, but from a social point of view they were a collection of time bombs. Their lifestyle was often bizarre, and their excesses of asceticism and religious zeal could create public disorders—a concern shared by both Theodosius and Nestorius. Monks chose celibacy, and above all they despised power and hierarchies: this was reason enough to cause unease among both the civil and the ecclesiastical authorities. They were accused of inciting slaves against their owners, and of forcing the rich to part with their property. Moreover, not all monks lived in monasteries, institutions that were easier to control: some lived on their own; others formed small groups. The empire's bishops were particularly fearful of itinerant monks, who practically lived on the road and, on the pretext of fighting for orthodoxy, constituted a constant risk to imperial government and public order in the cities. Their presence was especially awkward during the frequent periods of conflict over theological controversies. Nestorius prohibited their interference with laypeople during religious ceremonies.[43] This policy was inspired by his illustrious fellow citizen, Saint John Chrysostom, who a few years earlier had been persecuted and exiled precisely for such measures. It should come as no surprise, then, that Nestorius held a stately ceremony to commemorate this previous bishop of Constantinople on 26 September 428 (*Chronicle of Marcellinus*, Year 428).

Monasteries were relatively recent institutions in Constantinople, but they had dramatically increased in number due to Pulcheria's support, and their priors (*hēgoúmenoi*) were often influential figures. On his arrival, Nestorius had experienced the arrogance of Saint Hypatius, who could get away with such behavior because of the favor in which he was held by Pulcheria and the wider public.[44] On top of this, his relationship with Pulcheria herself was strained, as was reported in anecdotal form in later Nestorian traditions. The empress is supposed to have demanded a say on questions of liturgy and official ceremony, and Nestorius's followers spoke of this interference in fiercely misogynist tones (Pseudo-Nestorius, *Letter to Cosmas*, 5–8).[45]

This policy proved to be disastrous. Gilbert Dagron has observed that the monks' most dangerous characteristic was their ability to assimilate the social mechanisms of a constantly evolving city more quickly than the clergy. The prelates who came from rustic circles, such as Gregory of Nazianzus in the fourth century, or foreigners such as the Syrians John Chrysostom and Nestorius, were prisoners of protocol and court etiquette, which kept them apart from the faithful.[46]

The monks' opposition was greater than the bishop had expected, but it was not an insurmountable obstacle. At the end of the day, Nestorius shared a similar background with them and he had the talent to trounce them when it came to a public confrontation. His real adversaries were the much more formidable priests Proclus of Cyzicus and Philip of Side, brilliant preachers of the Church of Constantinople, who had aspired for some time to the episcopacy and therefore had good reason to hate and vilify their Syrian rival.[47] It is true that Nestorius had an uncommon talent as an orator, but eloquence alone was not enough to survive the court intrigues and the machinations of the capital's clergy, who accused him of having surrounded himself with clerics only from other regions of the empire (*Acts of the Councils*, I, i, p. 5).[48]

At the first opportunity, no more than a year after his election, Nestorius's enemies attacked him for his theological positions—his Achilles' heel. The controversy arose from his aversion to the Virgin's epithet, *Theotókos*, "she who gave birth to God." For this Syrian cleric, this term dangerously confused the divine nature of the Father with that of Christ: his mystic sensibility found repugnant and idolatrous the very idea that the divine Word could be incarnated in a baby. Consequently, he gave the priest Anastasius the task of correcting this tendency: if it was necessary to define Mary as the *Theotókos* because of popular religious belief that by then reflected a marked preference for this term, then it should at least be accompanied by the appellative *Christotókos*, "she who gave birth to Christ."

Nestorius suppressed the manifestations of popular piety linked to the cult of the *Theotókos* with intransigent zeal (Socrates, *Ecclesiastical History*, 7, 32). His adversaries could not have hoped for more: one of the first acts of hostility came from a layperson, a certain Eusebius of Dorylaeum, who dared to interrupt the bishop during his sermon, and shortly afterwards affixed his document accusing him of heresy to the wall of the church. On Sunday 23 December, the Feast of the Holy Fathers, Proclus attacked Nestorius's positions in an uncompromising sermon, which the faithful greeted with long applause. With his usual self-confidence, Nestorius attempted to interrupt Proclus with an immediate response, but he was not successful.[49]

From a doctrinal point of view, the debate over the term *Theotókos* was very much a side issue.[50] But the polemic against Nestorius triggered a series of doctrinal controversies that would continue for centuries.

·V·

The Anatomy of an Empire

In 428, the empire was close to reunification. Three years earlier, Theodosius had sent an army to free the Empire of the West from the usurper John and place on the western throne little Valentinian III, the grandson of Theodosius the Great and Theodosius II's cousin. The emperor was only nine years old, but belonged to the Theodosian dynasty and could therefore rule legitimately, albeit under the control of court officials. His coronation, which took place in 426, marked the end of the crisis between the Eastern Empire and the Western Empire.[1] There was an air of renewal, now that the house of the Valentinian-Theodosian family was back in favor and harmony was re-established between the two emperors, further consolidated by the official engagement between Valentinian III and Theodosius II's six-year-old daughter, Licinia Eudoxia (the wedding would take place in 439). The improved relationship between East and West was favorably received by many aristocratic families who had properties and interests in both parts of the empire.

The new understanding, which recalled the times of Theodosius the Great, was largely guaranteed by the skill and personality of that emperor's daughter, the queen mother Galla Placidia. However, the real architect of this understanding and goodwill was Theodosius II. Now that his aggressive policy in the East had been abandoned, he was able to devote himself to domestic affairs and the West. Constantinople's "passive disengagement" from the eastern question was inevitable if the empire was to strengthen its unity in the face of the barbarian threat. Unlike the Empire of the West, the Empire of the East now had greater military resources and the movement of barbarian peoples was lessening.[2]

At this particular moment, the Huns did not yet pose a threat, and in 427 their presence in the Danube basin decreased. According to the empire's official sources, the patrician Flavius Constantius Felix attacked the Huns, who had been occupying Pannonia for as long as fifty years, and had forced them out of the province (Marcellinus, *Chronicle*, Year 427; see Jordanes, *History of the Goths* or the *Getica*, 188).[3] Archeological evidence does not appear to show any signs of conflict, and Pannonia was probably evacuated peaceably following diplomatic negotiations.[4] The situation on the Danubian front remained under control until 434, the year in which Attila ascended to the throne.

In spite of political divisions, the imperial propaganda continued to impart a strongly unionist message. In his ambitious treatise *The City of God*, which he completed in 426, Saint Augustine always spoke of *a single* earthly city in opposition to the divine one. The earthly city was the Roman Empire and, in a sense, it was Rome. At the same time, the bishop of Hippo did not neglect earthly problems:

> For although there has been and still is no lack of enemies among foreign nations, against whom wars have always been waged and still are waged, yet the very extent of the Empire has given rise to wars of a worse kind, namely social and civil wars, by which mankind is more lamentably disquieted either when fighting is going on in the hope of bringing hostilities eventually to a peaceful end, or when there are fears that hostilities will break out again. (Augustine, *City of God*, 19, 7, from translation by H. Bettenson, Harmondsworth: Penguin, 1972, p. 861)

Saint Augustine's readers would have understood the allusion only too well: the conflicts between the Eastern and Western Roman Empires following the death of Theodosius I had caused a political crisis that gave rise to a fratricidal war that aided the rise of some barbarian elements, with various disastrous consequences for the material wealth and morale of the empire, starting with the sack of Rome in 410.

One of Saint Augustine's great admirers, Saint Prosper of Aquitaine, considered the Roman Empire still to be completely united:

> Divine providence preordained the Roman Empire in its full extension, so that the peoples destined to be united in the body of

Christ would be united in the law of a single empire; on the other hand, Christ's grace is not happy to share the borders of Rome, and has subjugated to the scepter of the Cross many peoples that Rome failed to subdue by force of arms. Besides, Rome has become greater as the religion's bulwark than as a seat of power. (Prosper, *On the Vocation of Peoples*, 2, 16)[5]

Prosper, a lay theologian with a singular passion for history, wrote these words in the mid-fifth century, while reviewing the political situation of the previous twenty/twenty-five years. At least officially, the western part of the empire (which included Rome and the imperial capital, Ravenna) was governed by Valentinian III, but in spite of the separation of the two parts desired by Theodosius the Great on his death in 395, the Roman Empire continued to be perceived as a single organism, and the separation of the two parts was referred to with embarrassment, or at least not without a degree of disapproval. Unsurprisingly, Olympiodorus of Thebes ended his historical work in 425 (the year of the acclamation of Valentinian III as emperor), while he started it in 408 with the death of Stilicho. Olympiodorus's history could thus be interpreted as an unhappy parenthesis of imperial division, which was to be replaced by a new era of *de facto*, although not *de iure*, unity between East and West.[6]

It was precisely because of his desire to reform a united and "catholic" empire that Theodosius ordered the formation of a commission of jurists to create a systematic corpus of laws. Proceedings started in 429, but the planning process had started at least as far back as the end of 425, following the rapprochement between Constantinople and Ravenna.[7] Initially, the idea was to compile two legal codes. The first, for use in the schools of jurisprudence, had to include all the general decrees issued from Constantine onwards, whether or not they were still in force. The other, of a more practical nature, would only examine the decrees that were still in force, but with the supplement of more ancient provisions and legal opinions, were to summarize "the rules to follow and the actions to avoid" and dictate the "direction of practical life" (*Code of Theodosius*, 1, 1, 5).[8]

The initial plan was considered too ambitious, and the commission restricted itself to compiling a single collection of the laws decreed since Constantine, with a considerable emphasis on public law. The result was the *Code of Theodosius*, which was completed in 438. The decision to have just one corpus was a good one. It is true that a century later the *Code of Theodosius* was replaced by Justinian's more systematic project, but as Mario Bretone has pointed out,

> His laws were transferred into or abbreviated by Romano-Visigothic legislation (as well as the Romano-Burgundian one), and further adopted in various ways. They were still be applied after the Carolingian age in the south of France (below the line running from the Charente to Saint-Claude), and in Spain throughout the centuries-long period of Arab domination.[9]

Theodosius' legislative plans were part of a wider global program that aimed at restoring order, and contrasted with barbarian disintegration and incoherence. The comprehensiveness of this juridical corpus enhanced the "catholic" image of the empire: the decisions taken during the decade 420–430—for instance the cooperation between the courts of the Western and Eastern Empires—appeared to be moving in the direction of a unitary system.

One of the more delicate problems was the definition of the border between the two "empires" or sections (*partes*) of an empire aiming at reunification. In the past, the Illyrian sector—today we would call it the Balkans—was considered part of the "West," partly because it was believed that the Danubian frontier was strategically essential for the defense of Italy. The established balance between the two parts was modified in 395, with the division of the empire and the creation of the new prefecture of Illyricum, which was added to the existing ones of the East, Gaul, and Italy/Africa. Theoretically, the jurisdiction of the Illyrian prefecture went from Greece to the Danube, but because of the ambiguity in Theodosius I's instructions, both the *partes* of the empire were quarreling over the new administrative sector. Now that relations between Ravenna and Constantinople had so much improved, the favored option was to divide Illyricum, which would have important consequences for centuries to come. While Ravenna controlled the upper and mid-Adriatic, Constantinople had consolidated its grip on eastern Illyria and, of course, Greece. The border on the River Drina, which Santo Mazzarino called an "iron curtain," separated two parts of the peninsula which up to that time had been considered a single geographic unit and perhaps also a strategic unit, but which now led to a cultural separation even in political terms—and that ongoing separation was between the Latin-speaking regions and the Greek-speaking ones.[10]

The agreement between the two *partes* had balanced the military situation which, in 428, appeared to be very settled, at least in Illyricum. With Felix's campaign against the Huns in 427, Ravenna had already obtained a success that guaranteed its control of the Adriatic-Danubian sector. In the meantime, Theodosius II, who had abandoned the eastern front and left Armenia to its fate, had been able to strengthen his defenses in Thrace, Dacia, and Macedonia, ensuring control of eastern Illyricum.[11] The agreement also confirmed the control of the Illyrian provinces by the Church of Constantinople, whose bishoprics prospered thanks to the tax exemptions they had been granted by central government.[12] In this way, a curb was put on Rome's ambitions, and at the same time it became easier to repress heretics and pagans.[13]

In spite of the climate of intolerance and the dominant image of triumphant Christianity presented by the Church Fathers, pagan traditions were surviving even in the East, where some pagan dignitaries were holding onto important positions.[14] One exemplary case was that of Cyrus of Panopolis, a pagan philosopher of Egyptian origin: he was a skilled administrator and a refined intellectual, and had been the prefect of Constantinople in 426.

The persistence of traditional cults should come as no surprise. Pagan intellectuals were useful to the empire, both as administrators and as teachers. They had been responsible for keeping the tradition of classical studies alive in Rome and especially Athens, which unlike Rome did not have any holy places or even a high-ranking bishop. The pagan past of the Greek city was not merely an "archeological" memory: it remained a reference point for classicism, particularly now that the advance of an intolerant Christianity made it difficult to hand on traditional learning.

Of course, Christianity was making inroads even in Athens, and the construction of the city's first church occurred in the second quarter of the fifth century. It was an imposing tetraconch structure, created within the public complex known as Hadrian's Library, which was restored followed the damage inflicted by the Visigoths.[15] However, Athens remained a blissful haven for pagans. Alison Frantz, the American archeologist who has revealed much about Athens in Late Antiquity, has demonstrated that the age of Arcadius and Theodosius II was one of prosperity for the city. Following Alaric's attacks towards the end of the fourth century, the city was subject to various restoration measures, and on the whole, it had been able to retain its own pagan identity, precisely because its tradition was so glorious.[16] But this was also in part the work of the Empress Eudocia, Theodosius's wife who, before her wedding and her conversion, had been called Athenais. She came from one of the city's leading pagan families, which may have been long established, and her father, Leontius, who died in 420, had held the *kathédra* in sophistics.

Eudocia's story is particularly interesting. The empress had become a fervent Christian who particularly prized the asceticism practiced by some kinds of monasticism.[17] Nevertheless, the Athenian schools of rhetoric and philosophy were to enjoy her protection for as long as she lived, and Athens was tolerated as a kind of pagan reservation. This tolerance was perhaps of political significance. During this time, Theodosius II was mainly concerned with avoiding rifts and resentments, and was probably interested in ensuring the services of intellectuals, in spite of radical opposition from many exponents in the Church. Judging by the legislation on heretics (and as we shall see later in the case of the Jews), we can assume that, at least during this particular period, imperial intolerance toward pagans was more a question of words than deeds.

For some years, the most distinguished Athenian school was the so-called Academy, which is more appropriately defined as the Neoplatonic school. Many of its exponents came from Alexandria, where a climate of increasing religious intolerance (typified by the dramatic killing of Hypatia during mob violence in 415) had forced the school to move to more welcoming Athens. Leontius himself may have had to leave Antioch for similar reasons.[18] The first "successor" to be master and reside in Athens was Plutarch, who was very old in 428 and was assisted by his disciple Syrianus of Alexandria and above all Proclus, the author of important commentaries on various works by Plato and on Aristotle's *On the Soul*.[19] The master's residence was close to the temples of Asclepius and of Dionysus: "this house ... could be seen, or at least made out, from the acropolis of Athens" (Marinus, *Life of Proclus*, 29). Students were probably also served by a group of lesser educational circles. We are talking then of an Athens that was a center for private teaching, with a group of internal students and another external group of listeners (Damascius, *Life of Isidore*, fr. 142).[20] One of these was the Syrian Odaenathus, perhaps a distant descendant of the homonymous ruler of Palmyra who governed the eastern part of the Roman Empire from 260 to 267.[21]

The presence of Neoplatonists in Athens helped to keep paganism alive in the city and the surrounding regions.[22] The leaders of the Neoplatonic school were not simply teachers, as they presented themselves as spiritual leaders and constituted a reference point for all Athenians and not just their own disciples.[23] Partly because of this, the local Christian community had not gained the necessary prestige to compete with the great pagan teachers. A master like Plutarch held a special authority which derived from his hieratic wisdom of the ancient magical and theurgic rites that made it possible for the Neoplatonist master, like the Persian or Chaldean magi, to communicate with the divine, invoke daemons and create horoscopes and calendars.

The Neoplatonists became the most important players in the pagan "resistance." In order to defend traditional cults from Christian attacks, they did not hesitate to abandon, at least in public, the vegetarian diet they had originally adhered to, and take part with other pagans in the cruel sacrifice of animals.[24] However, the persistence of traditional cults was not restricted to Athens and exclusive intellectual circles. In Greece, as in many other regions of the empire, paganism survived in many different forms.[25] Moreover, monasticism was a great deal less developed in the Balkans, and could not influence the process of Christianization as it had done in Syria and Anatolia.[26]

This situation guaranteed, for a period at least, the coexistence of pagans and Christians, whose religious activities could occasionally fuse together. One interesting example came from the archaeological dig at the "Spring of the Oil Lamps" in Corinth, on the site of the ancient complex of the Sanctuary of Asclepius (which collapsed as the result of an earthquake at the end of the fourth century). It was close to a natural spring where the pagan faithful placed thousands of votive lamps between the end of the fourth century and the middle of the fifth, in spite of the fact that Christians had chosen the surrounding area for a burial ground. Other lamps were found among the ruins of the temple, but the most striking feature was that many of them had wordings of Christian inspiration scratched on their surfaces. Typically these invoked the protection of the "angels who live in these waters"—angels who must have been a Christian interpretation of the ancient pagan cult of nymphs, documented by pagan inscriptions of the same era that have been found on the same site.[27]

·VI·

From Ravenna to Nola

ITALY IN TRANSITION

IN THE SYSTEM of power restored by Theodosius II, the Empire of the West was assigned to little Valentinian III. The emperor was still a child entrusted to the care of his tutor, one of those "child princes" that caused such outrage in senatorial circles.[1] But the world had changed, and traditional Roman values had been replaced by the "medieval" principle of dynastic legitimacy, which was in fact of eastern origin. The new emperor, who was anointed in 426, was the grandson of Theodosius the Great on his mother's side, and was therefore a first cousin of the emperor of the East.

Officially Valentinian was the absolute lord of the Western Empire: he signed the laws and played out his role at official ceremonies, but political power was administered by court dignitaries and above all by his mother, the forty-year-old Aelia Galla Placidia.[2] The unofficial involvement of a woman in political affairs was not unknown, but for traditionalists it was a sign of decadence. Modern historians have adhered to that enduring cliché of Otto Seeck's, the great historian of the late Roman Empire. He defined this period as a second-rate epoch and a "regimen of women": Placidia's regency in Ravenna and Pulcheria's influence in Constantinople.[3]

Placidia's power derived from her being the daughter of Theodosius I, but her real strength was her uncommon political experience. The queen mother knew the mechanisms of the western court, in which she had grown up and become empress, albeit for a brief period (421). Moreover, her recent exile to Constantinople, where she had lived at the court for about four years, had enriched her political and diplomatic experience. But most importantly, Placidia could boast personal knowledge of the barbarian world. She was taken hostage after the sack of Rome in 410, and had to follow the Visigoths back to Gaul. Following various negotiations, she ended up marrying King Ataulf in a sumptuous ceremony. Shortly afterwards there was a successful plot to kill Ataulf, and Placidia returned to Ravenna after having lived among the barbarians for five years, one of which was as a queen.

Clearly, her government was supervised by dignitaries loyal to Constantinople. The interests of the eastern court were safeguarded by the presence of Flavius Costantius Felix, a good military leader and a capable politician, who had just been promoted to the highly prestigious rank of *patricius*, and now, in the year 428, also held the coveted post of consul, a well-earned reward for having reconquered Pannonia. Felix's reputation is clearly demonstrated in the ivory diptych commissioned for his consulship. The left-hand panel, the only one to survive, is now held at the Bibliothèque Nationale de France. It is an extremely elegant artifact, but also a prestigious attribute of power. Felix is depicted frontally, dressed in the *trabea* (toga decorated with purple) of a victor, with his right hand on his heart, and his left hand holding a long scepter.[4]

Ravenna was a young capital. It had been the permanent seat of the western court since 402, and the principal base for the fleet. The city was well defended by a dense network of marshes and canals that made it less vulnerable to invasions, unlike the great cities of the Po Valley such as Milan or Verona, which were much more exposed if attacked by an army of horsemen.[5] Moreover it was much easier to send reinforcements and provisions through the nearby military port of Classis, which was not an inconsiderable advantage for an empire whose principal strength in its struggle against the barbarians was its control of the seas.[6] Ravenna had also been provided with new city walls, to a new design that signified important changes in the planning of a Roman city.[7]

The choice of a marshland city helped to diminish the negative image of the stagnant waters, typical of the classical view of such landscapes. In the past, there had been a tendency to exclude "marginal" scenery, such as forest or swampland, from literary descriptions.[8] This does not mean that these landscapes lost their negative connotations inherited from the classical tradition, but it was no longer considered unseemly to portray them. Thus the most effective description of fifth-century Ravenna and its unusual urban vistas can be inferred from a harsh judgment expressed by Sidonius Apollinaris in a letter of 468:

> In this marsh, where every norm is ceaselessly subverted, the walls fall and the waters stand firm, the towers shift on the water's surface and the ships do not move, you freeze in the public baths and you swelter in the private houses, the gods are thirsty and the buried swim, the thieves stand guard and the authorities sleep, the clerics charge interest on loans and the Syrians sing psalms, the traders serve our Lord and the monks engage in trade, the elderly think about playing ball and the youths about dice, the eunuchs are interested in warfare and the *foederati* in culture. What could you expect of a city ... that could more easily have a territory than it could have earth! [Clearly the original Latin played here on the words *territorium* and *terra* —*translator's note*] (Sidonius, *Epistle* 1, 8, 2ff)

For the aristocrat Sidonius, a major protagonist of the final throes of the Western Empire, Ravenna represented a world turned upside down, which contrasted with classical "urban" ideals. But this very description with its negativity allows us to revive the atmosphere of that fifth-century capital (in a way, it was a forerunner of Venice).[9] Ravenna in Late Antiquity is usually associated with solemn, priest-like figures portrayed in the church mosaics, who are "Byzantine" in their immobility. Like Constantinople and the other important metropolises, this city had its cosmopolitan population, court and associated ceremonies, but here the people lived in the midst of curious innovations, such as floating towers and firmly moored barges ("the ships that do not move"). All this contributed to creating an unusual and unsettling landscape, which marked a change in the very concept of the city, now very distant from the ancient ideals of the *polis*. Cities that did represent such ideals were like "corpses," mere monuments of the past that were now being dismantled, whereas large landowners like Sidonius from Gaul would describe their *latifundia* as rural microcosms that could boast all the features of "urbanity."[10]

With the restoration of the Theodosian dynasty, Ravenna had appointed a new bishop, clearly one suited to the importance of the post and sufficiently young and energetic. They chose Peter, an exceptional preacher and respected theologian who in the Middle Ages would be known as Chrysologus, from the Greek for "golden orator."[11] At the same time, Ravenna was also consolidating its own ecclesiastical position: the marshland city had already obtained control of the diocese of Eastern Emilia (it was this that gave rise to the distinction between Emilia and Romagna). Unlike the Eastern Empire, where religious controversies could determine the growth or decline of a diocese, the bishopric of Ravenna does not appear to have obscured the former capital, Milan, steadfastly proud of Saint Ambrose. Besides, in the West it had been Ambrose himself who increased the prestige of bishops and turned their role into one of pronouncing on all questions concerning the Christian faith, and by the period we are examining, this influence had in practice extended to all public matters.[12]

At the same time, the new capital was rapidly changing into a Christian city, as a result of an energetic policy to promote the establishment of churches, monasteries, and charitable foundations. Builders and their commissioners wished to break with the past. In fact, the monumental architecture of Ravenna is characterized by the dazzling ostentation of its interiors (particularly its mosaics) and the austerity of its exteriors. The upkeep of public buildings gradually became the prerogative of central government, while private individuals funded churches, which meant that pomp and wealth were no longer associated with the community of citizens, but rather with the community of the faithful.[13] One of the churches built during this period was the Basilica of Saint John the Evangelist, which today no longer exists, but was described along with its complex iconographical plan in the *Book of Pontiffs of the Church of Ravenna* and two anonymous medieval tracts. On the mosaics of the conch, the celebration of the supreme divine law of love promised a kingdom of merciful clemency, while the procession of emperors on the front of the triumphal arch and the apse wall secured loyalty to a policy of supporting the church, safeguarding orthodoxy, and generally maintaining harmony between the two *partes* of the empire.[14]

However, Ravenna had no ambitions for religious primacy, unlike Constantinople. On the contrary, the transfer of the imperial seat of government to Ravenna and the Milanese diocese's loss of political prestige had restored the balance between the north and the center of the peninsula, with considerable advantages for the Roman see. At the same time, the local aristocracies contributed to the development of the diocese in numerous towns within the province: some episcopal sees became so powerful that they could secure prestigious relics. The rapprochement between the Eastern and Western Empires led to the transfer of sacred remains, as probably occurred in the case of Ancona, which obtained some relics of the first martyr, Saint Stephen.[15]

We now move to Rome, the other pole of political power in Italy. In 428, the city was still suffering from the aftermath of the Visigoths' passing through. Of course, life had returned, but the massacres and exodus of its inhabitants had almost emptied it. Eighteen years after Alaric's sack of the city, its population was considerably reduced in spite of the return of many citizens.[16] The surrender of the Eternal City had had a powerful psychological impact on the entire empire, but perhaps its demographic decrease had given a certain respite to the economy of the western Mediterranean, which was so skewed by the problem of supplying that megalopolis.[17]

However, the memory of the sack was gradually fading. After all, Alaric had not killed many senators, and the destruction inflicted by the Visigoths had spared the Christian churches and most importantly the Holy Places, including the tombs of the apostles Peter and Paul. The fortifications of the Aurelian Wall had been restored and improved upon, and this defense system had been augmented by a kind of spiritual rampart made up of churches, oratories, and basilicas throughout the suburb. Rome succeeded in maintaining its long-held prestige both as a religious center and as a political one. This explains the magnificent ceremony that took place on 1 January 426 to celebrate the arrival of Valentinian III, which was skillfully managed by the court dignitary Helio, whom Theodosius II had sent to control the situation. Valentinian had already been officially awarded the title of Augustus by Theodosius (Prosper of Aquitaine, *Chronicle*, 1289).

The fifth century in Rome witnessed the final consolidation of a "Christian space" through a systematic reorganization of the territory, which reinforced the traditional balance between the city (*urbs*) and the suburb (*suburbium*—the city's surrounding territory covering a hundred

Roman miles in each direction) on a new, primarily religious basis.[18] Moreover, the devastation left by the Visigoths provided the Church with the opportunity for a radical program of urban renewal, which in the following years would indeed rise out of the ashes of the burnt-out buildings and bring new life to the ancient city.[19] One line of Olympiodorus alludes to this renewed grandeur: "Each of its houses is itself a stronghold, and a thousand strongholds the City holds in its embrace" (Olympiodorus, fr. 41.1).[20] The driving force behind this rebirth was primarily the bishop of Rome, who exercised great authority throughout the West, and was the administrator of enormous assets.[21] In this period he was already known as the pope or *papa*, although it should be remembered that this term of eastern origin simply meant "father" and did not yet constitute an official title.[22] The pope in 428 was Celestine, who had held the office for six years with the official title of "archbishop."[23] Peter Brown has summarized his role very effectively:

> The bishop of Rome was a *papa*—a Grand Old Man. He liked to play the elder statesman to less experienced regions. Throughout the fifth century, the *papa*, the pope of Rome could be relied upon to provide authoritative, reassuringly old-fashioned (and, for that very reason, largely inapplicable) advice on how a well-run church should function . . . .[24]

Like other popes of his time, Celestine worked hard to consolidate the authority of the Church. The Roman *Book of Pontiffs* briefly states: "He issued an edict relating to the whole Church, mainly concerning religious questions, which today are conserved in the Church archives" (p. 96, 8–9 Duchesne). For the most part, the "questions" concerned problems with the followers of Pelagius, a priest from Britannia or Ireland who had founded a religious movement at the beginning of the fifth century. The Pelagians proposed that Christians at all levels commit themselves to an active and ascetic life; they did not believe that asceticism should be restricted to monks, and argued that all the faithful should imitate Christ. Their doctrine, which was considered too radical, had been condemned on many occasions, but even after Pelagius's death in 427 and the exile of leading Pelagian figures, the movement continued to cause unrest in the Western Church. The movement was supported by various members of the aristocracy and some court officials.

Many Pelagians sought refuge in the East to escape the hostility of the Western Church. Previously, Nestorius's predecessors had upheld Celestine's complaints, but the new bishop of Constantinople was now acting in a more ambivalent manner (Celestine, "Epistle to Nestorius" in *Collectio Veronensis* 2, 1). Towards the end of 428, Nestorius asked for Rome's support in the dispute over the *Theotókos*.[25] The pope reflected on the question, but in the end links between Rome and Alexandria prevailed, and he joined adversaries of the bishop of Constantinople. Overcoming their communication problems (Celestine knew no Greek and was a rather crude theologian), the enemies of Nestorius managed to push forward their own arguments and above all to argue by analogy that Nestorius's doctrines resembled those of the Pelagians.[26]

The presence of religious tensions may have led to an increase in social violence. On 23 July 428, a certain Pyrrhus was assassinated in Rome: it is recalled without further details in the *Fasti Consulares Ravennates*. A symbolic illustration of the event has been preserved in MS 202 of the Chapterhouse Library of Merseburg, which portrays a corpse wrapped in a shroud.[27] Commenting on the images in the manuscript, W. Koehler argues that this iconography might allude to the "denial of the right to burial relating to a sentence for crimes against the state."[28] We know nothing else about Pyrrhus, but his murder must have been a fairly important event if it was included in a chronicle. Such acts of violence were not uncommon in this Rome far from the court and poisoned by religious conflicts: just two years earlier, a deacon had been killed while distributing alms to the poor, and the orthodox believed that the patrician Felix was the instigator of the crime (Prosper of Aquitaine, *Chronicle*, Year 426).

Although the Christianization had radically changed the *Urbs*, the Rome of the pope and the Holy Places had not entirely eclipsed the pomp of imperial Rome. The city was still the seat of the Senate, and many of its members were committed to defending its tradition, irrespective of their religious beliefs. The senators' political stage was much reduced in size, and the displays of paganism were limited to the actions of a small circle of senators who were keen to keep alive the city's historical memory and the places associated with it. However, the Senate had not been reduced to the rank of a municipal assembly of Rome.[29] The crisis of paganism does not appear to have touched the

forms for self-representation of their class, which we find in grandilo-
quent epigraphs or sophisticated artifacts such as ivory diptychs. On
the contrary, the machinery of senatorial ideology had been preserved
by ostentatious displays of their "pride in their survival," which was
linked to the memory of their traditions and therefore of paganism.[30]

This contradiction caused literary figures of the time to experience a
degree of discomfort. For example, the grammarian Servius, the author
of a learned commentary on Virgil, dwelt at length on the history of
monarchical and republican Rome, but devoted little space to the centuries of imperial rule.[31] Besides, even the most ancient pagan cults
were not only a bookish heritage for scholars and antiquarians, but also
testimony to the anxieties of a population looking for a solution to the
crisis in the revival of ancient soteriological cults.[32]

Many senators had converted to Christianity, but there were still some
important exceptions.[33] In 428, Antonius Volusianus from the powerful
family of the Ceionii was the prefect of the *praetorium*, and definitely
also a pagan. He was born around 380, when the Roman Empire had to
all intents and purposes become Christian, and he was considered an
"extreme" case.[34] As we have seen, the political situation favored a *de
facto* imperial tolerance of high officials who had not yet converted.
Moreover, the family of Volusianus included some Christians who were
both influential and fervent believers, such as his niece Melania the
Younger.[35] Ultimately, the authorities tolerated various degrees of understanding between Christians and the senatorial aristocracy during
the period immediately following the sack of Rome. As Giuseppe Zecchini has observed, the religious factor was no longer the object of ideological conflicts, and "Christians and pagans could equally find themselves allies, if they had a shared political ideal or a common enemy."[36]

Of course, the Christian empire had unleashed its campaign against
"pagan idols"—immortalized in the art of the catacombs—even in
Rome, in fact most appropriately in Rome.[37] However, the situation
was still confused, and the need to unite all forces during this difficult
time meant that the repression had to be relaxed. The *Code of Theodosius*
appears to reflect this confusion, by citing both examples of extreme
intolerance and of respect for pagan monuments (duly deconsecrated,
of course). On the other hand, the partiality of the sources means
that we cannot take all the accounts of Christian authors too literally.[38]

Paganism resisted as a conservative ideological system; this is demonstrated by such works as Macrobius's *Saturnalia*, which evokes the learned conversations of the cream of the senatorial aristocracy that believed in pagan ideas or at least sympathized with them—conversations that took place during the Saturnalia, a pagan festival that lasted from 17 to 19 December. The author was almost certainly Volusianus's successor as prefect of the *praetorium*, Macrobius Ambrosius Theodosius.[39] The intention of this literary project was to bring together the voices and fragments of a centuries-long tradition in a systematic manner using a "choral" structure (Macrobius, *Saturnalia*, preface, 8–10).

Ravenna and Rome, the two centers of power in the Western Empire, guaranteed the continued centrality of Italy in the geopolitical framework, even though Italy had for some time lost its traditional privileges that distinguished it from the rest of the Roman Empire, and was now effectively part of the provincial order.[40] Moreover, the authorities were worried about the situation in the Italian countryside. The Apennine regions had become particularly marginalized, in spite of their closeness to Rome. The economy of these areas was based on sheepherding, but the local aristocracies feared the shepherds, whose brigand-like lifestyle differed little from that of the barbarians who were pushing against the empire's external borders.[41] For this reason, only notables and specified officials had the right to travel by horse: imperial legislation, which was amended on several occasions during the second half of the fourth century, was intent upon finding the easiest way to identify bandits on horseback. Given that notables and officials were easily recognizable by their demeanor and dress, every other kind of horseman was immediately seen as a dangerous element and an enemy of public order.[42]

However, the economy of these territories was not stagnating, and still less was it abandoned. Of course, depopulation and invasions had left their mark, but archeological research has demonstrated that significant agricultural production continued in southern Italy, and was favored by the fact that political and military events had made communications between Italy and Africa more difficult. The crisis was primarily affecting the more delicate crops, such as winegrowing, and the small agricultural units. On the other hand, the structures of the *villae* of Late Antiquity were being extended and adopted once again.[43] On the eve of the fall of the Western Empire, Palladius (a landowner with estates in Italy and Sardinia) wrote an agricultural treatise in the form of a rural calendar, with the clear intention of demonstrating that time had never stopped for the peasantry.[44]

For Christian authors, the countryside was infested with superstitious pagans. In reality, Christianity was also advancing there. A great deal of land belonging to the emperor, which in Italy constituted a large part of the territory, was generously donated to the Church.[45] As time went by, monasteries and shrines favored increasing contacts between the countryside and the episcopal sees, as in the case of the Shrine of Saint Felix in a locality called the "Cemetery" (*Coemeterium*; today it is called Cimitile), close to the ancient city of Nola in the Italian region of Campania. This religious center, which attracted pilgrims and the faithful, was built close to the tomb of Felix, a "confessor" martyr of the third century, who was buried in the necropolis to the north of the city. The shrine was developed at the time of Constantine, reusing some ancient tombs and constructing new mausoleums.[46]

The spiritual authority of the shrine was the elderly and revered Paulinus, an aristocratic senator of Aquitaine, who at some stage in his life had abandoned all worldly activities and ended up in Nola, where in 395 he had organized an ascetic community around the restored Basilica of Saint Felix. Like other western monastic communities, the one in Cimitile had no proper set of rules, but merely followed the example of the former senator's austere life of self-denial. Many members of the monastery devoted themselves to doctrinal studies. Paulinus was not a great theologian, but he had an acute literary sensitivity, as demonstrated by his letters and above all his poetry.[47]

Although he no longer lived at the shrine but rather in Nola, of which he was now bishop, Paulinus came there to officiate at the main ceremonies, particularly the one in honor of Saint Felix, whose feast day is 14 January. Pilgrims poured into Cimitile in droves, drawn by the fame of the relics and the bishop's charisma. For a single day, the shrine experienced the illusion of becoming the center of the world (Paulinus, *Carmen* 14, 49ff).[48] According to Peter Brown, it was actually

> a joining place not only for the townsmen among themselves but between the townsmen and the alien, despised villagers on whose

foodstuffs the city depended.... The pilgrimage center could redress the balance between town and country in Campania.[49]

This depiction is evocative, but perhaps a little exaggerated. On the
other hand, such occasions would have helped Paulinus, now close to
death, to forget his own spiritual torments and personal vicissitudes.
Following years of uninterrupted warfare, the Italian peninsula could at
last relax a little. The barbarians were not far away, but in spite of widespread anxieties, people were beginning to recover their faith in the
empire and the idea of Rome. Of course, their Rome was a little less
eternal, and subject to violence and religious unrest, but the city had
survived its moments of crisis, and there was reason to hope for a recovery on this occasion too. The two parts of the empire appeared
united and willing to cooperate in keeping the barbarian threat at bay.
Even for the ageing Paulinus, the danger had passed: the only battles in
sight were those fought every day by the "soldiers of Christ," as he suggested in one of this poems:

> Those who do not fear God alone, fear everything.
> Let those who do not have faith in Christ our Savior
> flee behind the city walls and put their trust in legions.
> But we are protected by the invincible Cross;
> our spiritual armament is God.
> We are defenseless and vulnerable, but we do not want arms:
> Even in times of peace, we already have what is needed
> to fight against incorporeal enemies.
>   (Paulinus of Nola, *Carmen* 26, lines 100ff.)

Britannia

Verulamium
Londinium

FRANKS

Augusta
Treverorum

Colonia

Mogontiacum

Tournai

Belgica

Germania

Rhine

FRANKS

Metz

ALAMANNI

Lutetia

Troyes

Moselle

Danube

Auxerre

Imperial Provinces

BURGUNDIANS

Aquitania

Lyons

Burdigala

Alps

Visigothic Kingdom
(fullest possible extent in 428)

Toulouse

Arelate

Narbo Martius

Massilia

Lérins

Capraria

Tarragona

·VII·

Trial Runs for the Middle Ages

FOR THE MOMENT, Italy was not afraid of the barbarian menace, due to the rapprochement between Ravenna and Constantinople, and also the wisdom and competence of the determined and, it has to be said, utterly ruthless imperial generals. Not everyone, however, was willing to give them the recognition they deserved. First among these were the pompous and phlegmatic senators, whose feelings were ambivalent. The military men protected their lives and their property, but at the end of the day they were still coarse soldiers, often of barbarian origin. Moreover, the aristocrats were alarmed by the increasing influence of court officials. It was during this period that Macrobius wrote:

> What can we say of the generals and military leaders? They are only interested in bringing their own enterprises into the conversation, while they remain silent in fear of being accused of arrogance. But if by some chance they are asked to tell their stories, then you can be sure that they will feel rewarded for all their hard work! Indeed, it is recompense enough for them that someone wants to listen to their heroic deeds. The problem is that such tales evoke a climate of glory. Consequently any rivals or resentful persons among the public start to raise noisy objections or to tell other stories in order to prevent the orator from being praised for the deeds he speaks of. (Macrobius, *Saturnalia*, 7, 2, 7–8)

In the exclusive circles frequented by Macrobius, generals came into a room on tiptoes and kept a low profile to avoid some gossip complaining to the court about their uppishness. But it did not take much—perhaps an invitation to speak or the presence of a rival—for a military commander to remove his mask and to appear before his learned public as a "glorious soldier" of the kind Plautus used to write about.

The cleverer military leaders entrusted their image to writers who they could rely on to praise them in poems and panegyrics. There was no shortage of material for these writers: any one of the battles of varying degrees of importance on different fronts, which were fought to shore up the defenses against the continual barbarian incursions. Indeed, imperial territories in both the East and the West had been occupied by numerous external populations over the previous thirty years. During difficult periods, the empire had preferred to accept their presence and control it, but now the situation was more favorable and legions could be sent on the counterattack. The most important military sectors were in the prefecture of Gaul, where recent migrations of peoples had upset the structure of the territory. From 425, the supreme commander of this operational sector was the rising star of the Roman army, General Aetius.[1]

The invading peoples attempted to establish themselves in the Roman provinces primarily for the advantages provided by imperial organization. Their settlement was confirmed by a treaty with Rome called a *foedus*, which allocated them a territory to settle with their families. Moreover, the barbarian *foederati* were not entirely integrated, given that they did not have a right to Roman citizenship. They were used as settlers and soldiers, and constituted a separate social category.[2] In theory, they were distinct communities, whose customs and lifestyles set them apart from the Romans. In practice, many of these groups managed to preserve their ethnic identity to some extent, and this might explain a phenomenon observed by Peter Heather in the written documentation on the great migrations: some ethnic groups, which had apparently disappeared at a particular time, "reappeared" a few decades later. Of course, not all groups had such a strong identity, and in some cases they were simply absorbed into other, stronger groups.[3]

It was believed that these coalitions of peoples already had a well-defined ethnic identity at the time. This erroneous interpretation mainly derived from ideological trends in the modern era, which attributed precocious "national" identities to the barbarians.[4] In reality, the ethnic identity of a warrior or warrior clan in the fifth century often depended on the origins of the commander they chose to serve. Even the identification of a people with a language, which for us has become a self-evident truth, was a much more blurred reality for these peoples migrating across the continent. A degree of homogeneity could only be found in the dominant group, which gave its name to the ethnicity. Groups of "barbarians" were called either by their actual names—Goths, Huns, Swebians, Vandals, or Franks—or by some name with a more classical flavor—Scythians or Massagetes. However, various linguistic traces demonstrate elements of mixing between ethnic groups that came into contact with each other, as in the case of the Burgundians and the Huns in the first phase of the migrations.[5]

In spite of the integration of barbarian elements into the heart of the empire, these communities provoked feelings of terror among the native populations. Even today, the expression "barbarian invasions" is deeply rooted in the imagination of the Latin peoples.[6] Many authors expressed the anguish and fear of violence that the invaders had brought the heart of the empire by sacking Rome in 410. In Gaul, the local population had a terrible memory of the barbarian presence. The memory of the invasions began to fade, and the sufferings of many Christian martyrs in Gaul were attributed to a barbarian chief called Chrocus, but the sources do not agree on either his dates or his place of origin.[7] The most evocative description of the arrival of the barbarians is provided by Orientius, a cleric from Gaul who was probably a bishop in Gascony, and around 430 describes their arrival in a short poem to exhort his fellow men to a Christian life:

> Look at how death has swept through the entire world,
> at how many peoples have been affected by the madness of war.
> What use are thick forests or high and inaccessible mountains,
> what use the raging torrents with violent whirlpools,
> carefully located fortresses, cities protected by their walls,
> positions defended by the sea, the squalor of hiding places,
> the darkness of caves and the hovels among the rocks;
> nothing has been of use in avoiding the barbarians hunting in a
>   pack. . . .
> In the villages and the villas, in the fields and at the crossroads,
> in all the hamlets, on the roads and in every other place,

death, suffering, massacres, fire-raising, and mourning:
the whole of Gaul was burning in a single blaze.

(Orientius, *Commonitorium*, 2, 165ff.)

By using such images, authors like Orientius contributed to the creation of the myth about barbarian masses and innumerable hordes of invaders. Of course, the era of the great migrations did cause the mobilization of a fairly numerous population that was not made up solely of aristocrats and religious figures, but also included men, women, and children of all social backgrounds.[8] However, it is difficult to generalize about the data, partly because these encounters between populations did not always involve conflict, and the principal aim of the "barbarians" was not necessarily destruction (although the scarcity of sources can give the impression that some cities had been transformed into ghost towns).[9]

On the other hand, the Roman citizens who lived in the provinces besieged by barbarians or in the countryside bled dry by taxes and army requisitions, had many reasons for rejecting the patriotic ideals of imperial propaganda. In many western regions, the crisis had increased the phenomenon of social banditry. In Gaul and the Iberian Peninsula, bands of peasants and brigands were known by the Celtic name of *Bacaudae* or *Bagaudae*, and records of their existence go back to the end of the third century.[10] The last of this first wave of revolts, which broke out in the countryside between the Seine and the Loire, was quelled around 417. Repression made it possible to keep the situation under control for about twenty years, but the problem was not eliminated: the *Bacaudae* would take up arms again around 435 with even more violent consequences.[11] Around 428, the presence of Aetius's army must have discouraged any desires for rebellion.

The most notable problem was the cohabitation between barbarians and Romans, which the imperial citizens of Gaul viewed with apprehension: one of their most persistent fears was that they would turn into "semibarbarians."[12] Their anxieties were entirely justified, given that their lands had been partly occupied by the invaders with the emperor's consent. In 413, Emperor Honorius had granted the Burgundes an area of land between Bourgogne and the Rhineland, where they remained until 437.[13] As for the Visigoths, they had obtained recognition of their sovereignty from Ravenna: in 419 they settled in Aquitaine, and established their seat of government in Toulouse.[14]

Contacts with the Roman Empire and encounters between different tribes, such as the Visigoths and the Ostrogoths, changed the nature of these ethnic groups. For example, the language of power of the kings of Toulouse was inspired by Roman institutions.[15] This helps to explain why the Visigoths left so few traces of their presence in Aquitaine, unlike what would happen in Spain a few decades later.[16] At the time of the great migrations, some of the more resolute and politically intelligent chiefs helped to create multiethnic coalitions, in which the charisma of kings and warrior aristocracies counted much more than tribal and family identity. Moreover, the successes of a barbarian nation could cause the adoption of "fashions" and other forms of emulation by other peoples.[17]

Besides, not all the aristocracy of the Kingdom of Toulouse was of Visigothic origin. Some were warriors from other ethnic groups, who had taken advantage of the Huns' temporary withdrawal, following Felix's operations in Pannonia in 427. The mercenaries of the East would attempt to get themselves enrolled in the Roman army, but in some cases they preferred the Romano-barbarian kingdoms that were coming into existence: for example, Theoderic I, the first king of the Visigoths of Aquitaine, took in the Ostrogoth Beremod, who had fled Central Europe with his son Viteric.

Theoderic had been a good ally of the empire, but this did not mean that the Visigoths ceased to be a danger. In 425, the king took advantage of a political crisis in Ravenna to attack the great city of Arelate (Arles), an important river port on the Rhone estuary in order to lay his hands finally on an outlet into the Mediterranean. The Visigoths would probably have taken possession of the whole of Gaul, if Galla Placidia had not immediately dispatched Aetius to fight them.[18] Ravenna saved the western Mediterranean by blocking the Visigoths off from an access to the sea. Gothic and Vandal horsemen had in fact proved their superiority in the field of battle, and the empire could only maintain a degree of superiority by maintaining their dominion over the Mediterranean ports, which prevented the barbarians from taking control of the maritime trade (the barbarians had not yet abandoned Alaric's and Ataulf's dreams of greatness). It should come as no surprise that a law of 419 prescribed the death penalty for anyone caught teaching ship-building techniques to barbarians (*Code of Theodosius*, 9, 40, 24).[19]

By this stage a process of assimilation between Romans and barbarians had commenced in the West, in spite of the disputes and frequent conflicts.[20] The empire attempted to react, at least in the cases of a real threat. For example, the very severe measures against mixed marriages did not affect such unions in general, but the cases in which closeness between barbarians and provincials could put imperial authority at risk.[21] In any event, the identity of the Gothic community in 428 was sufficiently strong to justify its isolation from the Roman one, to their mutual advantage.

The identity of the barbarians was also defined by their religious choices. The best example is that of the Goths' Christianity, which was a particularly radical form of Arianism, to which they had in turn converted other Germanic peoples, such as the Vandals. It is argued that the barbarians' Arianism helped to preserve their identity, although not all the sources justify this interpretation; for instance, a chauvinist historian like Procopius would argue that the Goths were too ignorant to give any importance to doctrinal controversies (*Gothic War*, 4, 4, 11). Leaving aside the radical positions adopted in religious writings, it must not have been uncommon to find "catholics" among the Goths.[22]

While the Visigothic center in the region was Toulouse, the center for Roman culture and traditions was Arelate (now Arles). At the beginning of the fifth century, some people had been proposing that the imperial court should be moved there, paradoxically because of the Visigothic raids into Italy.[23] The capital was in fact shifted to Ravenna, but Arelate remained one of the empire's strongholds. Patroclus, the city's powerful bishop, had very effectively reorganized the Church of Gaul and transformed his see into a key post. Anyone who held that position had influence over the appointment of other bishops. This autonomy had however caused concern among the authorities, to the point that Felix had Patroclus killed in 426, and then had the diocese put under the direction of the monk Elladius (or Euladius), who was probably a man of straw preferred by both Rome and Ravenna.

In 428, the diocese of Arelate was once again in the hands of an important figure, the ageing and highly respected Honoratus, the founder of the community at Lérins, the monastery of the "Island of Saints."[24]

The establishment of monastic communities on small islands in the western Mediterranean was one of the western interpretations of the more radical monastic experiences developed in Egypt and Syria (other monks, like those of Jura, preferred the forest). Christians sought out alternative models, as shown by the enormous development of monastic foundations in Gaul: in the absence of deserts, small islands seemed ideal for a hermit's life. For some time, communities of ascetics had been established on various very small islands among the Balearics and in the Tyrrhenian Sea. Around 415, the poet Rutilius Namatianus contemptuously described the vulgar ascetics who "avoided the light" and lived alone on the Island of Capraria, off the coast of northern Etruria (Rutilius, *De reditu suo*, I, 439–52). Lérins, which was sufficiently far off the coast and infested with snakes, made it possible to recreate that climate of suffering and privation so beloved of eastern monks. In Roman legislation, banishment to an island (*relegatio in insulam*) was a severe punishment, considered much worse than exile.

The election of Honoratus confirmed the enormous influence of the Lérins community, in spite of the suspicions and accusations of heresy. The doctrines of so-called "semi-Pelagianism," which were disliked by both Rome and the court in Ravenna, were in fact circulating at Lérins.[25] The monks on the island also met with disapproval because of their origins: it was said that they came from distant and barbaric regions. The truth was that many aristocrats from northern Gaul had fled the advance of the barbarians and sought refuge in the monasteries of Provence, and their high level of education had contributed to the development of Lérins. However, these notables, who gave away their own property, were considered potential subversives, and alarmed the civil and ecclesiastical authorities by offending caste sensitivities.

The ecclesiastical authorities did not succeed in subduing the community and bringing it back to heel. On 25 July 428, in an attempt to reinforce his authority in a region that had become more or less independent under Patroclus, Pope Celestine sent a long letter to all the bishops of southern Gaul, which unsurprisingly started with an "image" problem: the pope censored the coarse habit worn by the monks at Lérins, even when they left the monastery to take up an episcopal see (Celestine, *Epistle* 4, 1). The authorities were alarmed by this trend: by continuing to wear a monk's habit, bishops like Honoratus emphasized their "subversive" decision to renounce their worldly lives, and more particularly they paraded their membership in a community that did not always accept the authority of Rome and Ravenna. The purpose of this preamble by Celestine was to demonstrate the importance of showing the Church to be united in its adherence to shared rules, and closely integrated into the framework of empire and its local communities. The epistle continued with a threat to apply more severe criteria in the recruitment and training of the higher ranks in the Church and a criticism of the election of "foreign" bishops without the support of the relevant city authorities.

Celestine's move may have set a precedent of some importance, one that heralded future developments in papal authority,[26] but the monastic communities were too strong to give in entirely to the directives from Rome. As with the Monastery of Saint Euprepius near Antioch in which Nestorius had been trained, or that of Hippo ("a Numidian Saint-Sulpice," as Franco Cordero has defined it), Lérins too was far too prestigious to be recalled to order merely by a letter.[27] Honoratus enjoyed the further advantage of belonging to an important senatorial family (Saint Hilary of Arles, *Sermo Sancti Honorati*, 4), and this guaranteed a support network in Rome and the most important cities. It is not impossible, as has recently been suggested, that Honoratus was the brother of Paulinus of Pella and therefore from the same family as the great Ausonius of Bordeaux.[28] Finally, the reaction to Nestorius's doctrinal positions, which soon involved the prelates of the West as well, required the support of the monks, and this allowed the school of Lérins to maintain a degree of political influence over the territory. Most religious figures trained in Lérins went on to govern important dioceses in Gaul, as in the case of Eucherius who became bishop of Lyons after 430.[29]

The same cultural environment could be found in Marseilles, another bustling port vital to trade.[30] The bishop of the city had benefited from the fall of Patroclus in Arles, and it appears that he took too much pleasure in it.[31] In 428, John Cassian, the founder of the extremely important Abbey of Saint-Victor, was still very much an active player. He was an exceptional religious figure in many ways, starting with his origins. Born around 365, he came from "Scythia" (Gennadius, *De viris illustribus*, 61): in other words, he was a barbarian, perhaps a Goth. Like so many monks of his time, he had been trained in the East, first in Bethlehem and later in the Egyptian desert, where they practiced an extremely radical asceticism. Driven out of Egypt and banned from Constantinople, Cassian took refuge in Rome, where he associated with important clerics like the deacon Leo, who would become famous as Pope Leo the Great. Later, perhaps after Alaric's sack of Rome, Cassian moved to Gaul.[32]

Cassian's most important work is made up of two complementary texts: a treatise on the *Institutes of Monastic Life* and the collection of twenty-four *Conferences* dedicated to Honoratus on his election. The *Institutes* had been commissioned by Castor, the bishop of a small diocese without any monasteries, so that "the lifestyle of the Egyptians and the Orientals can be organized" in these regions (Cassian, Introduction to *Institutes*, 3). Cassian was a superficial theologian, but he proved to be a talented popularizer: he suggested some simple meditations, inspired by his long experience in Egypt and based on the example of the ascetics he had frequented, to whom he attributed the spiritual arguments brought together in the *Conferences*. The bishops of Gaul spread his thought and raised it to a model of the monastic ideal.[33]

For Cassian, monks needed to examine doctrines by examining the substance without being dazzled by their apparent radiance, in the same manner that a money changer assays a coin (Cassian, *Conferences*, 1; 24). They had to follow the example of the Egyptian ascetics, whose simple and uncontaminated lives were largely inspired by the desert environment, which constituted a "special benefice" (*Conferences*, 17, 7). At the same time, however, the abbot criticized the radical exhibitionism of those who flaunted their own abstinence or, worse, considered obstinacy to be a virtue and refused to change their attitude (*Conferences*, 17, 21ff.). The perfect monk had to be "ambidextrous": with his "right" side he had to develop his spirituality, while his "left" one, which was exposed to the temptations of this world, provided him with a proper balance by avoiding both worldly sins and the false humility of a spectacular display of asceticism (*Conferences*, 6, 10). Cassian advised monks to learn by heart many passages from the Scriptures, even without understanding them. As a result of solitary meditation, they would appear in a new light, partly because they required an allegorical explanation (*Conferences*, 14, 10). All kinds of subjects can be found in the Scriptures, even for "minds lacking culture and incapable of a perfect penetration of mystical meaning" (*Conferences*, 8, 3).

Recollections of a classical education worried Cassian the "Scythian." He preferred an imperfect but "pure" knowledge of the Scriptures to an impeccable but not orthodox religious culture: there were many cases of ignorant and uncultured saints, while so many biblical experts were heretics, orthodox sinners, and obviously Jews (*Conferences*, 14, 14). It was better to follow the words of a wise Egyptian abbot:

> I find that my knowledge of literature is yet another obstacle to my salvation, over and above the problems of the spirit, which are common to everyone, and the temptations of the external world, which assail individuals when they are still weak. Because of the insistence of my teachers and my perseverance in my studies, I possess a fairly profound knowledge of the profane science. From when I was little and had only just started my studies, they have filled my head with poetic figures, foolish fairy tales, and warrior deeds. So now when I pray, all these things come back to mind. If I sing psalms or ask forgiveness for my sins, I remember the pagan poems and relive heroic battles. If these visions continue to deceive me, my soul will not be able to aspire to contemplate heavenly things. Therefore, I cry every day so that these images might disappear. (Cassian, *Conferences*, 14, 12)

While the monks of Provence preached meditation inspired by the most extreme eastern models, General Aetius was leading his *foederati* to defend an empire that was not yet with its back to the wall. But the relative vitality of the imperial system basically depended on raising taxes to finance the legions and the manufacture of weapons. And not only that, some imperial territories had had to make room for the numerous refugees from wars and invasions.[34] Many citizens no longer accepted the tax burden, and Rome was inexorably losing its authority: some refugees, who fled Aquitaine to escape the Visigoths, found the situation no better in Arles or Marseilles, and ultimately had to seek refuge elsewhere, as in the case of Prosper of Aquitaine, who finally had to move to Rome.[35] Others even thought about returning to their places of origin, even though they were occupied by the barbarians. This, at least, was the opinion of the restless Paulinus of Pella, the heir of a powerful family, whose properties were as far afield as Macedonia and Aquitaine.[36] Paulinus, who converted in 420, wrote an autobiographical poem many years later, in which he tells of all his misfortunes, which started with the expropriation of his lands during the Visigothic occupation of Aquitaine. Paulinus decided to seek refuge in Marseilles, where he owned an estate he called a "vegetable patch" and a number of slaves. In spite of all his efforts to get his finances in order, the "totally unstable times" to which he refers in his poems had reduced his wealth so much that he considered the idea of returning to Bordeaux, in Visigothic territory (Paulinus of Pella, *Eucharisticus*, 540–44).

The mood of the times is vividly described by Salvian of Marseilles, a monk trained in Lérins, who asserted that barbarian invasions were a scourge of God in his *De gubernatione Dei* (*On the Government of God*, which was written around the middle of the century), but even this was preferable to the rapaciousness of imperial taxation and the tyranny of local notables. The latter were considered to be on a par with brigands, as they were responsible for collecting taxes, a practice that barbarians were unaware of, at least according to the paradoxical Salvian (Salvian, *De gubernatione Dei*, 5, 36).[37] Thus the barbarian nations were idealized for their primitiveness but also their humility.[38] In reality, the "barbarians" wanted to be integrated into the imperial structures: even though they wanted an outlet into the Mediterranean, the Visigoths had chosen the prestigious and flourishing city of Toulouse as their capital.[39] As in the famous poem by Constantine Cavafy "Waiting for the Barbarians," the monks of Gaul seemed almost to perceive the barbarians as the solution to their problems, in the hope that the catastrophe would sweep away the representatives of a power that appeared increasingly weak but, in spite of this, no less arrogant. That power was accompanied by dissolute customs and even images of a civilization that they no longer acknowledged as their own.

The catastrophe was, however, delayed by Aetius, who at that time was starting his irresistible rise to prominence, and in 428 he achieved an important victory over the Franks, which was recorded in the chronicle of Prosper of Aquitaine: "The territory of Gaul close to the Rhine, which the Franks had occupied in order to take possession of it, was recovered by force of arms by Aetius" (Prosper, *Chronicle*, Year 428). We know from Cassiodorus that the general did not restrict himself to defeating the barbarians, but carried out a massacre (Cassiodorus, *Chronicle*, Year 428). The meager information provided by chroniclers does not do justice to the importance of the event: even thirty years after Aetius's death, this victory echoed through a poem by Sidonius Apollinaris, which even gives the location of the battle: the locality of *vicus Helenae* (Hélesmes, a village in Artois). In recalling the battles, Sidonius increases the pathos by telling us that a Frankish wedding was taking place on a hill close by:

> A barbarian wedding song resounded on a nearby hill,
> with Scythian [i.e., barbarian] dances and a blond young woman,
> who with a blond husband was being married.
>   (SIDONIUS APOLLINARIS, 5, 218–20)[40]

The "blond" bride and bridegroom were being united in marriage in accordance with the Frankish tradition, which was very different from the Roman one and still free of Christian elements (unlike the other Germanic populations, such as the Goths and the Vandals, the Franks had not yet been converted). Having little interest in the private life of barbarians, Sidonius does not specify the type of marriage that was being celebrated, and he restricts himself to defining the barbarian dances as "Scythian" on the basis of current literary usage, by which "Scythian" was the equivalent of "Goth," which in turn covered all foreigners of Germanic origin. The wedding ceremony probably concluded a process of *muntehe*, a kind of "gifting" of the young woman by the father to the bridegroom. However, the bride might also have been seduced or kidnapped (*raubehe*).[41]

The wedding ended in bloodshed as horsemen trampled the guests. The Franks who were crushed by Aetius had mainly settled on the right bank of the lower Rhine, and should not be confused with the Rhineland Franks, the Ripuarian Franks mentioned in the sources of the Merovingian age; these were the Salian Franks, led by King Chlodio, who settled in Artois at the beginning of the fifth century.[42] From 420, they had taken advantage of the political crisis in Ravenna to plunder the region between the Rhine and the Moselle.[43] Aetius had already concluded his campaign against the Visigoths, who had thus lost their hopes of obtaining a Mediterranean port. The purpose of the general's expedition in 428 was to drive the Franks from Cologne and Mainz, important cities in the Rhineland which had been occupied since 423.[44]

After his defeat by Aetius, Chlodio had to sign a treaty with Rome and he settled with his people in the "fiscal" territory of Tournai in what is now Belgium. It is not impossible that this defeat favored the emerging group of the Frankish aristocracy, that of the Salians. Within a century, this group would extend its territories to the detriment of the Visigoths. The Salian dynasty, better known as the Merovingian one, gradually consolidated its territory with important consequences for the history of Europe.

Aetius's victory marked a further step in his brilliant career; within a few years, he would become one of the great protagonists of the empire. Unlike other leading generals, Aetius was not of barbarian origin, but he had got to know both Goths and Huns in his youth, and because of this experience he had acquired all the characteristics of a warlord, feared and respected by imperial officials and barbarians alike. This provoked the envy of other court dignitaries, starting with Felix, a leading exponent of the court faction most hostile to the barbarization of the army.[45] But Aetius had the support of Galla Placidia, which, along with his military successes that had delayed the breakup of the empire, made him in some ways untouchable.[46]

Sidonius wanted to use the dramatic images he evoked to portray the clash of civilizations supposedly taking place. Reality was somewhat different: the two armies did not differ that much one from the other. The Franks Aetius defeated in 428 were not a single ethnic group, but a mixed group of often-heterogeneous populations, also swelled by some Roman deserters. But most importantly, the great majority of Aetius's horsemen were of barbarian origin. The presence of external populations within the Roman army was nothing new, but during this period the phenomenon had reached exceptional proportions. For at least thirty years, Roman policy had had to adapt to the constant presence of foreigners. These tribes, which had settled in the vast areas of western and central Europe, were largely of Germanic origin, as in the case of the Franks, but there were also Iranic tribes such as the Alans or Turkic tribes such as the Huns.[47] In exchange for the right to settlement, these *foederati* were required to fight for Rome against other barbarians.[48] For example, Aetius's horsemen were mainly Huns. This should come as no surprise, as following Felix's operations in Pannonia, the Huns were at peace with Rome. As they were not yet united under the authority of a single king, they found it more useful to serve the empire as *foederati* than to fight against it.[49]

Moreover, as Peter Brown has pointed out not without a trace of irony, Theodosius II was himself a quarter barbarian, given that his mother Eudoxia was the daughter of the Frankish official Bauto.[50] Most military power was in the hands of generals of barbarian origin: in the East an Alan called Ardabur, who had been consul in 427, was one of the powerful military leaders.[51] In spite of resistance from traditionalists, the integration of "external" elements was continuing apace. A few years earlier, Galla Placidia had married the Visigothic king Ataulf, by whom she had had a son; if that son had survived, he could have claimed descent from Theodosius the Great, with all the resulting dynastic implications.[52] As time went by, these "ethnic" groups developed sophisticated strategies to define their affinity with Rome. The Franks would trace their genealogy back to Troy, and the Goths would insist upon their superiority compared with the other invading peoples.[53] Using the same ideological arms as the Romans, the Franks could thus distinguish themselves from the other "barbarian" peoples of Germanic origin, without however wishing to confuse themselves with the Romans; indeed, they wished to put themselves on the same plane.

Nevertheless, Western Europe, involved as it was in armed conflict and political upheavals, was inevitably separating off from the "Mediterranean" world, even though the "Roman" identity and the "barbarian" one were much more confused and indistinct than would appear in our sources.[54] We encounter this at both the ideological level and the cultural one. For example, Salvian of Marseille, a radical critic of the empire, showed contempt for the traditions of Roman Gaul and introduced a kind of proto-medieval point of view.[55] In his rejection of the values of Roman civilization, which he considered the legacy of a lackluster form of paganism, Salvian praised the barbarians for being uncontaminated by such "civilized" practices as theatrical shows and circus games, which were both extravagant and unseemly (*De gubernatione Dei*, 6, 35ff.). These attitudes were by no means isolated ones. In the West, monastic culture fought and won the battle against Roman immorality and corruption (*Romana vitiositas*). Monks were not content with just objecting to the spectacle of circus games, but took to attacking other elements of ancient urban customs, such as public baths. The excess of personal hygiene, which had once distinguished the Roman from the barbarian, was now held in contempt and condemned as a symptom of sin and lasciviousness. Moreover, in Celtic areas, baths were associated with ancestral therapeutic practices, now considered forms of paganism.[56]

The abandonment of provincial territories by the Roman authorities accelerated this transformation. The most rapid changes occurred in many sites in Britannia where, around 420, the great *villae* appear to have lost their original function, and the final phases of occupation show a trend towards simpler settlements in which the existing facilities were adapted to more sober and, in many cases, more rudimentary lifestyles. Initially this reuse of *villae*, which British archeologists have called "squatter occupations," has been explained by the immiseration of the population. However, this phenomenon could be explained in another way. The increasingly austere, frugal, and spartan living spaces may have also been due to the adoption of the values of simple living promoted by monasticism. In any case, it went hand in hand with the abandonment of pagan places of worship, which appears to have started after 410, although in some cases they were transformed into monasteries.[57]

The situation in Britannia reflected the political and military upheavals in the western sector of the empire. The official demobilization of the island occurred around 410, but it was not entirely abandoned. Ravenna decided to discontinue its control of Hadrian's Wall and the western borders of Roman Britain, but it continued to garrison the forts to defend the eastern and southern coast known as the Saxon Shore. The administration of the former province was entrusted to leading figures in the local Celtic aristocracy, which had been Romanized to some degree. The medieval chronicles speak of the semilegendary figure of Vortigern or Guorthigirn (Welsh *Gwrtheyrn*, meaning "highest lord"), who was in control of Britannia around the mid-fifth century.[58] One of these sources, *History of the Britons* (*Historia Brittonum*), which has been attributed to a certain Nennius (9th c.), claims that 428 was the date of an epoch-making event for the island: Vortigern, in power since 425, is supposed to have summoned Saxon mercenaries, led by the brothers Hengist and Horsa, to assist him in defending the country from attacks by the Picts and the Scots.[59] Vortigern's decision proved to have disastrous consequences: the Angles and the Saxons were interested in the more Romanized territory, while the Celts were forced to abandon their lands and move to the current territories of Wales and Cornwall. Others crossed the channel and settled in Brittany (so-called because it had become *Britannia minor* or "Little Britain").[60]

The nature of the sources is such that we cannot produce a precise chronology for "sub-Roman" or "pre-Arthurian" Britain. The figure of Vortigern, although not entirely without historical foundation, has been transformed into a kind of negative precursor of King Arthur.[61] Even the archeologists do not reach the same conclusions: those who tend to uphold the tradition of Britannia's "splendid isolation" believe that the early Anglo-Saxon period caused an abandonment of the cities. Unlike Merovingian Gaul, where the Roman urban model was largely maintained by the new rulers, the cities of Britannia appear to have survived through inertia as "empty shells."[62] However, another tendency among scholars puts the emphasis on the elements of continuity, such as the *villae* of Roman tradition which can be found as late as the seventh century.[63] The new anthropological perspectives will make it possible in the future to clarify further the problems of the "Dark Ages."[64] Besides, Vortigern was not an isolated case: Celtic sources record a leader in northern Britannia during this period, who was known as Coel (from the Latin *Coelius* or *Coelestius*), and much later as the Old King Cole who appears in medieval literature.[65]

Some chronicles seem to date the first Saxon incursions to the time of the military crisis in the first decade of the century.[66] In 428, however, the empire appears to have shown a renewed interest in Britannia, at least for strategic reasons. Following operations against the Franks, Aetius could then attend to the defense of the coast along the Channel and the North Sea.[67] Ravenna's reawakened concern for Britannia coincided with the interests of the Church, which was worried about the presence of Pelagians, who had been persecuted as heretics since 418, and had found a safe haven in Britain, Pelagius's native land (Prosper of Aquitaine, *Contra collatorem*, 21). During this period, Germanus, the energetic bishop of Auxerre, was preparing a "catholic" mission to Britannia, which would take place in 429 and have important military repercussions: the cleric is supposed to have routed both the Picts and the Saxons while leading the army in person (Prosper of Aquitaine, *Chronicle*, Year 429; Constantius, *Life of Saint Germanus*, 16–18). Like

Rabbula in Syria, Germanus was an imperial notable who had been put in charge of a diocese.[68] Thanks to his military education, he knew how to line up an army and direct a battle.[69]

The strategy for Germanus's campaign in Britannia was very probably put together by Aetius in line with papal directives.[70] It should not surprise us that information of this kind is lacking in the biography of the saint written by Constantius of Lyons.[71] According to Constantius, Germanus and his associate Lupus of Troyes were both sent as missionaries following the decisions of the council of bishops held in Gaul. Unlike Prosper of Aquitaine, who put a proper emphasis on the role of Pope Celestine, the hagiographer attempted to demonstrate that the merit of Germanus's mission went entirely to the Gaulish bishops, while there was probably a need to note the influence of figures such as the deacon Palladius, who was mentioned by Prosper.[72] Ultimately, the activities of evangelizers like Germanus (and, shortly afterwards, Palladius in Ireland) were very much affected by Roman policy: even the far west did not yet constitute a self-contained reality.

·VIII·

Waiting for the Vandals

AETIUS'S OPERATIONS in 428 managed to regain ground in the Rhineland and on the Channel, but the far West remained in the hands of barbarians who had settled in the Iberian Peninsula twenty years earlier. Many of these events were recorded in the chronicle of the Galician Hydatius, which covered the years 379–469. Having spent his youth in the East, Hydatius became bishop of his native land, "Galicia, situated at the end of the world."[1] The cleric was obsessed with chronology, which he used to justify his eschatological beliefs: basing himself on an apocryphal letter sent by the apostle Thomas to Christ, he firmly believed that the end of the world would occur on 27 May 482.[2]

For Hydatius, the "third year of Valentinian Augustus" (i.e., 428) was the rift. Before this date, the chronicler had been able to draw on other sources, but after it, he was cast out to "the pokiest part of the Roman Empire" and therefore forced to narrow his horizons dramatically (Hydatius, Preface, *Chronicle*, 7).[3] His Galicia was officially administered by the Roman Empire, but the situation was increasingly unstable. It would shortly be invaded by the *Suebi* or Swabians, who held the region until 585. They had enlarged their area of operations because of an event that had been under preparation for some years: the migration of the Vandals from Spain to Africa, which occurred during 429.

The Vandals, descendants of one of the most ancient Germanic tribal groups (who were in turn divided into two ethnic groups: the *Hasdingi* and the *Silingi*), entered the Iberian Peninsula in October 409, along with the Swabians and the Iranic Alans.[4] This coalition of barbarians appears to have followed a well worked-out plan to take advantage of the weakness of Roman central government and settle in new territories with the intention of colonizing them (Hydatius, 35). The wars and diplomatic activity of the following years helped to confirm their position in Iberia which, around 428, was divided more or less into three large territories: the Tarraconensis, which remained under Roman control, Galicia, which was officially Roman but in reality territory disputed between the Swabians and the Hasdingian Vandals, and Baetica (i.e., southern Spain), which was occupied by the Silingian Vandals.[5] Hydatius and other chroniclers of the time depict a dreadful scene of uninterrupted conflicts, rebellions, and invasions. However, unlike other regions, the sites and necropolises of Spain do not provide any indications of migrating peoples. Clearly, the Vandals, Alans, and Swabians assimilated the local culture in terms of physical artifacts.[6]

Many Christian authors of Late Antiquity and the Middle Ages helped to create the well-known image of a fierce and destructive people, which is still associated with the Vandals. In reality, however, they were no more "barbarian" than the other peoples.[7] Their reputation for being uncouth, ill-disciplined, and thuggish warriors is documented by this fifth-century epigram, conserved in the collection known as the *Latin Anthology*:

> With the Goths who say *eils* or *scapia, matzia ia drincan*,
> no one dares to produce poetry of any worth.
>
> (*Latin Anthology*, 285)

The German words in the epigram are not Gothic, but have been identified as one of the rare examples of the Vandalic language (the term "Goths" used in the epigram is synonymous with "barbarians"). The poet lists what were for him the key words in the Vandalic lifestyle: apart from the greeting *eils* (*Heil*), the expression *scapia, matzia ia drincan* is of considerable interest, and appears to refer to the favorite pastimes of the barbarian soldiers: "produce" or "create" (an erotic allusion?), "eat" and "drink."[8]

The year 428 was crucial for the Vandals as well. Their king, Gunderic, conquered the important city of Hispalis (Seville), and then died "in the clutches of a demon," which was, according to Hydatius (89), a just punishment for having profaned a local church.[9] The throne then passed to his half-brother (or possibly stepbrother), Gaiseric or

Genseric, probably through a law of succession based on seniority.[10] We have been left a very effective literary portrait of this great warrior, who reigned for nearly fifty years over the Vandals and the Alans:

> He was of medium stature, and lame because of a riding accident. Thoughtful and taciturn, he despised comforts; he was avaricious and irascible, a capable leader of peoples, a sower of discord, and always ready to spread hate. (Jordanes, *History of the Goths*, 168)[11]

In the meantime, his men were preparing for the invasion of Africa. An expedition of this kind required the fitting out or confiscation of a considerable number of ships (between 500 and 1000), and certainly could not be done overnight.[12] The Vandals had already carried out some preliminary sorties to the African continent from their strategic bases in Baetica and the Balearics.[13] They undoubtedly had the support of the *Mauri*, who controlled large tracts of northwestern Africa that had been abandoned by the Romans for more than a century. In 428, when everything was ready for the final attack, Gaiseric was informed of the immediate reaction of the Swabians, who with their king, Heremigarius (or Hermigarius), set about plundering Lusitania.[14] Close to Emerita (Mérida), they were halted and killed; Heremigarius fled and perished in the River Anas (now the Guadiana), while the Swabians continued to sack Galicia. The Vandals were now ready for their African adventure.

The empire looked on anxiously at these movements of peoples, and in recent years had tried to stem the rise of this new menace. In 422, Ravenna had supported the Swabians in their struggle with the Vandals by sending General Castinus along with Gothic reinforcements. He was accompanied by a highly experienced official, the military tribune Bonifacius, who was also a protégé of Galla Placidia's. However, the court intrigues and the rivalries between Castinus and Bonifacius had compromised the operation from the very beginning. Bonifacius had taken his troops back to Italy, while Castinus, who left on his own to fight the Vandals, was defeated and had to withdraw to Tarragona. To avoid further disputes, Placidia sent Bonifacius to Africa with the rank of *comes*, or in other words as the principal military leader.[15]

It very much appears that no one was expecting the attack in Africa, which would lead in a very short time to the formation of the Vandalic

Kingdom. Subsequent events proved that Gaiseric had made the right decision. Of course, the Iberian Peninsula also contained fertile territories, with extensive urban developments particularly in the south. But the Maghreb had great advantages, because it allowed the Vandals to control the maritime trade with Italy. From the Straits of Gibraltar to Cyrenaica, these lands were the richest and most fertile sector of the Western Roman Empire, and the key to domination of the western Mediterranean. The metropolis of Carthage, which long ago lost its associations with the Punic Empire, was one of the richest ports in the Mediterranean, from which cargo ships sailed laden with grain to supply Italy and Rome, especially after the foundation of Constantinople: the needs of the new capital had diverted most of the produce from Egypt and transformed the provinces of North Africa into the "granary of Rome."

In Africa, the imperial estates had grown to cover vast areas, including the land on which cities were built and property confiscated from pagan temples.[16] Apart from the enormous estates, which comprised a great variety of rural holdings, there were also the properties of rich and influential senatorial families. These agrarian complexes brought considerable financial advantages for their owners, because of the fertility of the land and the low cost of labor in the form of the impoverished *coloni* often mentioned in Saint Augustine's correspondence.[17] There was no shortage of the usual cases of oppressive taxation by corrupt local officials. Ravenna tried to rein them in with two laws against the excesses of tax collectors, who connived with the local administrations. According to the provisions of these laws issued on 27 April 429, tax arrears could be paid directly to the provincial tax office. The empire was not only trying to fight injustice by introducing these laws; it wanted to recover funds needed to pay soldiers. Indeed, taxes would be collected by the military if the deadline of four months was not observed in accordance with the provisions of the edict (*Code of Theodosius*, 12, 1, 185 and 186).

Ravenna was thus attempting to resolve the problems of an overextended territory that was increasingly difficult to control. Besides, the real lord of Africa was the extremely powerful *comes* Bonifacius. This general, who was possibly a native of the Balkan provinces, had enormous experience behind him: he had fought against the Goths (at the command of other Gothic *foederati*), and on various occasions he had routed the indigenous tribes who terrorized the cities of Africa. A military man of such caliber obviously had many political enemies. His greatest adversary was the patrician Felix, the dignitary in Ravenna most closely linked to Constantinople.[18] In 426, Bonifacius lost Placidia's support because of his rivalry with Aetius and perhaps his marriage to Pelagia, a wealthy barbarian who had not entirely repudiated the Arian faith in spite of her conversion to Catholicism. In fact, their daughter was baptized by an Arian priest, which caused some anxiety to Saint Augustine (*Epistle* 220). Moreover, Bonifacius was accused of excessive indulgence to heretics: it appears that his men (mainly Goths and therefore Arians) had been allies of the followers of Donatus of Carthage, who had been putting themselves forward as an alternative to the official Church for more than a century. In 411, the "Donatists" had been outlawed, but a few communities, particularly in the Numidian countryside, managed to avoid the harsh repression.[19]

Placidia, possibly incited by Aetius, was unhappy with the increasing autonomy of the *comes* of Africa, who enjoyed the support of many influential western senators (Theophanes, *Chronicle*, 1, 95).[20] Such a powerful general could have become a danger to the new imperial unity. In 427 Placidia, probably on advice from Felix, recalled him to Ravenna. Suspecting a plot to eliminate him, Bonifacius refused, and by way of reply Ravenna sent an army against him under the command of three generals. However, the western court had underestimated the military skills of the *comes* of Africa and the loyalty of his men, mainly Gothic *foederati* who had entered into some kind of direct pact with their commander. It was one of the first recorded examples of the semiprivate militias that would later be called *buccellarii*.[21] The troops sent by Ravenna were defeated and the three generals killed (Prosper, *Chronicle*, Year 427).[22]

In 427 and 428, the empire entrusted the command of the operations in this new civil war to another Goth, the commander Sigisvult, who managed to take Carthage, while Bonifacius withdrew to the hinterland. The conflict is recorded in an apocryphal correspondence, which attempts to rehabilitate the general by presenting the events in rather a simplistic manner. In one of these letters, Saint Augustine alludes to the public enemy who came from Italy and exhorts Bonifacius to fear "neither Goth nor Hun" (Pseudo-Bonifacius, *Epistle* 4).[23]

The situation suddenly changed during 428. The imminent Vandal attack forced Ravenna to suspend the hostilities. The Italian aristocracy, who had supported Sigisvult, now wanted an agreement with the *comes* of Africa. Felix himself, now facing the increasing power of Aetius (who had taken advantage of the imbalance in power), had no interest in maintaining the rivalry with Bonifacius, the man most suited to take on the invasion with an army that in recent years had been drastically reduced in size while many African territories were gradually being occupied by the *Mauri*.[24] Darius, an eminent figure, was sent from Italy to negotiate the peace and reassure Bonifacius of the senate's benevolence (Augustine, *Epistles* 229 and 230).[25] As a guarantee, the general sent Darius a hostage called Verimodus, probably his son.[26]

At the same time, the Church was bringing its influence to bear on the African provinces, by exploiting the prestige of the most respected cleric in the West: Augustine of Tagaste, who for many years was the bishop of the vast diocese of Hippo (now Annaba/Bona on the coast of eastern Algeria).[27] In 428, Augustine was seventy-four; two years earlier he had finished writing one of his most ambitious works: the twenty-two books of *The City of God*, a meditation that mixed theology and history. The same spirit animated some contemporary projects in monastic communities, such as the *Theopolis* located on the Gaulish side of the southern Alps, to which Dardanus, the former prefect of Gaul, had retired a few years earlier.[28] We do not know if this community-microcosm was founded before or after its literary formulation, *The City of God*. We do know that Dardanus and Augustine were writing to each other, and in their different ways, both were trying to find answers to the misgivings that pervaded the empire.

The search for an ideal community reflected African discontent with Rome, which was no longer able to protect the region, but continued to impose taxes and demand obedience. In Africa, Punic was widely spoken as well as Latin, and in a famous passage of *The City of God* Augustine reminds the reader that the imperious Roman capital had not only placed the yoke of its dominion on defeated peoples; it had also imposed Latin as the official language (Augustine, *The City of God*, 19, 7).

Among Augustine's letters that can be dated to 428, one of the most interesting is part of a group of twenty-nine epistles discovered in 1975 by the scholar Johannes Divjak in two manuscripts in Paris and

Marseilles.[29] It denounces the frequent abduction of women and children on behalf of slave traders (*mangones*), a relatively widespread practice in the ancient world, but one that Augustine perceived as a sign of the empire's decadence. The problem was not so much that the Christian empire condemned the practice of slavery, as that the suppliers of slaves no longer restricted themselves to obtaining slaves from the barbarians and had taken to attacking the cities and countryside of Numidia, such was the demand (Augustine, *Epistle* 199). With the backing of powerful and influential figures, they acted with complete impunity, partly because the abducted children (or in some case those sold by their parents) were taken to distant regions where there was little opportunity to prove their status as free people.[30] The victims were taken by force or trickery, and in some cases because their families feared reprisals:

> From what I have heard, one of these raids was carried out a few days ago against a small farm, in which the men were killed and the women and children taken away. Let us put aside this account, which might not be true as we are not told where the event was supposed to have taken place. I have, however, carried out my own personal investigation among those who have been ransomed by our Church from that miserable state of slavery. A young girl replied that she had been sold by the *mangones* after having been kidnapped in her parents' house. When I asked her if she was alone in the house, she replied that she was taken away in the presence of her parents, brothers, and sisters. She was too small to explain properly what had happened, but this was done by her brother who had come to take her home. These brigands had come during the night, and as they took them for barbarians, everyone preferred to hide, given that they dare not put up any resistance. (Augustine, *Epistle* 10*, 3)

While still dealing with the numerous problems of his diocese, Saint Augustine was at this time primarily involved in the defense of orthodoxy, which was threatened by social and political tensions. The complex reflections expressed in *The City of God* were formulated immediately after the sack of Rome in 410. But now, as the empire recovered, he needed to review at least partially the political aspects of the question, which were not restricted to Africa and the Empire of the West, but also concerned matters that only appeared to be distant, such as the abandonment of an aggressive policy towards Iran. Augustine wanted to demonstrate that a traditional god like *Terminus*, the protector of the Roman frontier, was in fact impotent: history had shown that the empire's frontiers were not inviolable.[31]

However, a just emperor who feared God could save his empire and defend its unity and borders. The examples to be followed were Constantine and Theodosius I (*City of God*, 5, 25ff.). Peter Brown considers these chapters to be "in themselves, some of the most shoddy in the *City of God*."[32] In truth, praise for the two Christian emperors (particularly Theodosius) seems artificial and unconvincing in a work of such philosophical depth, which purposefully avoids topical politics. But these apparently "shoddy" pages present an eloquent message: although in command of an earthly city and therefore subject to divine will, Constantine remained the ideal model of an *imperator felix*, which needed to be emulated or at least mourned. Long-lived, victorious and fortunate, he "had a long reign, and as the sole Augustus he ruled and defended the whole Roman world."[33] Moreover, "God even granted him the honor of founding a city, associated with the Roman Empire, the daughter, one might say, of Rome herself, but a city that contained not a single temple or image of any demon (*City of God*, 5, 25). Earthly salvation therefore came from Constantinople.

Towards the end of his life, Augustine was too tired and too disenchanted to hope for a new Constantine to rally his troops and lead Rome to recovery. The references to recent history in *The City of God* still reflected the crisis that had pitted one part of the empire against the other, but for Augustine, the idea of a Christian empire was a contradictory one. Of course, the emperors were Christian, and they fought to guarantee the unity of a territory that was also that of the Church, but the organization they commanded was founded on different values. After all, Augustine was mainly interested in the role of the Church in the fight against corrupt customs and the demons of profanity, and it was therefore necessary to be on one's guard against dangerous centrifugal forces fueled by the pressures coming from the barbarians and the lack of trust in imperial institutions. In 428, Prosper of Aquitaine and his lay friend from Arles, Hilary, wrote to their African mentor to report the horrors of "semi-Pelagianism" which was spreading through southern Gaul, and asked him to dispatch his most recent works (Augustine, *Epistles* 225 and 226).[34] In the same year in which Theodosius II issued new provisions against the heretics, Augustine decided to write a summary of this question in the first and only book of a treatise *On Heresies*, which has been dated to 428 or at the latest 429—a work that was never completed.[35]

The brief correspondence between Augustine and Quodvultdeus, the deacon and future bishop of Carthage (*Epistles* 221–224), reveals the reasons that drove the ageing Augustine to write the first part of the treatise at a time when he was overburdened with work (he was, among many other things, drawing up an inventory of his own works). The correspondence took place after the end of 427. Quodvultdeus asked his mentor to compose a compendium on heresies. Even in a metropolis like Carthage, wrote the deacon, "there are ignorant members of the clergy," who have no need of learned treatises, "but rather a more light-weight handbook (*commonitorium*) which simply lists all the heresies and the arguments against them. This would therefore be quite suffi-cient" (*Epistle* 221, 2–3). Augustine probably intended to complete the work later and develop a definition of heresy from a more systematic theological perspective.

Augustine was very aware of the problem of heresy from the mo-ment of his conversion to Christianity. Indeed, he had been sympa-thetic to the Manichaeans in his youth, and for many years, until as late as 387, he had frequented not only the "listeners" but also the "elect" of that sect (*Confessions*, 5, 10, 18), whose intelligence and insight he ad-mired.[36] Moreover this opinion was fairly widespread: a few years ear-lier, Pelagius had attempted to distinguish the "heretics" from the "fools" (Augustine, *De gestis Pelagii*, 6, 16). In the sixteenth book of *The City of God*, Augustine uses a reference to Saint Paul to attribute to the heretics a necessary function in the development of the true Christian doctrine. Even in an empire apparently subject to orthodoxy, the heretics dem-onstrated an "animated disorderliness on many questions relating to the Catholic faith."[37] In other words, a well-instructed Christian, provoked by the disputes, could better defend the true faith once the theological questions had been "more carefully examined, more clearly understood, and more earnestly propounded" (*City of God*, 16, 2, 1).[38] This, however, did not prevent the former Manichaean sympathizer from contributing to the repression by giving credence to foul slanders, such as the accusation that the Manichaean "elect" took a "Eucharist sprinkled with human semen," and accompanied these rites with the rape of young girls and other iniquities (*On Heresies*, 46, 9).

The first part of the treatise *On Heresies* is simply a list and classification of the endless variants of Christianity, drawing on fourth-century authors, particularly Philastrius of Brescia and Epiphanius of Salamis. The former had listed 180 heresies (apart from the pre-Christian ones in the Judaic tradition), and latter came up with "only" 80 (*Epistle* 222, 2). Epiphanius's treatise, written in Greek about half a century earlier, was entitled *Panarion*, which could be translated, with a slight distortion, as a "first-aid kit." The one by Philastrius, which was written in Latin a little later, expanded Epiphanius's catalogue by adding the heresies proclaimed by schismatic movements and other religious tendencies that were not necessarily heretical. But Quodvultdeus wanted something different for the Christians of Carthage. New heresies had appeared since the death of the two heresiologist bishops, but the main problem was that their works were far too long. And then, Epiphanius's was in Greek. Using a metaphor that emphasized the practical nature of this request, Quodvultdeus asked his mentor to put aside all "exotic flavors," for he preferred the "bread of Africa" (*Epistle* 223, 2–3).[39] Augustine decided to please the young deacon by compiling a list of heresies that supplemented Epiphanius's, without challenging Philastrius's record-breaking figure. Saint Augustine came up with eighty-eight heresies from the origins of Christianity to the year 428, and he put them in order of appearance, starting with Simon Magus and ending with Pelagius, whose heresy he particularly abhorred. Augustine also flavored the "bread of Africa" with a little "peasant" heresy (*rusticana*) that he had encountered in his own diocese—the Abelians. However, this group had long since been returned to orthodoxy.

As in the legislation enacted by Theodosius II, Augustine strove to formulate a definition at least of a heretic, if not of a heresy. Someone who spread false and perverse opinions was not necessarily a heretic: this much more dangerous individual was one who propagated and stubbornly maintained new opinions, while constantly parading the cardinal points of the faith.[40] Paradoxically, this was exactly the basis for the accusations against Nestorius, the man Theodosius II had wanted for the reaffirmation of orthodoxy in the East. Shortly afterwards, the bishop of Constantinople would be attacked by Greek and Latin bishops alike for his blundering attacks on the epithet *Theotókos* for the Virgin.

While they were burning down Arian places of worship in Constantinople, Bonifacius's Arian militias were preparing to defend Augustine's Africa. "According to some," the king of the Vandals is supposed to have converted his people, who until then had been orthodox Christians, to Arianism in 428 (Hydatius, 89). This was a decisive move in religious terms, but also in terms of its political and military aims. By converting to Arianism, the Vandals could dispossess the wealthy local churches without any qualms. These included the Church of Hispalis (Seville), which was desecrated by Gunderic (or perhaps more simply transformed into an Arian church). This would shortly also be the fate of the church in Carthage. By an irony of fate, it was Saint Augustine, a Carthaginian, who developed a new interpretation of the Roman concept of *bellum iustum* which was closer to modern thought. According to him, it was no longer a "legal war" in the original sense, but the concept of a genuinely "just war," which in effect meant a war desired by God.[41]

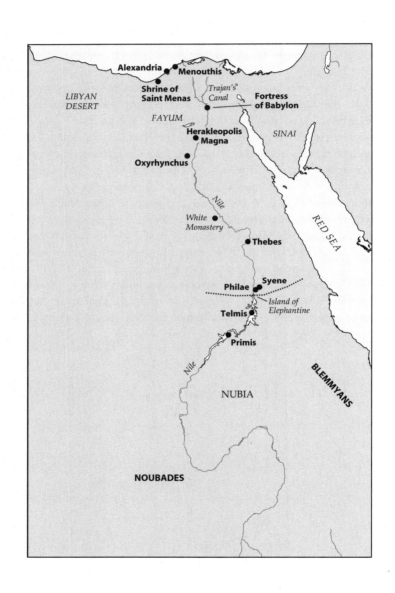

· IX ·

Pagans and Christians on the Nile

EGYPT was the most populous territory in the entire Mediterranean. Because of the exceptional fertility of its soil, the Nile Valley provided most of the grain that was shipped to Constantinople.[1] For about half a century, the province had been enjoying a special degree of autonomy. Power was divided between a multitude of civil, military, and ecclesiastical officials. The governor of the diocese, called the "Augustan Prefect," shared power with the military leaders each in charge of one of three areas: Thebais, Lower Egypt, and parts of the Libyan desert. Wars and invasions had strengthened the army's role, and thus the *comes* of Egypt who was in command of the army of the Lower Nile gradually acquired some prerogatives of a civil nature (*Code of Theodosius*, 6, 28, 8).[2] It was always a risk to give the military such power to the detriment of the civil authorities, and Theodosius II was aware of this, but there were such serious problems in the region that in the following decades it was even decided that all civil and military authority should be concentrated in the hands of a single official. Besides, the imperial presence had not gone beyond the borders of Egypt for more than a century—no further than the First Cataract. In 298, Diocletian had ordered the withdrawal of troops from their outposts in Nubian territory, and fixed the frontier at the Isle of Philae.

The most important fortress of the time was Babylon, whose walls have now been incorporated into the old Coptic district of Cairo. It was modified under Diocletian, and controlled navigation along Trajan's Canal, which linked the Nile to the Red Sea. This *Traiános potamós* was abandoned under the Arabs, but in the first half of the fifth century was still in working order: some papyri dated to 421–423 report that the canal was being cleaned every year in the spring, when the Nile was at its lowest level.[3] Thebes (Luxor), the capital of Thebais, was a crossroads for merchants and travelers. This Christianized world had not lost its curiosity for distant and exotic peoples, such as can be found in *De Gentibus Indiae et de Bragmanibus* (*Of the Peoples of India and the Brahmans*), a short ethnographic work which was an enormous success with the Byzantines and has been attributed to Palladius, the Galatian author of the *Lausiac History*. At some point *De Gentibus* was incorporated into the *Alexander Romance* and also translated into Latin. The work does present some problems in terms of dating and attribution, but it seems possible that the first part could be attributed to Palladius, who is thought to have relied on an account by an anonymous *scholastikós* (lawyer or rather imperial official) whom he met in Thebes. This person is supposed to have spent six years in India and held in slavery in a region not too far from the Bay of Bengal, where he was able to discover the wonders and curiosities of the country, particularly the asceticism of the Brahmans, who could be considered an example for Christian monks.[4]

However, the most important city was still the metropolis of Alexandria, an extremely important religious center, and the reference point for orthodoxy. The bishop of Alexandria, who in 428 was the great theologian Saint Cyril, had the privilege of sending permanent envoys to Constantinople, the so-called *apochrysárioi*, who were in fact ambassadors who ensured a channel of communication to the emperor and his court. In this manner, the patriarch could resist the rivalry of emerging episcopacies and intervene immediately in the event of theological disputes. From the end of 428, it was Cyril, with the pope's support, who provided the theological basis for condemning Nestorius.

The advance of Christianity was one of the things that kept the emperors away from Egypt, because they no longer needed to pay homage to its pharaonic past. In spite of the esteem in which great founders of monasticism were held, Constantinople had not forgotten the Arian crisis of the fourth century, when orthodox Alexandria distanced itself from the capital. The restoration of orthodoxy did not improve the situation, because the consolidation of the New Rome was damaging the fortunes of the Alexandrian church.

Cyril was a fierce adversary of heretics, Jews, and pagans, against whom he fought with every available means.[5] On the emperor's orders he undertook to destroy Emperor Julian's writings, which were circulating as a literary model (*Coptic History of the Church of Alexandria*, II, p. 42 Orlandi).[6] His power even extended to public order: the patriarch had a squad of about five hundred men under his command. These *parabalani* were part clergymen and part Praetorian Guard, and constituted a formidable deterrent against pagans in public spaces such as theaters and tribunals. These groups of bravoes were recruited among the trade associations, and there are records of such organizations in Rome and Antioch as well. Using violence and intimidation, they helped reinforce the authority of bishops, and in some cases they could artfully foment riots involving the poorer strata of the population and the most radical elements of monastic circles. In 415, the *parabalani* were the principal perpetrators of the lynching of Hypatia, a famous Neoplatonic philosopher and scientist, which aroused the indignation of pagan, semipagan and Christian intellectuals.[7] In the name of religious controversies, powerful groups therefore succeeded in steering popular discontent and identifying the pagans as a scapegoat in critical moments, such as famine or when the increasing needs of the imperial leviathan caused inflationary pressures (general expenses, money for troops, tributes and gifts to barbarians).[8] To escape these persecutions, pagan intellectuals had no choice but to seek a safer home, such as Athens or other more tolerant cities.

The Egyptian bishops, who were appointed by the patriarch, had the right to resolve religious disputes and could also rule on matters of private law, when they concerned the Christian community or just individual members of it. As it was their duty to look after the poor, they could requisition and channel funds for their assistance. This often hit the smaller landowners, who could, however, seek the protection of more powerful figures in the area in accordance with a law passed in 415 (*Code of Theodosius*, 11, 24, 6). Alan Bowman has described the situation as follows:

> The fragmentation of authority, the polarization of institutions which developed their own internal strength and coherence in a situation where lines of demarcation either did not exist or were in practice frequently ignored, is accompanied by the adaptation of

the imperial authority to circumstance and goes along with the gradual reduction of the area under administration to smaller and smaller units whose boundaries, geographical and administrative, were not impermeable.[9]

Egyptian Christianity had spread among the less Hellenized classes who spoke and wrote in Coptic, a language that derived from ancient Egyptian.[10] The development of a Coptic Church and the establishment of Coptic as a liturgical language in the monastic communities of the oasis and the Nile Valley had certainly favored the Christianization of the countryside, but at the same time it had separated the region culturally from the rest of the empire.

Shenute, a leading figure in Coptic monasticism, played a commanding role in the Egypt of Late Antiquity. He was the revered abbot of what is today known as the White Monastery, situated about ninety kilometers north of Luxor.[11] His works and the hagiography written in Coptic by his disciple Besa, contain numerous details on everyday life of the time, but unfortunately we cannot date them with the desired accuracy, as often occurs in literature of this kind. The exception is the reference to his participation in the Council of Ephesus, at which the abbot is supposed to have supported Cyril against Nestorius, although we cannot be certain that this was in fact the case. Besa portrays his spiritual father as a smallholder's son who was profoundly attached to his land. This is demonstrated by his reaction to the arrival of a messenger of Theodosius's. The emperor wished to have the holy man's blessing for himself and for Constantinople, and is supposed to have sent an official to bring him to the palace. But Shenute did not like to leave his land, particularly when he was ordered to. So God, the biographer tells us, had him perform a mystical flight to appear before Theodosius, bless him and convince him to discharge the military escort that had been sent to bring him to the palace.[12]

Shenute, author of numerous works in a complex and obscure Coptic, loved to play the part of the true representative of the Egyptian people and defender of the oppressed in the struggle against the local notables, who were the last members of a dwindling pagan aristocracy. He boasted that he had ransacked the home of a powerful landowner, subjected him to all kinds of humiliation, and repeatedly vilified him even after his death.[13] We have attempted to verify this episode histori-cally, but the fact is that we cannot take all these details literally. Such stories, provided with further details by Shenute's biographer, mainly served to increase the abbot's prestige.[14]

Charismatic religious figures like Shenute addressed the peasant masses of Egypt and preached the redemption of the humble and the dispossessed. However, Egyptian monasticism was less "rural" than we might think, and many monasteries were built in cities or more espe-cially on the outskirts of cities.[15] Members of these communities, who challenged episcopal authority just as they did in Constantinople, came from all social groups and not only from the *fellahin*. On the other hand, both the Greek and the Coptic hagiographies contributed con-siderably to the creation of this historical model, because of their wide circulation. Even though they were at least partly inaccurate, they did not lose any of their ideological significance. Of course, monasticism needs to be perceived as it really was historically, and therefore the rural social character attributed to the monastic movement in Egypt has to be somewhat diluted. The texts themselves are the principal evidence of the relationship between these social groups and the rural world, which was contrasted with the urban world of Alexandria, the bearer of "Hel-lenic" values and paganism that was far from silenced.

The Coptic monks zealously undertook to suppress traditional cults, whether Egyptian or foreign. A veritable surge of antipagan fanaticism spread throughout Egypt from 391 (the date of the destruction of the Serapeum of Alexandria) until at least 420. A law of 423 (*Code of Theo-dosius*, 16, 10, 24) attempted to mitigate these excesses in the eastern prefecture, but we do not know to what extent it was observed in all the provinces. It has long been believed that the advent of Christianity in Egypt was the result of an almost natural evolution, but study of the sources—particularly the hagiographies—does not support this the-ory.[16] Of course, Egyptian paganism had too many shades to be consid-ered a unitary tradition, but the more fanatical Christians, especially the monks, harassed all the cults without making any real distinctions. It should come as no surprise that the Coptic word for "pagan" is *hel-lene*. By considering paganism to be an essentially Greek culture and therefore foreign, the descendants of the ancient Egyptians were claim-ing a kind of national identity.[17]

This situation explains the heavy-handed treatment of ancient sites of the pharaonic period. Many magnificent temples were transformed into churches or other places of Christian worship.[18] Depictions of gods and monarchs were usually covered with a layer of plaster, but in many cases they were systematically destroyed in order to exorcize the magic power attributed to ancient depictions of gods.[19] Hieroglyphics were seen as suspect, and Shenute, who was well aware of their symbolic power, tried to convince the faithful that they were blasphemous writings carried out "with blood and not just ink," and therefore needed to be replaced with images of God, Christ, angels, and saints.[20]

The establishment of a Christian community did not always bring such forms of fanaticism with it. One example is the temple of Ramesses II at Deir el-Medineh, which is now known as the Ramesseum. The complex was subjected to hammer blows and covered with graffiti in the form of crosses. The colossal statues in the external courtyard were also destroyed, but in spite of this attack, the temple was not transformed into a church, and the industrious wreckers restricted themselves to using a modest area for prayer within one of the rooms.[21] In other Christianized sites, the reuse of the ancient monument can appear casual or in some way the result of practical requirements.[22]

Some places of worship acquired increasing importance, such as Karm Abū Mina, a small town with a shrine not far from Alexandria but also on the outer limits of the Libyan Desert. The shrine contained the tomb of Saint Menas, martyred at the time of Diocletian's persecutions. According to one of the traditions, Menas was martyred in Phrygia, but his remains were taken to this area by a devout imperial official who was sent from Phrygia to put down a revolt (the saint's relics would guarantee the victory for the Roman soldiers). Pilgrims also visited the shrine for the practice of "incubation," which involved sleeping in a specific environment to obtain revelatory dreams. This was typical of many Mediterranean pagan cults, and the religious authorities therefore disapproved of it.[23] A complex for receiving pilgrims grew up around the church which was dedicated to the saint, and was enlarged and renovated on several occasions in the fourth, fifth, and sixth centuries. There was a hostel for pilgrims, housing, and a cemetery.[24] The cult of Saint Menas became extremely popular and spread beyond Egypt: churches and shrines were established in various Mediterranean cities, and there is even proof of a church dedicated to the saint in Constantinople as far back as the fifth century.

In spite of the massive progress of Christianity, around 428 there were still clear remains of the pre-Christian religions along the Nile Valley. The people were keen to preserve their traditional festivals such as the *panegyrís* in honor of the river at flood level, which was still being held in 424 (*Oxyrhynchus Papyri* 43, 3148, concerning the provision of wine for the festival). A text discovered in Herakleopolis Magna—but written in the nearby city of Oxyrhynchus—has been dated to 426 and demonstrates the existence of "pagan confraternities" (*paganikaì syntéleiai*).[25] The existence of such associations in all imperial territories or, at least in the Empire of the East, is confirmed by Theodosius's reference to "surviving pagans" in decrees of 423, which also corroborate the repression of Jews and heretics, although there is an attempt to avoid the excesses carried out by monks. The pagans in question, who were guilty of carrying out "execrable sacrifices" to demons, were condemned to exile and confiscation of their assets (*Code of Theodosius*, 16, 10, 23; cf. 22). In any event, the harsh imperial legislation affected all public manifestations of traditional cults, even where paganism still had deep roots. There had long been a tendency to transform paganism's public spaces into private ones, but under Theodosius I paganism entered a period of underground activity.[26]

The repression of traditional cults in all the territories was an attempt to reestablish the necessary unity in an empire threatened by incursions from outside its borders. The attacks on Egypt came from the west and the south. To the west, the Libyan Desert area had, since the end of the fourth century, been affected by repeated incursions by Berber tribes, the Macae and the Austurians. In 398, these peoples participated in the revolt of Gildo, the *comes* of Africa (who, unlike Bonifacius, was of local origin) and the subsequent imperial repression had forced them to move east. Saint Jerome referred to these movements in a letter dated 411 (Saint Jerome, *Epistle* 126, 1), which some scholars have incorrectly linked to attacks by Arab nomads.[27]

The greatest danger, however, came from Nubia, where the imperial crisis had strengthened the position of the local kingdoms. It appears that the inscription on the facade of the hypostyle hall of the temple dedicated to Mandulis at Telmis (Kalabsha) was carried out around 428.

It is one of the longest inscriptions in Meroitic, the language of the ancient Kingdom of Kush (fourth century BC to 325 AD), and its name derived from the kingdom's capital, Meroe, in modern-day Sudan. Meroitic (which so far has only been partially deciphered) was also used by the Nubian dynasties that controlled these territories after the kingdom fell. The Kalabsha inscription mentions a King Kharamadoye, who could perhaps be one of the princes buried in the necropolis of Ballana, whose royal charisma is represented by the crowns placed in the tombs. If the chronology suggested by Laszlo Török is right, the text describes events that occurred after the period 410–420. Kharama-doye supposedly came into conflict with King Ysemneye, who might be the same person as Isemnē mentioned in a Greek inscription also in Kalabsha.[28]

Ysemneye/Isemnē was "king" of the Blemmyans, a population that had invaded the ancient frontier land that divided Egypt and Nubia. This was recorded by the historian Olympiodorus, who came from the ancient pharaonic capital of Thebes, and visited Upper Egypt in 421 (Olympiodorus, fr. 1, 37). The Blemmyans were probably ancestors of the Sudanese tribe of the Beja, whose raids have been recorded since the second half of the third century. After the withdrawal of Roman troops from Lower Nubia, they occupied the territory on the other side of the First Cataract, which included the citadels of Telmis and Primis (Qasr Ibrīm), and the territory called the "twelve *schoinoí*" (a *schoinós*, meaning "rope," was a unit of measurement equal to 137 kilo-meters), famous for its emerald mines. Using their bases, the Blemmy-ans frequently plundered Upper Egypt, and often pushed further north as far as such sites as the White Monastery. The biography of Shenute contains a rather distorted version of these attacks, which mainly emphasizes the miraculous powers the abbot used to reduce the Blemmyans to impotence by withering their hands and blocking their movements.[29] This was clearly wishful thinking: the anguished inhabitants of the Thebais trusted in the charisma of his holiness, who would free them from the barbarian threat. Indeed, the barbarians were perceived as horrible monsters, similar to those of the visions of Saint Anthony. A writer of the time, the African Martianus Capella, could quite happily take up themes of Pliny the Elder's *Natural History* in his great encyclopedic *Marriage of Philology and Mercury*, and assert that "the Blemmyans have no head, and their mouths and ears are on their chests" (Martianus Capella, VI 674).

The Blemmyans were not alone in aspiring to dominate Lower Nubia; there were also the Noubades or Annoubades. Their presence was recorded on an inscription in the Temple to Mandulis in Kalab-sha, although the date is uncertain, in any case before 450. A certain Silkō, chief of the Noubades, commemorated a victory that proclaimed him "prince (*basilískos*) of the Nubians and all the Ethiopians." The in-scription is in Greek and is accompanied by an engraved portrait of him in ceremonial uniform. The use of Greek and the modest term *basilískos* demonstrate the recognition of some form of vassalage to Theodosius II.

The relative scarcity of sources does not allow us to resolve the ques-tion definitively; nor does it reveal the sequence of events with any great clarity. Moreover, the building of the Aswan Dam and subsequent formation of Lake Nasser has covered most of the archeological sites with water. We do know, however, that the Christian communities were often attacked by the Nubian peoples. The *Zeta Papyrus* of Leiden, which has been dated to between 425 and 450, contains Bishop Appi-on's plea to Theodosius II. This is a particularly important document, given that it contains Latin text in the emperor's own hand: *bene valere te cupimus* ("we wish you good health").[30] The ecclesiastical jurisdiction of Appion included the district of the city of Syene (Aswan), the adja-cent island of Elephantine, and a town on the other side of the Nile. Following the usual preamble, the bishop starts on the substance of his request:

My churches and I find ourselves in the midst of depraved barbar-ians, the Blemmyans and the Noubades, who inflict endless incur-sions upon us and seem to appear out of nowhere. This happens without there being a single soldier to protect our lands. Conse-quently, the churches under my direction have been humiliated, and cannot help those who seek refuge in them. I prostrate myself before the divine and immaculate footprints left by your passing, in the hope that you shall be so kind as to order that our holy churches be protected by our soldiers, who shall obey me and fol-low my orders, just as the soldiers garrisoned at the said fortress of

Philae, in your province of Upper Thebais, are in the service of the holy churches of God in Philae. (*Leiden Papyrus Zeta = Fontes Historiae Nubiorum*, III, no. 311)[31]

The reference to Philae is significant: this locality, the site throughout the entire imperial era of an extremely famous temple dedicated to Isis, was located on an island at the far end of Upper Egypt on the border established after Diocletian's withdrawal from Lower Nubia. On the adjacent bank there was an important garrison (actually an entire legion), which was connected to Syene's city walls at some unspecified time during the period of the late empire. Besides, the *Notitia dignitatum* (*Oriens*, 31, 35–65) demonstrates that there was a military presence in Syene and Elephantine, the "region" controlled by Appion, which continued until the fall of Byzantine rule in Egypt. As has been observed by the expert on Roman military history Michael Speidel, this was an "extraordinary example of strategic continuity" which, however, must have been suspended at the time of Appion, purely because of some momentary crisis.[32]

Whereas pagan temples had been despoiled, ransacked, or turned into churches in the rest of Egypt, the temple at Philae long remained a pagan outpost. It should not surprise us that it was there that we find the last hieroglyphic inscription, a bilingual graffito of 394 AD (hieroglyphic and demotic) inscribed by Esmētakhom, a priest of Isis (*Fontes Historiae Nubiorum*, III, no. 306). The graffito was not, however, dedicated to Isis but to Mandulis, the god of Lower Nubia worshipped in Telmis. The priests were thus attempting to ingratiate themselves with the Blemmyan "rulers" (or rather the warlords) who had occupied the city of Telmis and its temple and, in all probability, had transformed the site into a fortress from which to make the sudden attacks that in Appion's heartfelt appeal "seemed to appear from nowhere."

The temple of Philae probably survived because of the support of the populations in conflict with Rome. The treaty of 453 was actually agreed upon within the temple area, and there does not appear to be any record of a conversion of the shrine before the time of Justinian, when the complex was finally transformed into a church (*Fontes Historiae Nubiorum*, III, no. 324). This led the papyrologist Ulrich Wilcken to speak of a "Christiano-pagan" period in Philae. Under Theodosius II, Egypt is supposed to have gone through a period of cohabitation.[33] This was not however the opinion of the religious authorities, whose representatives, like Shenute, a zealous destroyer of idols, were openly in conflict with large sections of the population who were determined to defend their own traditions.[34] Moreover, in the region of the First Cataract, the Nubians were rather similar to the barbarians who lived beyond the border, such as the Blemmyans.[35]

· X ·

Easter in Jerusalem

THE DATE for Easter, Christianity's most important festival at the time, clearly had to be carefully calculated for each year, and in Egypt, the patriarch of Alexandria sent a letter as early as Epiphany to all the communities announcing the start of Lent and the date of Easter (Cassian, *Conferences*, 10, 2). This calculation was not at all easy, and gave rise to endless debate, which led to improvements in the calendar (in the East, it was finally settled under Justinian). In 428, the calculation was already established: Easter fell on the first Sunday after the full moon that followed the spring equinox, which meant a date between 22 March and 22 April.[1]

The desire for a uniform date resulted from the need to have all the faithful in the empire—and hopefully also beyond—celebrating the event on the same day. For the ecclesiastic community, it must have been exhilarating to know that Christians of all Churches were intent upon the same ritual, listening to the passages from the New Testament and sacred hymns in their own liturgical languages: Greek, Latin, Syriac, Gothic, and Armenian.

The ceremony of *Anástasis* ("Resurrection") was particularly moving. Around 428, the reading of the Gospel was not restricted to the story of the resurrection, but also included an evocation of Christ's suffering and death on the cross.[2] A bishop's personality had an important role in this. The success of the ceremony depended on his oratorical and perhaps even theatrical skills in enthralling the crowd and making it relive those dramatic moments. The reading of the Gospel was accompanied by hymns such as the following:

> When, King of Justice, you stretched out your hands on the Cross,
> Your mother tearfully leaned on the Cross,
> the sepulcher had been prepared,
> God had foreseen it.
> And when you entered,
> Your divine and human being
> and Your angels, without body, did not recognize it.
> But on the third day You rose again, because of Your power,
> You who have brought about the death of death.
> And with your Resurrection, You have once more lifted up
> us who had fallen.[3]

The most important Easter celebration was held in Jerusalem. It was there that the festival was transformed into the complex ritual that would eventually evolve into Holy Week. It started with the Thursday-night vigil on the Mount of Olives and Gethsemane. Then Good Friday was spent in reviving the memory of the trial of Jesus and his flagellation; at midday, the relic of the True Cross was put on display, and there followed another vigil. Saturday was devoted to fasting and resting while awaiting the Easter vigil. Then the bishop went to the entrance of the Holy Sepulcher and told the story of the resurrection in the same place that the miracle had occurred. Here, the suggestive power of the sacred places provoked powerful reactions. As soon as the bishop started to read the Gospel, all the faithful burst into tears and started to scream and shout in what can only be called a collective trance.[4] In 428, the bishop was the energetic Juvenal, who undoubtedly celebrated the ritual with the appropriate degree of rapture.[5]

The community in Jerusalem had every reason to celebrate. Following the destruction of the Temple and the subsequent Jewish diaspora at the time of Hadrian, the city had lost its supremacy to Caesarea. Jerusalem was turned into a Roman colony under the name of Aelia Capitolina, and entered a long period of decline.[6] The Christianization of the empire had, however, restored its fortunes, and the development of the Holy Places for pilgrimage had caught the imagination of the more devout members of the imperial household, such as Saint Helena (Constantine's mother) and Theodosius I.

In the second half of the fourth century, the great Bishop Cyril of Jerusalem played a key role in the promotion of the city and transformed it into a cosmopolitan and multilingual metropolis.[7] The increasing importance of religious affairs in the Empire of the East did not stop at promoting the rebirth of the city, but also marked the restoration of its former glory. From the moment of his election in 422, Bishop Juvenal set about promoting his episcopal see in any way he could, and elevated it to a much more powerful and prestigious position.[8] This was a fundamental privilege, if you consider that the recent division of Palestine into three provinces had weakened the economic importance of Caesarea and therefore its episcopal see as well.

Juvenal, whose Latin name suggests Roman or in any case western origins, believed that Jerusalem had to become even more powerful than Antioch.[9] This plan met with imperial support, as demonstrated by his reference to "pragmatic letters" or "divine letters," which meant letters rewritten by the emperor in support of his demands.[10] The imperial household took his side, starting with Eudocia, who went on a long pilgrimage in 438/9 and became particularly involved in protecting and developing the Holy Places. Pulcheria was not to be outdone, and in 428 (if the chronology is correct), the religious authorities gave her the right hand of Saint Stephen, the Church's first martyr, whose remains had been discovered in 415 at Kefar Gamala, a locality about twenty kilometers from Jerusalem.[11] To celebrate the acquisition of this important relic, she had a church built in the palace in Constantinople.[12]

At the Easter celebration, there followed the usual period of eight days in which the newly baptized were instructed in the sacraments. On 7 May 428, Juvenal started to walk eastwards. He was accompanied by Passarion, a cleric whose official title was "corepiscopus-archimandrite," and the famous "Master of the Church" Hesychius, who wrote a commentary on the Book of Job.[13] After about ten kilometers, the holy men reached the *láura*, which the monk Euthymius had founded in the desert of Judea, and consecrated the church.

Láura means "narrow way" in Greek, but the term had come to mean a monastic institution that was halfway between a hermitage and a monastery. The monks could pray and meditate in their cells, which were not isolated like those of a hermitage; indeed they were adjacent to each other. Moreover, a *láura* was built around a central complex that included a church, an administration, a hospice for visitors and pilgrims, and other shared facilities (the most important of which was the bread oven).[14] All this created a kind of village of monks. For most of the week, the *kelliōtai* (the inhabitants of the cells) devoted their time to prayer and also material activities such as basketwork that did not require contact with the outside (world). In the meantime, the steward with the help of other monks dealt with the community's material needs, and all this came under the direction of the abbot (*hēgoúmenos*). On Saturday and Sunday, everyone took part in divine worship, but the practice of a shared meal does not appear to have been proven.[15]

A native of the most westerly regions of Armenia that were under Roman rule, Euthymius had been practicing his religious duties for more than twenty years (in 428, at the time of the *láura*'s foundation, he was over fifty). Although he completed his apprenticeship in his native city of Melitene (now Malatya in Turkey), Euthymius moved to Palestine shortly after his ordination, and there he set out on his long monastic career that more or less took in all the experiences that this type of life could offer a penitent. His monastery was an important training center for monks, who like him came from various regions of the eastern Mediterranean. Those who were considered most suitable were ordained as priests and sent to other ecclesiastic institutions in Palestine and beyond, where they worked as deacons, priests, and even bishops.

Euthymius's *láura* was halfway between the Holy City and the Dead Sea, and not far from the road for Jericho.[16] The abbot, now on his third foundation, set himself up as a hermit, although the site did not lend itself to the isolated life of an anchorite as it was teeming with pilgrims.[17] The road between Jerusalem and Jericho was literally strewn with memorable places, such as the Mount of Olives and the depression that surrounds the Dead Sea. A pilgrim could travel through an extraordinary variety of desert areas and pass through a series of key places in biblical geography. However, travelers over this twenty-kilometer stretch would not have been on their own: unlike the deserts of Egypt and Syria, those of Judea were too close to the city to offer the experience of true ascetic isolation.[18]

Connected by a dense network of roads, the monasteries of Palestine contributed to the development of the economy.[19] For example, an extensive irrigation system had been developed in the Negev, starting in the fifth century. Very probably, the region's prosperity was due to imperial interest in religious centers that attracted pilgrims, such as the Monastery of Saint Catherine in the Sinai. In the settlements of Avdat (ancient Oboda), Elusa, and Shivta, Israeli archeologists have discovered very large buildings for pressing grapes, which confirms the situation reported in written sources from the mid-fourth century. It was once believed that viticulture was introduced to Palestine by Christian monks who were followers of Saint Hilarion. The truth is that wine was already part of the culture and economy of the Nabataean Arabs, who had been prospering in the region since the Hellenistic Age. The rejection of wine was not therefore anything to do with Arab culture, but was associated with the ascetic practices of some Christian communities, as has been demonstrated in nearby Syria.[20]

The development of vineyards in the Negev was mainly due to the new market requirements, which channeled middle-eastern products towards Constantinople through the ports of Gaza and Ascalon (Ashqelon). These regions, which had once been threatened by nomadic raids, were now protected by the imperial army. This guaranteed greater stability and also considerable demographic growth, evidence of which covers the entire middle-eastern area.[21] The prosperity of the monasteries favored good relations with the local Arab populations: for example, the church of Euthymius's *láura* had been built by Peter, a converted "Saracen,"[22] and one of its two water tanks was reserved for the Saracens (Cyril of Scythopolis, *Life of Euthymius*, 51).[23] During these years, there were three prominent bishops of Palestine who had typically Arab names: Abdelas (Abdullah) of Elousa, Saidas (Sa'id) of Phaeno, and Natiras (Nadir) of Gaza.[24]

There was a considerable increase in the number of pilgrims, who came from all parts to visit the Holy Places. Around 428, the time when Euthymius founded his *láura*, the biography of the saint recorded the sojourn of as many as four hundred Armenian pilgrims on their way from Jerusalem to the Jordan, who had decided to take a detour. Domitian, the steward, had told Euthymius of his concerns: how was such a crowd to be fed? The *láura*'s scarce resources—bread, oil, wine—were multiplied miraculously. This definitively established Euthymius's fame: the population of the *láura* reached fifty monks (Cyril of Scythopolis, *Life of Euthymius*, 17–18). The presence of Armenian pilgrims was not surprising: at the end of the fourth century, Saint Jerome had praised the melting pot of Christians who rushed to Palestine from such distant lands as Gaul and India to take part in the dissonant but extremely devout chorus of monks and virgins (*Epistle* 46, 10). In the same period, around 429, a hermit who lived in a cave near Livias, on the east bank of the Jordan, received a visit from Nabarnugi, a prince of the Iberians of the Caucasus. The noble was stunned when the monk addressed him by name and then made references to his genealogy (*Syriac Life of Peter of Iberia*, 85–87).

Apart from recalling Christ's feeding of the five thousand in the New Testament, Euthymius's miracle reveals the wealth of the monasteries in the Desert of Judea, where wheat grew with difficulty and had to be transported on camelback from Transjordania.[25] The monks had to abstain from eating meat and fish, but when they were not undergoing ascetic exercises, their diet did not differ that much from the other inhabitants of the eastern Mediterranean.[26] The monasteries benefited from donations from the rich and devout, and also from the imperial household itself. These fundamental assets were then enlarged by other economic activities such as crafts.

The monasteries of Palestine often took in highly respected figures. Melania the Younger, her husband Pinianus, and her mother Albina had been living in the Holy Land since 417. These young aristocrats, who had already abandoned the luxuries and society life of Rome following the death of their children, now set out on the path of asceticism. Having sold off their immense estates that could be found in all the western provinces, they chose the "angelic" life of chastity and temperance.[27] Once she was in the Holy Land, Melania the Younger followed the example of her grandmother, Melania the Elder, who in 372 left Rome to undergo an extreme monastic experience. Her forbear had lived in Palestine for twenty-seven years, founded a monastery on the Mount of Olives, and died around 410. The young couple went to Jerusalem; Melania, however, recoiled from the city life, and soon withdrew to a female monastery also on the Mount of Olives. This was also a means to cut all ties with her aristocratic past; besides, the black sheep of her family, the powerful pagan uncle Volusianus, was living in Rome and in 428 became the prefect of the *praetorium* of Italy and Africa.

In her convent, Melania devoted herself to intellectual activities, such as the transcription and reading of sacred texts.[28] This approach was typical of most aristocrats who found urban life indecorous and disreputable, and preferred to withdraw to country estates, as Melania did first—before taking her final decision. But, as Andrea Giardina has pointed out, it was only isolation in the relative sense:

> These religious communities of saintly women, however, both in the city and in the countryside, were constantly under the scrutiny of the entire Christian world: under the eyes of the local people, of pilgrims, of the faithful who flocked to Palestine from all over the earth, and to whom these wonderful tales were told of aristocratic ladies who abandoned their gilded palaces for humble convents in the Holy Land.[29]

The conversion of the cream of senatorial aristocracy provided the monastic movement with charismatic associations that were much admired even at the royal palace, particularly by Empress Eudocia (*Life of Melania the Younger*, 54–56).

In the Holy Land, the Jewish tradition meant that Christianization was undoubtedly less traumatic than elsewhere. Yet the fanaticism of Christians produced its victims here too: in 402, the pagan shrine to Marneion in Gaza was razed to the ground. Bishop Porphyry had a church built in its place: his hagiographer smugly observed that the paving stones of the church square, which had been cut from the temple ruins, were being trodden on by men and animals (Mark the Deacon, *Life of Porphyry of Gaza*, 76).[30] As in other regions, monasteries often took over existing buildings and facilities: the most interesting example is that of the glorious fortress of Masada, the symbol of Jewish resistance to Rome, which was transformed into a monastery and renamed Marda.[31]

Although Jerusalem had become a place of memory for Christian identity and Palestine overrun with monks and pilgrims, the Jewish community was not yet subject to systematic persecutions, but it must have felt threatened. Jews and Samaritans, who were profoundly upset about the proliferation of Christian places of worship throughout

Palestine, found their hopes renewed in 363, when the nostalgic and utopian Emperor Julian granted them express permission to rebuild the Temple in Jerusalem. But Julian's reign turned out to be a brief interlude, and after that, imperial legislation became increasingly repressive towards them, and eventually defined the Jewish religion as a *superstitio* and no longer a *religio*. The Jews of Jerusalem basically experienced conditions similar to those living in the diaspora, while many Jews and Samaritans converted to Christianity. If, however, Jews converted non-Jews to their religion or even just favored proselytizing by other Jews, they could be severely punished.

Under Theodosius II, the empire attempted to avoid the excesses of Christian fanaticism that had only created disorder and discontent. However, he also did all he could to restrict the room for maneuver of Jewish communities. So while it was lawful to repair synagogues damaged by frenzied monks, they were not allowed to build new ones. However, the empire showed clemency to those Jews who, having converted to Christianity, wished to return to their community (*Code of Theodosius*, 16, 8, 23): the law, issued in 416, annulled those conversions taken for opportunistic reasons or to escape difficult situations.[32]

Many elements of this story remain obscure—primarily the presence of the Samaritans. This religious community, which was created by a split within Judaism around the fifth century BC and still exists today (but with a tiny number of adherents divided between Israel and the Palestinian Authority), has many similarities with traditional Judaism, but also differs on several points: the Samaritans only accept the Pentateuch (the first five books of the Bible) as part of their tradition, and they read it in a different version. Moreover they interpret various points of Mosaic Law in a different fashion. Because of this, they do not have the right to marry Jews or share in their worship. Their sacred mountain is not Zion, but Mount Gerizim close to what is now Nablus (formerly Neapolis). Theodosius II's legislation did not distinguish between Jews and Samaritans, and the latter, who were mainly of rural and highland extraction, did not have a good reputation. However, some of then became wealthy and gained positions of prestige, partly because they were more likely to convert to Christianity.[33]

The "orthodox" Jewish community (which included various currents) was also going through a critical period. Under pressure from the

Church authorities, the empire was gradually but inexorably removing its members from positions in the administration and the legal system. Just before 429, as stated in decree in the *Code of Theodosius* (16, 8, 9), the position of patriarch (*nāsī'* in Hebrew) ceased to exist. The holder of this hereditary post appointed the president of the Sanhedrin, a figure of great religious authority for all Jews (see *Code of Justinian*, 1, 9, 17).[34] Over the centuries, the *nāsī'* had been a point of reference for all the diaspora, particularly after the destruction of the Temple in 70 AD. Every year, the faithful were required to send him a special tribute. In order to ensure his control of the entire community, the patriarch sent trusted emissaries, called "apostles," to all the synagogues, and the emissaries were entitled to raise taxes.[35] Even if these activities were often subject to restrictive measures by the empire, the patriarchs were honored with a high-ranking title.

The abolition of the patriarch does not appear to have been an act of repression. The empire was simply acknowledging the death without heirs of the last *nāsī'*, who was probably still the Gamaliel VI who had been affected by a restrictive measure in 415. Theodosius II took advantage of this death to decentralize religious authority to the leaders of the individual Jewish communities, while diverting taxes on the diaspora communities to the imperial treasury.[36] These measures marked the beginning of the slow decline of the Jewish community in Palestine. However, the Israeli archeologist Zeev Safrai suggests that in some areas Judaism resisted Christianity, which only became a mass religion in Palestine during the second half of the fifth century.[37] In the areas furthest away from the coastal centers, such as the Galilee Plateau, traditional cults were maintained, as appears to be demonstrated by the more "oriental" nature of the material culture.[38] Jewish traditionalism was in fact favored by imperial legislation, which aimed to keep a check on contaminations between Judaism and Christianity in order to stem the proliferation of heresies. In fact, it is not always easy to come up with a definition of "Judaism" for the fifth century. The empire viewed religious minorities such as the Manichaeans in loose and simplistic terms, and the Jews were no exception. Besides, some terms used to define particular groups within Judaism, such as the mysterious *minim* (heretics) who were criticized on many occasions in rabbinical literature, do not appear to have equivalent categories in modern thought or indeed in classical or contemporary Christian thought.[39]

In the first half of the fifth century, the final version of what is called the Palestinian Talmud was completed, and this followed the same path set out two centuries earlier by the Mishnah. Talmudic texts, although concerned with religious questions, reveal important features of the history of the Jewish community, strategies for retaining identity and "a rich and complex world of *latent* history" (J. Neusner); in other words, they are a key for entering the Jewish universe of the imagination and emotions in the fifth century, as seen by learned interpreters of the Scriptures.[40] The particular feature of the Palestinian Talmud, compared with the Mishnah, is the development of an historical perspective on relations between Jews and the Roman Empire, expressed as a kind of dialectic between Israel's weakness and Rome's power. According to the Talmudic rabbis, God ordered the archangel Michael to found Rome in order to punish Solomon, guilty of a dynastic marriage with the family of the Pharaoh Neccho. The sins of the Jews are supposed to have caused the greatness of the Roman Empire (Palestinian Talmud, '*Avodah Zarah*, 1, 2). The history of Rome was therefore interpreted as an anti-history of Israel.[41] The sins of the Jews had brought about the victory of the idolaters and the darkness that fell on the chosen people. While waiting for Israel to see the error of its ways and thus bring about the arrival of the Messiah, it was necessary to resign oneself to one's fate and to ask forgiveness for one's own sins (Palestinian Talmud, *Ta'anīt*, 1, 1).

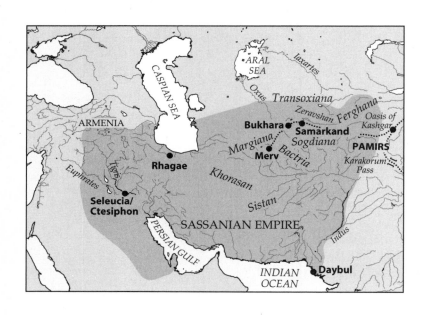

·XI·

The Great King and the

Seven Princesses

IN SPITE of the now irreversible changes triggered by the migrations of peoples and political instability, there was still an entity that could be defined as "Rome," which was acknowledged as such by its subjects and its enemies, and maintained its ancient authority over the Mediterranean world and, to a lesser extent, Europe too. But the Roman Empire was not the only empire. Beyond the Euphrates another sovereign, or rather the "King of Kings" (*shāhanshāh*), reigned over the great Sassanian Empire which extended as far as Central Asia.

Direct contacts between the two empires were rare, but this did not mean that Constantinople and Ravenna ignored the problem. Of course, Theodosius II had had to renounce the traditional Roman policy towards the east to concentrate on recovering a unified empire, and this had led to the permanent loss of the Kingdom of Armenia and a stronger position for the rival empire. Nevertheless, the emperor continued to ruminate on possible strategies for regaining the initiative. In this period, war against the Persians was of particular concern to the emperor, and Nestorius has been exploring these anxieties (see Socrates, *Ecclesiastical History*, 7, 29, 5).

Moreover, the problems of the Euphrates were not only disturbing military leaders and the court at Constantinople: even the African Quodvultdeus, who had humbly declared to Saint Augustine that he knew no Greek and did not even know how to read Latin very well, would thirty years later prove to be fully aware of the crisis of the Eastern

Roman Empire in the 420s, when speaking specifically about the "Armenians" who were seeking refuge from the emperor against the will of the Persians (Quodvultdeus, *Book of God's Promises and Predictions*, 3, 36). During the same period in Ravenna, Bishop Peter Chrysologus referred in his sermons to the symbols of royalty in the Sassanian Empire (Peter Chrysologus, *Sermons*, 120, 2).[1]

The Great King of Iran was the Sassanid Bahrām V, the son of Yazdegerd I, and about the same age as Theodosius II. Arab authors are in agreement in claiming that the future emperor had been educated as an Arab at the Oasis of Hīra (close to the current town of Kūfa in southern Iraq), and this may have been to avoid plots in the court. This story, which was developed in the Islamic tradition, was embellished with important details in the poem *Haft Paikar* ("The Seven Beauties") by the Persian poet Nezāmī, who lived from 1141 to 1209 in the Caucasian city of Ganja (now Gyandzha in Azerbaijan).[2] Hīra was one of the great centers of pre-Islamic Bedouin culture. Nezāmī describes it as a city fit for *A Thousand and One Nights*, with decorated palaces, hanging gardens, and, above all, the marvelous castle of Khawarnaq, built by the great architect Semnār and commissioned by Prince No'mān (in Arabic al-Nu'mān).[3] It was said that the Arabs developed their own writing in this city, and the most ancient historical inscription in Arabic does indeed date from the first half of the fourth century and was written on behalf of one of the first Lakhmids, the princes who had set up the structures of an autonomous kingdom.[4] Initially, the Lakhmids sided with Rome, but very soon became vassals of the Sassanian Empire, and governed the oasis—until the Great King Khusro II suppressed the dynasty in 602. In the fifth century, the Bedouins of Hīra were the guardians of the Sassanian border. When Flavius Dionysius carried out his embassy, his Persian opposite number was probably escorted by these warriors. In 428, their leader was al-Nu'mān's son, Prince al-Mundhir, who in the past had taken in and protected Bahrām, who had studied alongside the prince's own son, Nu'mān the Younger. Like other "Saracens," al-Mundhir was close to Christianity: he was a worshiper of Saint Sergius, whose shrine was in a place known as the "Plain of the Barbarians," close to the desert frontier with Iran.[5] However, in 421/2 this lord of the desert fought alongside Iran against the most Christian Roman Empire, and clashed with the Roman Empire's Alan general,

Ardabur, on the Mesopotamian front where he deployed a large number of elephants.[6] According to al-Tha'alibī, an Arab historian of the eleventh century, Bahrām granted al-Mundhir control of all the lands from Mesopotamia to the Fertile Crescent. This was a kind of *foedus*, the similar situation established by the Romans in relation to the barbarians settled in their provinces.[7]

In medieval Islamic culture, which revived and reworked the epic traditions and chronicles of the heroic deeds of the Sassanid kings, Bahrām V was known as *Bahrām Gor*, or "Bahrām the Onager." It may seem strange to name an emperor after a wild ass, but it is thought that, at least originally, the epithet meant "great" or "powerful."[8] These members of the horse family were in fact the fastest animals in the deserts of Central Asia. Pursuing an onager was a difficult undertaking even for an expert horseman, and this meant that their herds survived until hunters could use motorized transport. The onager's ability to bolt or produce a burst of speed was also known in the West, and so when Greek military technicians came up with a machine for launching large stones during a siege, they named it after these wild asses of Central Asia.

Bahrām's time with the Bedouins explains his skill in hunting animals in the desert, and also the particular attention he paid to the frontier world and the ethnic and religious diversity of his empire. The education of the young prince in Hīra is supposed to have provided him with the necessary expertise to command both peoples. The medieval legend of Bahrām "the Wild Ass" drew on lost works of Pahlavi literature, such as the *Khoday-nāmak (Book of Sovereigns)*.[9] As Michael Barry has observed, such an idealized figure of the king represents a kind of archetypal hero in Iranic literature.[10] In fact, the very ancient tradition of the Hunter King goes back at least as far as the epic story of Gilgamesh, and was associated in the Iranic world with the god of the same name, Bahrām or *Vahrām*, whom the ancient Mazdean [Zoroastrian] sacred texts called *Verethragna*, and who was known to the Armenians as *Vahagn*.[11] The charisma of the Iranic peoples determined their superiority among other nations who had made different religious choices, such as Christianized Iberia (now part of Georgia), for whose population Iran remained the country they looked to and considered the "land of heroes and giants" (*Life of King Vakhtang Gorgasal*, p. 170 Qauchishvili).[12]

The Sassanid iconography of the Hunter King had struck the more attentive Roman observers. At the time of Emperor Julian's expedition in 363, the historian Ammianus Marcellinus had personally observed the paintings in the Great King's hunting lodge in the middle of a pleasant cypress wood close to the River Tigris:

> In every part of the small palace you could see the pictures typical of this people (*gentiles picturas*), which depicted the king in the act of killing wild animals in every kind of hunting. Indeed, Persians only depict wars and massacres, whether in literature or in art. (Ammianus Marcellinus, 24, 6, 3)

The tradition that attributes to Bahrām the development of a hunting bow is perhaps not too far from the truth, nor can it be discounted that he learnt Greek, Sanskrit, and Hebrew, as claimed by al-Thaʿalibī. These three languages were in fact the three pillars on which culture in the East was built: representing respectively astronomy, medicine, and religious law in the tradition of Solomon. Such knowledge, together with the valor learned from the Arabs and the charismatic glory (*khwarrah*) of the Sassanid monarchy, would have made him an extremely powerful emperor capable of competing with Theodosius II.

This image of Bahrām, which had currency in medieval Arab and Persian literature, was immortalized most notably in Nezāmī's poem *The Seven Beauties*. The illustrated manuscripts of this work, often masterpieces of Islamic art, depict the emperor in the act of chasing onagers to brand them, or of shooting a single arrow through an onager and a lion—and of course there had to be the most fabulous enterprise of all, the killing of a dragon. The poet tells us that, at the end of one of his frenzied hunting trips, the king saw a stupendous female onager which he followed throughout the day, until he found himself before a terrifying dragon. At this stage, he understood that the female onager had led him there so that he could kill the monster. After he had decapitated and eviscerated the dragon, Bahrām found a baby onager that it had devoured. Having thus taken revenge, the mother then led him to a nearby cave where he discovered an enormous treasure. Nezāmī's poem, which is also known as *The Seven Princesses*, is made up of the stories told to the king by his seven wives. The princesses came from the "seven continents of the world": India, Byzantium, Khwarezm (Central Asia), the land of the Slavs, the "West" (roughly speaking, the Germanic king-doms), China, and Iran itself. The Persian princess descended from the most ancient royal line; the Slav princess and the one from Khwarezm had been chosen for their beauty, whereas the "Western" princess and Chinese one, who was the daughter of the "Great Khan," had been claimed together with other tributes. Only the Byzantine princess had been taken by force: Bahrām "attacked the land of the *Rūm* leaving des-olation in his path. The terrified Byzantine emperor did not raise objec-tions and handed over his daughter with profuse apologies."

The description of the "seven continents," which is intentionally vague, is clearly also anachronistic. The heroic depiction of Sassanid kings found in Nezāmī and other authors came long after the fall of the Sassanid monarchy in the seventh century. However, the manner in which the fictional Bahrām managed to obtain his Byzantine princess does in some ways echo the historical Bahrām's victories over the East-ern Roman Empire. Even in the Middle Ages, it was asserted that under his reign, Iran had experienced its period of greatest splendor. In the Iranic religious tradition, he was known for good reason as the in-carnation of the figure that the Zoroastrian tradition called the *Sōshāns*, "Savior" of the world and the enemy of the Lie. An echo of this apoca-lyptic interpretation of history can be found in the Persian cosmologi-cal text known as *Bundahishn*. In one of the final chapters, written when the Sassanid Empire was only a glorious memory for Zoroastrian sur-vivors, there is a reference to an ancient prophecy that heralded the coming of a Great King called *Wahrām*:

> All men shall follow him. He shall take command of India, Rome, the land of the Turks, and all the countries. He shall remove all mistaken beliefs and shall establish the religion of Zoroaster, for no other belief shall come out into the open. (*Bundahishn*, 33, 27f)[13]

The redemptive role of the emperor was justified by his agreement with the priests of the Zoroastrian religion. Indeed, Bahrām V was the first Sassanid king who was not crowned by a noble, but by the *mōbadān mōbad*, the high priest of the magi. The investiture ceremony was there-fore transformed into a genuine process of sanctification.[14]

Bahrām proved to have excellent political gifts. We have seen how Theodosius was obliged to surrender Armenia in 428, a move that would have repercussions for the entire Mediterranean world. In order to understand fully the treaty of 428, we need to examine the situation in its entirety, and attempt to rediscover Sassanid policy of the previous years. Back in 421/2, Theodosius II forced Bahrām to fight a war from a position of weakness, but nevertheless the latter was able to bring it to an honorable conclusion. The Romans were obliged to withdraw quickly in response to a Hun invasion of Thrace, practically on Constantinople's doorstep.[15] This sudden migration appears a little suspect: perhaps the barbarians were colluding with the Great King.

Indeed, Bahrām had been in dialogue with the Huns from the beginning of his reign, when a powerful army under the command of a *khagan* or king of the Huns had crossed the River Oxus to invade the rich oasis of Merv. The horde then moved westwards as far as Rhagae (now Tehran). Its soldiers probably belonged to a single tribe, that of the Hephthalites, which Byzantine sources distinguish from the tribes of the Chionites and the Kidarites (but Persian and Indian sources simply talk of "White Huns" and "Red Huns").[16] The Persians were not new to these kinds of attack, and knew their enemy's weaknesses very well. However, Bahrām was forced to seek an agreement and pay a tribute in order to end the hostilities. The eastern sources present the war against the Huns as a single campaign in which the Great King managed to overcome misfortune and defeat the enemy, but this story perhaps condenses the developments of a more complex conflict. The first phase, which ended with the acceptance of the *khagan*'s demands, probably coincided with the war against Rome in 421/2, which, as we have seen, ended because of a Hun attack on Thrace, although it is not clear which tribe was involved. The second phase, which strengthened the Persian hand, ended around 427.

Bahrām was not only interested in controlling Central Asia for military reasons. The "Silk Road" was at stake.[17] This was a series of caravan routes along the axis that connects the Middle East to China through the steppes and deserts of central Asia. Starting from the city of Chang' an (Xi'an), the Silk Road heads off northwest through the region of Gansu as far as the oasis of Dunhuang. From there it carries on through the Jade Gate (Yumenguan), and at this stage caravans could choose from two routes to avoid the Taklamakan Desert: the northern route that went towards Hami and then skirted the Tien Shan (Celestial

Mountains) as far as the oasis of Kashgar, or the southern route that also reached Kashgar but by skirting the slopes of the Tibetan Mountains, a little north of the Karakorum Pass.

From Kashgar, the caravans had to tackle the Pamir Plateau or "roof of the world," and from there they went through the cities of Samarkand, Bukhara, and Merv, entered Sassanian territory and headed for the Mediterranean. The mountains of Central Asia opened up to many other routes to important markets in what is now Afghanistan and Northern India. While the ancient *Xiongnu* (the name of the Huns in Chinese sources) were marching to the west, the "shadow empire" of Rouran established itself on the Central Asian steppe in 428. Meanwhile China was going through a long period of internal divisions (it would last until 581) which ended its control of the Silk Road. During the period we are concerned with, the trade routes were contested by the Huns and the Persians: a papyrus of the fifth century even speaks of "Hunnish silk" with reference to Chinese silk that had to pass through regions dominated by the Huns in order to reach the trading centers of the Mediterranean.[18]

Even in northern Afghanistan, once ancient Bactria, we have discovered many documents written in the numerous languages spoken within the region at the time. The commencement of the Bactrian era has been dated to 233 AD by Nicholas Sims-Williams, and we have an administrative document dated 428: a receipt that certifies the production of sixty-four measures of grain (*tasko*, literally "quarter"), sent to the landowner Keraw by the factors Soras and Aspand.[19] This land appears to have had less importance than Sogdiana, and archeological data suggests a period of economic decline, although the Buddhist monasteries continued to maintain a degree of vitality.[20]

The ancient splendor of Bactria was losing ground to a hardened group of merchants from Sogdiana, a region of eastern Iran between Amu-Darya and Syr Darya. Like the Bactrians, the Sogdians spoke an Iranic language which has survived in numerous texts, some of a commercial nature but most of a religious one. They were responsible for founding extremely important cities in Central Asia, such as Bukhara and Samarkand. Sogdian merchants were also responsible for the spread of Buddhism in China in the second and third centuries of the Common Era. In 428, official relations between Sogdians and Chinese were still suspended: only in 435 would they resume the political and commercial contacts with the court of the Wei in the north, and a few years later with the court of the Song in the south.[21]

During the fifth century, the Sogdians merged with the Hun nation, as can be shown by the frequency of the name *hwn* in inscriptions. The Huns had invaded Sogdiana during the second half of the fourth century. A Chinese chronicle records the presence of a *Xiongnu* dynasty in Samarkand. In 437, the dynasty was already at its third representative, who the source defines as *Huni*.[22] The sources are not sufficient to clarify the historical context completely, but it appears to have been a period of relative calm at least until the war between the Huns and the Persians under Bahrām V. The Great King issued coinage demonstrating that he was active at Merv in Margiana, where he reinforced the city's defenses.[23]

There is also mention of the city of Maymurgh, which developed in the same era from a more ancient site, after the Dargom Canal had been built, while archeological data provides evidence of a concentration of sites in the valley of the Zeravshan—the "river of the caravan guides" in Chinese sources—and the foundation of new cities.[24] Unlike their cousins settled in Central Europe, the Central-Asian Huns in Sogdiana brought wealth and monopolized trade in the interior, while their Persian rivals continued to control the sea trade in the Indian Ocean.

This real geography contrasted with a mythical geography, made up of distant and fantastic lands, where perfect and magical lands could be found. A year earlier, in 427 AD, Tao Yuanming, the Taoist author of *Record of the Peach Blossom Valley*, died. He had described the Land of Peach Trees as a world populated by immortals, a refuge from life's hardships that existed outside time.[25] The Tibetan tradition assimilated these legends and merged them with its own about a lost paradise. Eventually it developed the myth of the Hidden Valley, which came into the Western imagination as the "Shangri-La" of James Hilton's novel *Lost Horizon*.[26] An echo of these traditions was also to be found in the Christian Mediterranean, where descriptions started to circulate of the imagined lands of the East as transitional areas in direct contract with the Earthly Paradise.

But let us return to Bahrām's wars. In order to resume the conflict, the Great King embarked on his counterattack in Azerbaijan, after having recruited more troops in Armenia. The Sassanid army skirted the mountain chain that follows the southern shore of the Caspian Sea, until it reached Merv. The final battle ended with the death of the Hun leader, the rout of the horde which crossed the Oxus (Amu Darya), widespread looting, and the capture of the *khagan*'s wife. While one of his generals was pursuing the Huns into Transoxiana and engaging them in another bloody and victorious battle, the Great King was able to adorn his crown with a great number of pearls, the universal symbol of purity and associated with royalty.[27] A column was erected to mark the border close to the River Oxus, and the surrounding region, which was named Khorasan, was entrusted to Bahrām's brother, Narseh. This confirmed the role of the Oxus in demarcating the border between Iran and Turan, between sedentary peoples and peoples of the steppes—a distinction that in the Zoroastrian tradition recalled the cosmic separation between Good and Evil, and between the Kingdom of Light and the Kingdom of Darkness and Mendacity (*drūj*). The inhabitants of these lands would long remember the figure of Bahrām: the *dirham* with his head on it would later serve as the prototype of the coinage issued in the oasis of Bukhara.[28]

Eastern sources tell of further campaigns waged by Bahrām in India, albeit based on highly fictionalized traditions. The king, dressed as a low-ranking officer (exactly like Alexander the Great in the *Alexander Romance*), is supposed to have visited the court of "Shangal," the king of Sind known historically as Chandragupta II (375–415), to further his heroic exploits as a slayer of monsters. Al-Thaʿālibī reports that in the countryside, Bahrām defeated Shangal's worst enemy, and Shangal rewarded him by giving him his daughter in marriage. The properties and riches that made up the dowry included the port of Daybul (Banbhore) on the Indus delta, fifty-five kilometers from modern-day Karachi, and the acquisition of this trading post allowed the king to consolidate Persian trade in the Indian Ocean.[29] According to Ferdowsī's *Book of Kings*, Bahrām returned to Iran and brought with him *lūlī* musicians, the ancestors of the Gypsies, to entertain the court. For scholars of the Rom civilization, this is the first record of the Gypsy migration, and the anecdote probably contains an element of truth.

Bahrām's next move was to incorporate Armenia into the Sassanian Empire by exploiting the difficulties of the Western Roman Empire.

Because this enterprise was not carried out by military means, but by diplomatic negotiations instead, it would have been difficult to include it in the epic tales and *chansons de geste* produced by the court poets. But the Persians knew that the annexation of the Armenian Kingdom was Bahrām's true political masterpiece. After centuries of failed attempts that often ended in bloody conflicts, the Iranic king had taken possession of a territory that belonged to the Iranic tradition. It is true that Armenia was now Christian, and one and a half centuries of evangelization had eliminated the ancient beliefs. The only remaining pagan temple was that of Garni, which had been built with the aid of the Romans after a peace treaty in 63 AD, and had survived the fanaticism of the new religion only because it acted as a shrine for the dynastic cult of the Arsacids of Armenia.[30]

The Christians in Persia itself had been well integrated into the Sassanian Empire, in spite of the hostility of the Zoroastrian clergy. The empire's trust in the Christians is demonstrated by the fact that their clergy's highest representatives were given important missions as, for instance, when the leading prelate Akhai was sent as an impartial investigator into whether a cargo sent from India had really been stolen by pirates or simply misappropriated by the local governor, one of the emperor's nephews (*Patrologia Orientalis*, V, pp. 324–26). In 428, the head of the Church of Persia was the influential Dādīshōʻ, previously the bishop of the eastern region of Khorasan, and he had played a significant role in defending his land from the Huns' recent attack.[31] The Persian Church, which was protected by Bahrām and integrated into the Sassanian Empire, was now separate from the "catholic" one and was no longer the object of persecutions.[32] According to an anecdote recorded by Theophanes (*Chronographia*, Year 5916), Marouthas, the bishop of Mesopotamia, gained the benevolence of the Great King by freeing his son, the future Yazdegerd II, from a demon who possessed him.[33]

The Church of Persia appears to have sent some missionaries to the east along the most important trade routes. The episcopal see of Merv in Margiana on the border of the Sassanian Empire was established in 424.[34] Moreover, central Asia was at the time a refuge for many Manichaeans, who had themselves fled Roman repression and the bloody persecutions organized by the Zoroastrian clergy of the Sassanian

Empire. Nestorius could not have imagined when he took office in Constantinople that, a few years later, followers of his interpretation of Christianity would be forced to abandon the territories of the Roman Empire and seek refuge in the Sassanian Empire, and that from there they would spread as far as Mongolia, China, and Indonesia.

· EPILOGUE ·

OUR JOURNEY ends here. It is well known what would happen next. The western part of the Roman Empire survived for about a half century, and the new Rome would take on the mantle of the old one. We must, however, secure the image of 428 AD and its aftermath. The year 428 of the Common Era was of course also the year of the consuls Felix and Taurus and 1181 from the foundation of Rome (and we could go on, given that several calendars and chronological systems existed at the time).[1] We will restrict ourselves to recalling the fate of some of the main characters we have encountered.

Artashes of Armenia ended his days on Persian soil, probably in the notorious "Fortress of Oblivion," where some of his predecessors had also been locked up.[2] The Sassanids did not persecute the Armenian Church and did not encroach upon its privileges, but rather they tried to control it in the same way as they had controlled the Christians of Iran. The elderly *katholikós* Sahak was restored to his position, but shortly afterwards he retired to a hermitage, where he died around 439. The loyal ambassador Flavius Dionysius continued his diplomatic activities after having held the position of consul. A few years later, Theodosius sent him to King Ruga of the Huns, who was Attila's uncle and predecessor. Nestorius was repudiated in 431 at the Council of Ephesus, and summoned to appear before Theodosius, whose decision met with the support of Pope Celestine and Cyril of Alexandria. The pope died in 432, a year after Paulinus of Nola.

Following a period in which Nestorius and his remaining loyal supporters put up some resistance, the former bishop's works were publicly burnt. They eventually deported him to Egypt, where he was kidnapped by the Blemmyans, but managed somehow to return to Thebais in a rather poor state, and ended his days in the governor's custody. In the meantime, the wars between Rome, the Blemmyans, and Noubades continued until 453, when a peace treaty was signed with Governor Maximinus (Priscus of Panion, fr. 21).[3]

Abbot Hypatius continued to impose his own brand of charismatic intransigence. Around 434 he managed to stop Leontius, the prefect of Constantinople, from restoring the Olympics. The games, which had regularly taken place until the fourth century, had been suspended because of the antipagan campaign. Leontius's idea was to bring them closer to the capital by moving them from Olympia to Chalcedon, and the plan did not encounter any opposition from Nestorius; after all, the games at the hippodrome, which dominated life in Constantinople, followed the traditional pagan calendar. But Hypatius's zeal against the "this terrible feast of Satan" (Callinicus, *Life of Saint Hypatius*, 33) meant that the games had no future, and would not have one until Baron de Coubertin successfully restored them in 1896.

In May 429, Gaiseric led his people into Mauretania, and from there to the Roman provinces of Numidia and Africa: the sources talk of eighty thousand men.[4] Saint Augustine died of an illness in 430, a year before the fall of Hippo. Other clerics, such as Quodvultdeus and Salvian of Marseilles, would witness the barbarian government. Bonifacius, the count of Africa, stayed on in Africa until 432 in an attempt to halt the Vandal advance. On his return to Italy, he was killed in battle by his rival, Aetius,[5] and after his death, his enemies spread rumors that he had been responsible for inviting the Vandals for some unspecified Machiavellian reason.[6] This version, which was taken up in Byzantine sources such as Procopius and Jordanes, came to be believed: after all, Vortigern had done the same thing in Britannia when he invited the Saxons. The Vandal kingdom lasted for nearly a century, and in 455, Gaiseric led a contingent of Vandals and *Mauri* against Rome, which was plundered once again.

Theodosius died at the age of fifty after falling from a horse. He never gave up on the idea of a war against Iran, which he did in fact launch in 441, but then had to suspend hostilities to go to the assistance of Valentinian III, who had been attacked by Vandal forces now stationed in Sicily.[7] In 441, the virgin Pulcheria finally managed to free herself of her rival Eudocia, who in 440 withdrew to a convent. After her brother's death, she attempted to maintain the legitimacy of the Theodosian dynasty by marrying General Marcian (without, however, consummating the marriage), thus making him Theodosius's successor. She died shortly afterwards in 453, and is today venerated as a saint.

Galla Placidia died in 450, in the same year as Theodosius II. Her mausoleum, which is decorated with splendid mosaics, is one of Ravenna's most important monuments. Valentinian III clashed with the increasingly powerful Aetius, who in 451 succeeded in defeating Attila's Huns and driving off the threat. In 454, Valentinian managed to eliminate him in a duplicitous manner, but the following year his followers were to murder the emperor. Aetius would long be remembered by the Romans and more especially the barbarians. It appears that he was the inspiration for Hagen, one of the more important characters in the *Nibelungenlied* cycle.[8]

Melania the Younger's persistence finally succeeded in converting her uncle Volusianus in 437, when he was visiting Constantinople. The philosopher Cyrus, who remained a pagan, was removed from all his positions because of this. The Christian mob gathered and forced him to convert so that he could continue to serve the public interest (Malalas, *Chronography*, pp. 361ff., Theophanes, *Chronography*, 1, 96–97). In Athens, Proclus continued to teach Platonic philosophy until his death in 486. The Academy would not be definitively closed until Emperor Justinian in 532. The Platonists had to leave the Roman Empire for the more tolerant Sassanid territories, which had already provided refuge to the followers of Nestorius.

In the Eastern Roman Empire, the ascetic lifestyle contributed to the long life of many religious leaders. The coarse Rabbula died in 435, while Simeon Stylites had his column raised to sixteen meters, where he remained until his death in 459.[9] Telanissos continued to be visited by pilgrims, even when the saint's remains were taken to Antioch, which clearly demonstrates that the column itself was considered a relic. Already advanced in years, Nilus of Ancyra died in 430, at the same time as his fellow monk Palladius. Cyril of Alexandria died in 444; Juvenal continued to devote his time to increasing the prestige of Jerusalem until 458. Shenute died in 465 over the age of a hundred. Euthymius died in 473, having almost reached a hundred, and his *láura*, which was transformed into a monastery, continued as such until the thirteenth century.

Our journey has made it possible to encounter and often bring together historical figures whose lives are separated in much of the specialist and populist literature. The examination of people belonging to different and distant worlds like King Artashes of Armenia, Euthymius, and Vortigern within the same work almost seems the kind of expedient that would be used in the popular novels of Christian Jacq or film scripts for a particularly fantastic sword-and-sandal movie. But this is one of the characteristics of Late Antiquity: the imperial crisis and the arrival of new peoples were responsible for bringing the various and previously hidden elements of a complex and multiethnic world to the surface. The men of the fifth century appear more sensitive to this variety and this complexity, which had once been dismissed as things of marginal concern. It is true that the Mediterranean was no longer a shared geographical space. Yet, the empire left behind a clearly defined political dimension, which would continue for many generations. Whatever their evident conflicts, all the voices we have heard—whether imperial or foreign—continued to express views in which the Roman Empire remained the key reference point. Subsequent events would undermine this viewpoint and accelerate the centrifugal tendencies in the Mediterranean, but in 428, Rome, although a little less eternal, was still very much a real entity and had not yet been reduced to a mere concept.

· NOTES ·

PREFACE

1. As in G. W. Bowersock, P. Brown, and O. Grabar (eds.), *Late Antiquity. A Guide to the Post-Classical World* (Cambridge, Mass., 1999).

2. For an overall perspective see Arnaldo Marcone, "A Long Late Antiquity? Considerations on a Controversial Periodization," *Journal of Late Antiquity* Vol. 1, 1, Spring 2008, pp. 4–19.

INTRODUCTION

1. The Current Era (Common Era), which is the politically correct term, was actually introduced in the mid-sixth century, but did not become widespread until many centuries later.

2. G. Duby, *L'An Mil*, Paris: Julliard, 1993; P. Magdalino (ed.), *Byzantium in the Year 1000 AD*, Leiden: Brill, 2002; B. Vincent, *1492. L'«année admirable»*, Paris: Aubier, 1991; S. Bernstein and P. Milza (eds.), *L'année 1947*, Paris: Presses de Sciences Po, 1999; J. E. Wills Jr., *1688 A.D. A Global History*, New York: W. W. Norton & Co., 2001.

3. As Arnaldo Momigliano has observed, the overthrow of Romulus Augustulus was "the inaudible end of an empire": A. Momigliano, "La caduta senza rumore di un impero nel 476 d.C." (1973), in *Sesto contributo alla storia degli studi classici e del mondo antico*, Rome: Ed. di Storia e Letteratura, 1980, pp. 159–79); and yet this judgment, however distinguished, did not challenge the by then well-established historiographical tradition that took this event to be the dividing line between the ancient world and the Middle Ages (in the West). At the very most, it encouraged further reflection on the appropriateness of the criteria used in periodization. See G. W. Bowersock, "The Vanishing Paradigm of the Fall of Rome" (1996), in *Selected Papers on Late Antiquity*, Bari: Edipuglia, 2000, pp. 187–97, and A. Marcone, "A Long Late Antiquity? . . . ; C. Ando, "Decline, Fall and Transformation," ibid., pp. 31–60. A. Marcone refers to the

Italian edition of this book, and finds my own position "impossible to share," but fails to explain why (p. 7, note 11).

4. G. Traina, "La fine del regno d'Armenia," in *La Persia e Bisanzio*, Rome: Accademia dei Lincei, 2004, pp. 353–72.

5. G. Dagron, "Aux origines de la civilisation byzantine: langue de culture et langue d'État" (1969), in *La romanité chrétienne en Orient. Héritages et mutations*, London: Variorum, 1984, III, pp. 23–56. For a new assessment of this emperor, see F. Millar, *A Greek Roman Empire: Power and Belief under Theodosius II (408–450)*, Berkeley: Univ. of California Press, 2006.

6. Using a bold comparison, the jurist Stefan Verosta has suggested a situation similar to that of Austria and Hungary between 1867 and 1918: the Roman Empire is therefore supposed to have become, in effect, a federal state that was only temporarily decentralized into two autonomous units, the eastern and the western *partes*. For this reason, Constantinople continued to think of the regions governed by barbarian kingdoms as "Roman" territory, even after the fall of the Empire of the West in 476. This juridical pretense would affect international politics for centuries to come: S. Verosta, "International Law in Europe and Western Asia between 100 and 650 A.D.," *Académie de droit international. Recueil des cours*, 3, 1964 [1966], pp. 491–617, particularly 564.

7. For general information, see W. E. Kaegi Jr., *Byzantium and the Decline of Rome*, Princeton: Princeton University Press, 1968, pp. 3–27; H. Montgomery, "The Parting of the Ways: Byzantium and Italy in the Fifth Century," in L. Rydén and O. Rosenqvist (eds.), *Aspects of Late Antiquity and Early Byzantium*, Stockholm: Swedish Research Institute, 1993, pp. 11–19. For a work that is still fundamental, see S. Mazzarino, *Stilicone. La crisi imperiale dopo Teodosio* (1942), Milan: Rizzoli, 1990², with an introduction by A. Giardina, "Stilicone o l'antico destino degli uomini vinti," pp. vii–xxxvii.

8. S. Mazzarino, *Stilicone* . . . , p. 87. For Mazzarino, this was the second great era of human crises in the Mediterranean: the first one was in 1200 BC, and the third was the "short century" in which Mazzarino himself lived: see F. Tessitore, *Mazzarino e lo storicismo degli storici*, Catania: Università degli Studi, 2003 (http://www.unict.it/mazzarino).

9. For these questions, see A. Giardina, "Esplosione di tardoantico," *Studi Storici*, 40, 1999, pp. 157–80; G. Fowden, "Elefantiasi del tardoantico?" *Journal of Roman Archaeology*, 15, 2002, pp. 681–86, and the roundtable debate recorded in E. Lo Cascio (ed.) "Gli spazi del tardoantico," *Studi Storici*, 45, 2004, pp. 5–46. Lo Cascio explains the problems very well in his introduction to S. Mazzarino, *Aspetti sociali del IV secolo*, Milan: Rizzoli, 2002², pp. i–xxix, particularly xxviii. For the limitations of periodization, see K. L. Noethlichs, "Kaisertum und Heidentum im 5. Jahrhundert," in J. van Oort and D. Wyrwa (eds.), *Heiden*

und Christen im 5. Jahrhundert, Louvain: Peeters, 1998, pp. 1–31. The medieval-ist's point of view is ably summarized in S. Gasparri, "Tardoantico e alto Me-dioevo: metodologie di ricerca e modelli interpretative," in S. Carocci (ed.), *Storia d'Europa e del Mediterraneo*, VIII, *Il Medioevo. Popoli, poteri, dinamiche*, Rome: Salerno, 2006, pp. 27–61.

10. See A. Schiavone, *The End of the Past: Ancient Rome and the Modern West*, trans. by M. J. Schneider, Cambridge (Mass.): Harvard University Press, 2000 (original title: *La storia spezzata. Roma antica e Occidente moderno*, Rome-Bari: Laterza, 1996), which is discussed in L. Cracco Ruggini, "The Italian city from the third to the sixth century: «broken history» or ever-changing kalei-doscope?" in C. Straw and R. Lim (eds.), *The Past Before Us. The challenge of historiographies of Late Antiquity*, Turnhout: Brepols, 2004, pp. 33–48.

11. The difficulty in combining archeological data with the various eastern and western sources emerges from a recent historical overview by A. Cameron, *The Mediterranean World in Late Antiquity, AD 395–600*, London: Routledge, 1993. Also by A. Cameron, "Ideology and agendas in late antique studies," in L. Lavan and W. Bowden (eds.), *Theory and practice in late antique archaeology*, Leiden: Brill, 2003, pp. 3–21. See also M. G. Morony, "Economic Boundaries? Late An-tiquity and Early Islam," *Journal of Economic and Social History of the Orient*, 47, 2004, pp. 166–94; P. Sarris, "The Origins of the Manorial Economy: New In-sights from Late Antiquity," *English Historical Review*, 119, 2004, pp. 279–311.

12. E. Patlagean, "Lingue e confessioni religiose fra Oriente e Occidente," in *Storia di Roma*, III. *L'età tardoantica*, 1. *Crisi e trasformazioni*, Turin: Einaudi, 1993, pp. 975–89, particularly 989.

13. A. Harris, *Byzantium, Britain and the West. The Archaeology of Cultural Identity, AD 400–650*, Stroud: Tempus Publishing, 2003.

14. C. Wickham, *Framing the Early Middle Ages*, Oxford: Oxford University Press, 2005.

15. R. Bianchi Bandinelli, *Roma. La fine dell'arte antica*, Milan: Rizzoli, 2005², pp. 23ff.

16. "Inscriptions grecques et latines de Syrie," IV, 1439, in D. Feissel, "Notes d'épigraphie chrétienne" (X), *Bulletin de correspondance hellénique*, 119, 1995, pp. 386–89.

17. K. Flasch, *Was ist Zeit? Augustinus von Hippo. Das XI. Buch der Confessio-nes*, Frankfurt am Main: V. Klostermann, 1993; G. O'Daly, "Remembering and forgetting in Augustine, Confessions, X," in A. Haverkamp and R. Lachmann (eds.), *Memoria. Vergessen und Erinnern*, Munich: Fink, 1993, pp. 31–46.

18. Late Antiquity had certain features that are similar to those remarked upon by Pierre Nora more generally for premodern societies: "For established powers, existing religions tended to eliminate new developments, reduce their

corrosive power, and regulate it by means of ritual. All established societies thus attempt to perpetuate themselves through a system of knowledge whose ultimate aim is that of denying the event, given that the event is precisely the schism that would challenge the stability on which they are founded." See P. Nora, "Le retour de l'événement," in J. Le Goff and P. Nora (eds.), *Faire de l'histoire*. I. *Nouveaux problèmes*, Paris: Gallimard, 1974, pp. 285–308, particularly 298.

19. The mainstream approach to Late Antiquity has ended up creating an alternative periodization which is somewhat arguable: for the counterargument, see Giardina, "Esplosione . . ." For the reactions to Giardina's article, see in particular G. W. Bowersock, "Centrifugal force in Late Antique historiography," in Straw and Lim (eds.), *The Past Before Us* . . . , pp. 19–23. For a response in favor of discontinuity, see B. Ward-Perkins, *The Fall of Rome and the End of Civilization*, Oxford: Oxford University Press, 2005, which adopts a stylistic approach similar to the one used by Brown in his books. See now the criticisms in L. Canetti (ed.), «La caduta di Roma: "fine della civiltà" o fine del tardoantico? Una discussione con Bryan Ward-Perkins», *Storica*, 46, 2010, pp. 101–35.

20. For this definition of *De aedificiis*, I am indebted to my student Federico Montinaro, whose graduate thesis, which was examined in July 2005, is currently being further developed. For the *Expositio*, see the recent translation with comment by M. Di Branco and U. Livadiotti, *Anonimo del IV secolo. Descrizione del mondo e delle sue genti*, Rome: Salerno, 2005.

I

THE TRAVELS OF FLAVIUS DIONYSIUS AND THE END OF ARMENIA

1. Sources in J. R. Martindale, *The Prosopography of the Later Roman Empire*, vol. II, *A.D. 395–527*, Cambridge: Cambridge University Press, 1980 [from here on it will be referred to as *PLRE* II], pp. 365ff.

2. For information on the site, see J.-P. Sodini, "La hiérarchisation des espaces à Qal'at Sem'an," in M. Kaplan (ed.), *Le sacré et son inscription dans l'espace à Byzance et en Occident*, Paris: Publ. de la Sorbonne, 2001, pp. 251–62 (the shrine that can now be seen was built after Saint Simeon's death in 459). For more general information, see S. A. Harvey, "The Stylite's Liturgy: Ritual and Religious Identity in Late Antiquity," *Journal of Early Christian Studies*, 6, 1998, pp. 523–39.

3. "Syrische Lebensbeschreibung des hl. Symeon," ed. by H. Hilgenfeld, in H. Lietzmann, *Das Leben des heiligen Symeon Stylites*, Leipzig: Hinrichs, 1908, p. 118 (for a more recent translation, see R. Doran, *The Lives of Symeon Stylites*, Kalamazoo: Cistercian Publications, 1992). Dionysius is already mentioned in

chapter seventy, but this does not necessarily mean that the story refers to an earlier time. For the importance of the *Syriac Life* . . . , see B. Flusin, "Syméon et les philologues, ou la mort du stylite," in *Les saints et leur sanctuaire à Byzance*, Paris: Publ. de la Sorbonne, 1993, pp. 1–23 (also bibliography).

4. For a general overview, see A. D. Lee, *Information and frontiers: Roman foreign relations in late antiquity*, Cambridge: Cambridge University Press, 1993, passim. See also A. D. Lee, "Embassies as evidence for the movement of military intelligence between the Roman and Sasanian empires," in P. Freeman and D. Kennedy (eds.), *The Defence of the Roman and Byzantine East*, Oxford: British Arch. Reports, 1986, pp. 455–61; Z. Rubin, "Diplomacy and war in the relations between Byzantium and the Sassanids in the fifth century AD," in *The Defence of the Roman* . . . , pp. 677–95.

5. See A. Cutler, "Silver across the Euphrates. Forms of Exchange between Sasanian Persia and the Late Roman Empire," *Mitteil. spätant. Archäologie und byz. Kunstgeschichte*, 4, 2005, pp. 9–37; J. Engemann, "Diplomatische «Geschenke»—Objekte aus der Spätantike?" in *Mitteil. Spätant. Archäologie* . . . , pp. 39–64.

6. On the presence of the clergy in diplomatic missions, see N. G. Garsoian, "Le rôle de la hiérarchie chrétienne dans les rapports diplomatiques entre Byzance et les Sassanides" (first published 1973/4), in *Armenia between Byzantium and the Sasanians*, London: Variorum Reprints, 1985, VIII, pp. 119–38. On the role of merchants, see G. Traina, "La frontiera armena dell'impero romano: i due punti di vista," in C. Moatti (ed.), *La mobilité des personnes en Méditerranée de l'Antiquité à l'époque moderne*, Rome: École Française de Rome, 2004, pp. 205–23.

7. See A. Panaino, "'Guerra' e 'pace' nella tradizione religiosa iranica preislamica," in M. Perani (ed.), *Guerra santa, guerra e pace dal vicino oriente antico alle tradizioni ebraica, cristiana e islamica*, Florence: Giuntina, 2005, pp. 27–44.

8. The conflict ended with a relatively advantageous situation for Theodosius: see K. G. Holum, "Pulcheria's Crusade A.D. 421–22 and the Ideology of Imperial Victory," *Greek, Roman and Byzantine Studies*, 18, 1977, pp. 153–72.

9. The two Armenian sources (which have similar content, except for a few minor details) appear in an English translation by R. W. Thomson, *Moses Khorenats'i. History of the Armenians*, Cambridge (Mass.): Harvard University Press, 1978, and a revised edition, Ann Arbor: Caravan Books, 2006; *The History of Lazar P'arpec'i*, Atlanta: Scholars Press, 1991. For problems in dating Moses's *History of the Armenians*, see the introduction by A. and J.-P. Mahé in *Histoire de l'Arménie par Moïse de Khorène. Nouvelle traduction de l'arménien classique (d'après Victor Langlois)*, Paris: Gallimard, 1993. For the historical context, see Traina, *La fine del regno d'Armenia* . . .

10. The shift in the balance of power is confirmed by a contemporary document, which lists the *nakharark'* on the fall of the Armenian kingdom. This list (*gahnamak*), which according to tradition had to be ratified by the king and the *katholikós* (the head of the Christian Church of Armenia), only came into effect when it was lodged with the imperial archives in Ctesiphon, a clear sign of the "limited sovereignty" of the kingdom. The document, which was discovered in the nineteenth century, can be consulted in N. Adontz, *Armenia in the Period of Justinian. The Political Conditions based on the naxarar System*, ed. by N. G. Garsoian, Lisbon: Fundação Gulbenkian, 1970, pp. 67ff.

11. Contrary to the custom in other Christian Churches, the Armenian patriarch (*katholikós*) was not elected by a council of bishops, but was chosen by the Parthian family of Saint Gregory the Illuminator, who was the evangelizer of the Armenian lands. The hereditary principle limited the bishops' scope for initiative, avoided dangerous doctrinal controversies, and above all guaranteed the Armenian Church a greater degree of autonomy from Constantinople and Rome, which was clearly also an advantage for the Sassanian Empire. The Parthian ancestry of the *katholikós* helped to reinforce his charisma and obviously guaranteed a dependable relationship with the royal family. For information on the Armenian Church, see N. G. Garsoian, *L'Église arménienne et le Grand Schisme d'Orient*, Louvain: Peeters, 1999.

12. The clause was not particularly damaging to western merchants, given that the city had maintained a degree of economic importance and had acquired a prominence in the collective religious memory due to the cult of Saint Gregory, which attracted many pilgrims. At the same time, however, they were barred from Dvin, the nearby capital of the kingdom, unless they were in the retinue of an official diplomatic mission. This was to prevent them from coming into contact with court circles. See Traina, "La frontiera armena ..."

13. H. Manandyan, "Critical Interpretation of the History of the Armenian People" (in Armenian), Part II (first published 1945), facsimile reprint in *Opere*, Yerevan: Academy of Sciences, 1978, Vol. II, pp. 287ff. The text by Ełishē can be consulted in the English translation by R. W. Thomson, *Ełishē. History of Vardan and the Armenian War*, Cambridge (Mass.): Harvard University Press, 1982. See also Adontz, *Armenian in the Period of Justinian* ... ; C. Toumanoff, *Studies in Christian Caucasian History*, Washington (D.C.): Georgetown Univ. Press, 1963.

14. The Arsacids of Armenia were a local branch of the great dynasty of the Arsacids of Parthia, who in turn had long ruled over Iran. Their imperialist policies clashed with those of Rome, and this rivalry had favored the independence of Armenia. Around 225, however, the Parthian Arsacids were deposed

by the Sassanid dynasty, and this dynastic change had triggered a series of conflicts which had also involved the Armenians. Towards the beginning of the fourth century, the latter embraced Christianity, precisely in order to distance themselves from the Sassanids. Following various vicissitudes, the geopolitical balance shifted around 387 in Persia's favor. With the exception of the more western provinces, which had been ceded to the Romans, the Armenia of the Arsacids was still nominally independent, but under the vigilant control of Sassanian Persia. The treaty of 422 had confirmed these conditions. For fourth-century Armenia, see especially the essays in N. G. Garsoian, *Armenia between Byzantium and the Sasanians* ..., and Garsoian, *Church and Culture in Early Medieval Armenia*, Aldershot: Variorum, 1999. More generally, see R. C. Blockley, *East Roman Foreign Policy. Formation and Conduct from Diocletian to Anastasius*, Leeds: Francis Cairns, 1992.

15. At that time, the Sassanids did not restrict themselves to the persecution of Christians in Iran, but also attempted to impose their own king on Armenia, one who followed the Zoroastrian religion (Moses Khorenatsʻi, 3, 55–56).

16. Unfortunately folklore is not a great help. For the period after 425, the historical documentation is particularly sketchy. There is no genuine historical guide, and in any event there are only fragments of the contemporary Greek and Latin historical works, or in other words, just scanty information selected by uninspiring chroniclers. For general information, see G. Marasco (ed.), *Greek and Roman Historiography in Late Antiquity*, Leiden: Brill, 2003.

17. Dionysius was probably the nameless ambassador mentioned by Theodoret of Cyrrhus (*The Ecclesiastical History*, 5, 39) who, when charged with a mission to Persia under Theodosius II, attempted to save Deacon Benjamin, who had been imprisoned for two years. Martindale, *PLRE* II, p. 1236, suggests that this episode may have occurred during the war of 421/2.

18. According to the *Syriac Life of Saint Simeon the Stylite*, Dionysius "negotiated brilliantly and achieved everything he had wanted, and was able to return with full honors and to a grand parade." Moreover, the two manuscripts contain a significant variant, which can undoubtedly be attributed to a pro-Sassanian tradition: in place of "negotiated," it says "was received."

II
The World of Nestorius: Bishops, Monks, and Saracens

1. The acts of this council reflect the political changes that had occurred in recent years, and without doubt the great political sensitivity of the patriarch Dādīshōʼ, about whom more information can be found below on p. 126. From

this time on, the Church of Iran was considered independent: it was no longer necessary to appeal to the authority of Constantinople, and the "protection of the Fathers of the West" was no longer admissible (*Synodicon Orientale*, pp. 295ff.): V. Erhart, "The Development of Syriac Christian Canon Law in the Sasanian Empire," in R. W. Mathisen (ed.), *Law, Society, and Authority in Late Antiquity*, Oxford: Oxford University Press, 2001, pp. 15–29.

2. In reality, the Sassanid Empire had halted the wave of persecutions of Christians by 410, and issued the political decree to establish a Christian Church of Iran. This move, which was unpopular with the Zoroastrian clergy, proved to be successful at least in appearance, as it brought reconciliation between the Great King and the Christians, and therefore a return of public order. But above all it founded a national "Church" free from the authority of the most powerful Christian bishoprics of the Roman Empire. The Persian Church looked to the Armenian Church for its inspiration. Its foundation in 410 led to the establishment of a number of bishoprics, which consolidated the Christian faith in various provinces of the empire. Unlike the Armenian Church, the Persian Church did not, however, have any nationalist characteristics, given that the Christians of Iran were always a minority. The "Western" influences on the establishment of the Church of Persia are still a matter for debate; for current positions on this question, see A. Panaino, "La Chiesa di Persia e l'impero sasanide. Conflitto e integrazione," in *Cristianità d'Occidente e Cristianità d'Oriente (secoli VI–XI)*, Spoleto: Centro Italiano di Studi sull'Alto Medioevo, 2004, pp. 765–863, particularly 808.

3. See P. Peeters, *Orient et Byzance. Le tréfonds oriental de l'hagiographie byzantine*, Brussels: Société des Bollandistes, 1950, pp. 49–70; S. Brock, "Greek and Syriac in Late Antique Syria" (first published 1994), in *From Ephrem to Romanos. Interactions between Syriac and Greek in Late Antiquity*, London: Variorum, 1999, I, pp. 149–60.

4. For a biography of Nestorius, see M. Jugie, *Nestorius et la controverse nestorienne*, Paris: Beauchesne, 1912, pp. 18ff.

5. *The Ecclesiastical History* was written around 449/50. A few years later, Theodoret wrote the *Compendium of Heretical Accounts*, which also included a section on his former friend Nestorius, who had just died: the decision to include Nestorius was unavoidable, as failure to do so would have led to accusations of heresy.

6. For a summary of Nestorius's theology, see C. Fraisse-Coué, "Le débat théologique au temps de Théodose II: Nestorius," in *Histoire du christianisme*, 2. *Naissance d'une chrétienté (250–450)*, Paris: Desclée, 1995, pp. 499–555.

7. Most of the information on Antioch comes from literary texts. The site of the city (now in Turkey, close to the Syrian border) has never been the object

of systematic archaeological digs. See I. Sandwell and J. Huskinson (eds.), *Culture and Society in Later Roman Antioch*, Oxford: Oxbow, 2004.

8. The expression comes from A.-J. Festugière, *Antioche païenne et chrétienne. Libanius, Chrysostome et les moines de Syrie*, Paris: de Boccard, 1959, p. 403.

9. P. Brown, *Power and Persuasion in Late Antiquity. Towards a Christian Empire*, Madison: University of Wisconsin Press, 1992, p. 12.

10. On Antioch, see G. Downey, *A History of Antioch in Syria*, Princeton: Princeton University Press, 1961; W. Liebeschuetz, *Antioch, City and Imperial Administration in the Later Roman Empire*, Oxford: Clarendon Press, 1972; W. Liebeschuetz and H. Kennedy, "Antioch and the Villages of Northern Syria in the Fifth and Sixth Centuries A.D.: Trends and Problems" (first published 1988), in *From Diocletian to the Arab conquest: change in the late Roman empire*, Aldershot: Variorum, 1990, XVI, pp. 65–90.

11. See L. Lavan, "The political topography of the late antique city," in *Theory and practice . . .* , pp. 314–37, particularly 315ff.

12. G. Tate, "La Syrie-Palestine," in C. Morrisson (ed.), *Le monde byzantin*, I. *L'empire romain d'Orient (330–641)*, Paris: Presses Universitaires de France, 2004, pp. 373–401, particularly 392.

13. See M. Sartre, "Les *metrokomiai* de Syrie du sud," *Syria*, 76, 1999, pp. 197–222; see also M. Kaplan, *Les hommes et la terre à Byzance*, Paris: Publ. de la Sorbonne, 1992, pp. 90ff.

14. Peter Brown has emphasized the social implications of this phenomenon in three important works: *The Cult of Saints: Its Rise and Function in Latin Christianity* (new edition), Chicago: University of Chicago Press, 1982; "Town, Village and Holy Man: The Case of Syria," in *Society and the Holy in Late Antiquity*, Berkeley: University of California Press, 1982, pp. 153–65; and "The Rise and Function of the Holy Man in Late Antiquity," *Journal of Early Christian Studies*, 6, 1998, pp. 353–76.

15. The expression comes from S. Mazzarino, "La democratizzazione della cultura nel 'basso impero'" (first published 1960), in *Antico, tardoantico ed èra costantiniana*, I, Bari: Dedalo, 1974, pp. 74–98. For the implications of this important concept, see G. Cantino Wataghin and J.-M. Carrié (eds.), "Antiquité tardive et «démocratisation de la culture»: mise à l'épreuve du paradigme," *Antiquité tardive*, 9, 2001, pp. 25–295.

16. M.-Y. Perrin, "Théodoret de Cyr et la représentation de l'espace ascétique: imaginaire classique et nouveauté socio-religieuse," in R. B. Finazzi and A. Valvo (eds.), *Pensiero e istituzioni del mondo classico nelle culture del Vicino Oriente*, Alessandria: Edizioni dell'Orso, 2001, pp. 211–35.

17. Later, Theodoret would recall his efforts in his *Epistle* 139 to Anatolius, to which Brown refers in *Power and Persuasion . . .* , pp. 218ff.

18. C. Mango, "Aspects of Syrian Piety," in S. A. Boyd and M. M. Mango (eds.), *Ecclesiastical Silver Plate in Sixth-Century Byzantium*, Washington (D.C.): Dumbarton Oaks, 1993, pp. 99–105.

19. It is more difficult to agree with Mango's views on radicalism among Syrian monks. He argues that the theatricality of these extreme forms of asceticism was due no so much to rustic fanaticism as to the "expression of an inventive and mercantile nation": Mango, "Aspects . . . ," p. 105.

20. Saint Simeon's fame reached the court. In 423, Theodosius intended to adopt a moderate line against the widespread Judaeophobia and expropriation of synagogues in the Syriac area, but he decided not to apply these measures because of pressure from the saint (*Syriac Life of Simeon Stylites*, 130–31). Leaving aside the question of its actual truth, this anecdote clearly shows the authority of Syriac monks. By electing Nestorius, the emperor probably wished to gain better control of their fanatical excesses.

21. We should not forget Luis Buñuel's film *Simón del desierto* (Mexico, 1965). The monk, played by Claudio Brook, resists the temptations of the devil, but in the end gives in, after being taken to a modern nightclub in New York.

22. P. Maraval, *Lieux saints et pèlerinages d'Orient. Histoire et géographie des origines à la conquête arabe*, Paris: Éd. du Cerf, 1985, pp. 87 and 342–44.

23. E. K. Fowden, *The Barbarian Plain. Saint Sergius between Rome and Iran*, Berkeley: University of California Press, 1999.

24. For an analysis of this passage, see G. Traina, "Materiali per un commento a Movsēs Xorenac'i, *Patmut'iwn Hayoc'*, II, *Le Muséon*, III," 1998, pp. 95–138, particularly 125ff.

25. H.J.W. Drijvers, "The Persistence of Pagan Cults and Practices in Christian Syria," in N. G. Garsoian, T. F. Mathews, and R. W. Thomson (eds.), *East of Byzantium. Syria and Armenia in the Formative Period*, Washington (D.C.): Dumbarton Oaks, 1982, pp. 35–43.

26. Edessa was also home to the followers of Bardesanes, the third-century philosopher and poet who created his own school. Bardesanes's doctrines and his school were viewed with suspicion by Christian theologians who fervently opposed his legacy; see the summary in A. Camplani, "Rivisitando Bardesane. Note sulle fonti siriache del bardesanismo e sulla sua collocazione storico-religiosa," *Cristianesimo nella Storia*, 19, 1998, pp. 519–96. For Eznik, see A. Orengo, *Eznik di Kołb. Confutazione delle sette*, Pisa: ETS, 1996.

27. For the authority of bishops in Late Antiquity, see C. Rapp, *Holy Bishops in Late Antiquity. The Nature of Christian Leadership in an Age of Transition*, Berkeley: University of California Press, 2005.

28. H.J.W. Drijvers, "Rabbula, bishop of Edessa: spiritual authority and secular power," in H.J.W. Drijvers and J. W. Watt (eds.), *Portraits of Spiritual*

Authority. Religious Power in Early Christianity, Byzantium and the Christian Orient, Leiden: Brill, 1999, pp. 139–54.

29. This could explain Rabbula's tactical decisions following the Council of Ephesus in 431. When Nestorius was condemned, the Bishop of Urha/Edessa was united with the other eastern bishops in condemning the positions of Cyril of Alexandria, but when Cyril emerged the victor and Theodosius II abandoned Nestorius, the bishop rapidly joined the "orthodox" forces and successfully managed to hold on to his own see, unlike many other bishops close to Nestorius, who became victims of a far-reaching purge. It is probable, as Drijvers has suggested (*Portraits of Spiritual Authority . . .* , p. 151), that his aristocratic origins helped him to keep the necessary support at the court, but it would be an oversimplification to view Rabbula as merely an opportunist.

30. P. Rousseau, "Eccentrics and Coenobites in the Late Roman East," *Byz. Forschungen*, 24, 1997, pp. 35–50.

31. This name has been connected to homonymous "Saracen," queen of the fourth century (*Année épigraphique*, 1947, 193). The hypothesis, which is certainly a suggestive one, is not unfortunately supported by other evidence. For the text of the inscription, I have followed D. Feissel, "Les «martyria» d'Anasartha," *Travaux et mémoires*, 14, 2002 (Mélanges Gilbert Dagron), pp. 201–20.

32. According to another theory, the term derives from the Arabic *sherqiyye*, which means the act of migrating towards the desert interior. For the bibliography, see T. Gnoli, "Dalla «hypateia» ai «phylarchoi»: per una storia istituzionale del «limes Arabicus» fino a Giustiniano," in *Ravenna da capitale imperiale a capitale esarcale*, Spoleto: Centro Italiano di Studi sull'Alto Medioevo, 2005, pp. 495–536, particularly 515.

33. For the arguments against this stereotype, which has proved to be very resilient and is still very much alive, see D. F. Graf, "Rome and the Saracens: reassessing the nomadic menace," in T. Fahd (ed.), *L'Arabie préislamique et son environnement historique et culturel*, Leiden: Brill, 1989, pp. 341–400, particularly 351–56.

III
On The Pilgrim's Road

1. L. Di Paola, *Viaggi, trasporti e istituzioni. Studi sul* cursus publicus, Messina: Di.Sc.A.M., 1999, pp. 33–40.

2. Messengers working on the *cursus publicus* could travel extremely quickly: in 422, a certain Palladius is supposed to have taken only three days to announce

the victory over the Persians (Socrates, *Ecclesiastical History*, 7, 19). Clearly this was an exaggeration. See A. Chauvot, "Guerre et diffusion des nouvelles au Bas-Empire," *Ktema*, 13, 1988, pp. 125–35; Lee, *Information and frontiers....*

3. The expression belongs to W. M. Ramsay, *The Historical Geography of Asia Minor*, London: John Murray, 1890, pp. 197, 242. Nestorius's itinerary is only reliably documented in its final stage from Chalcedon to Constantinople (see below, pp. 23ff.).

4. On the practicability of roads in Anatolia in Late Antiquity, see the brief study, J.-P. Sodini, "L'Asie mineure," in Morrisson, *Le monde byzantin ...* , pp. 353ff. For the *Itinerarium*, see J. Elsner, "The «Itinerarium Burdigalense»: Politics and Salvation in the Geography of Constantine's Empire," *Journal of Roman Studies*, 90, 2000, pp. 181–95.

5. For the discomforts of traveling with the *cursus publicus*, see Di Paola, *Viaggi, trasporti e istituzioni ...* , pp. 99–103. According to the *Syriac Legend of Nestorius* (Brière p. 5), Nestorius is supposed to have actually ridden a messenger's horse throughout the journey: M. Brière, "La légende syriaque de Nestorius," *Revue de l'Orient chrétien*, 15, 1910, pp. 1–25.

6. There are some doubts about this information, given that the eighty-year-old Theodore died that very year—428—but it is not definitely false.

7. G. Dagron, *Vie et miracles de sainte Thècle. Texte grec, traduction et commentaire*, Brussels: Société des Bollandistes, 1978, pp. 55–79.

8. The tomb of Emperor Julian was in Tarsus, but understandably it was somewhat neglected (Libanius, *Orations* 17, 306).

9. See *Apocalypse of Paul*, 17, and the comment in C. Kelly, *Ruling the Later Roman Empire*, Cambridge (Mass.): Harvard University Press, 2004, pp. 239–41.

10. The Isaurians were a kind of "political fossil." B. D. Shaw, "Bandit Highlands and Lowland Peace: The Mountains of Isauria-Cilicia," *Journal of the Economic and Social Hist. of the Orient*, 33, 1990, pp. 199–233 and 237–70, particularly 263. See K. Feld, *Barbarische Bürger. Die Isaurier und das Römische Reich*, Berlin: de Gruyter, 2005.

11. Dagron, *Vie et miracles ...* , pp. 119–23.

12. There is a reversal of the usual *topos* in Christian literature, that associates brigands with demons: see G.J.M. Bartelink, "Les démons comme brigands," *Vigiliae Christianae*, 21, 1967, pp. 12–24.

13. E. A. Thompson, "The Isaurians under Theodosius II," *Hermathena*, 68, 1946, pp. 18–31; Millar, *A Greek Roman Empire ...* , p. 50.

14. M.-A. Calvet-Sebasti and P.-L. Gatier (eds.), *Firmus de Césarée. Lettres* [Sources chrétiennes 350], Paris: Éd. du Cerf, 1989, pp. 37ff. A further clue to the closure of the frontier can be found in the tradition on Honorius's constitution

relating to the transit of merchants (see above, p. 26): this law appears in the *Code of Justinian* but not in the *Code of Theodosius*, which was published in 438, but work on drawing it up started in 429.

15. See Calvet-Sebasti and Gatier, *Firmus de Césarée* . . . , p. 52. For Cappadocia's defense problems, see S. Métivier, *La Cappadoce (IVᵉ–VIᵉ siècle). Une histoire provinciale de l'Empire romain d'Orient*, Paris: Publ. de la Sorbonne, 2005, p. 413.

16. Calvet-Sebasti and Gatier, *Firmus de Césarée* . . . , p. 43. Parochial rivalry between neighboring bishoprics is one of the characteristics of the doctrinal disputes discussed in the great ecumenical councils. At the council of Ephesus, Euterius also adopted a position hostile to Firmus in defense of Nestorius. Following the condemnation of Nestorius, he managed to stop Firmus from appointing another bishop of Tyana thanks to the support he received from his fellow citizens (*Synodicon*, p. 87). In the end, however, he paid for his loyalty to Nestorius with disgrace and exile.

17. For the surviving works of Theodotus, see M. Aubineau, "Une Homélie grecque inédite, attribuée à Théodote d'Ancyre, sur le Baptême du Seigneur" (1969), in *Recherches patristiques*, Amsterdam: Hakkert, 1974, pp. 93–118.

18. C. Foss, "Late antique and Byzantine Ankara" (first published 1977), in *History and Archaeology of Byzantine Asia Minor*, Aldershot: Variorum, 1990, VI, pp. 28–87, particularly 65ff.

19. See S. Mitchell, *Anatolia. Land, Men, and Gods in Asia Minor. I. The Celts and the Impact on Roman Rule*; II. *The Rise of the Church*, Oxford: Clarendon Press, 1993, I, pp. 50ff. and 175; II, p. 93.

20. Of course, monks had to avoid distractions and temptations, particularly if they lived in towns, something Nilus complained of in *De monachorum praestantia*. See Foss, "Late antique and Byzantine Ankara . . . ," pp. 53ff.

21. Nilus's works had great resonance within Nestorian circles, and were translated into Syriac. The Greek corpus was in turn reworked in the sixth century: see A. Cameron, "The Authenticity of the Letters of Nilus of Ancyra" (first published 1976), in *Literature and Society in the Early Byzantine World*, London: Variorum Reprints, 1985, VI, pp. 181–96.

22. Hypatius's activity was documented in the biography written by the monk Callinicus, who was already in the monastery in 426. See the recent article by R. Kosiłski, "A Few Remarks on the Author of the *Vita Hypatii*," *Electrum*, 8, 2004, pp. 143–51.

23. Dagron, *Vie et miracles* . . . , pp. 85ff.

24. On the survival of paganism in western Asia Minor, see A.-V. Pont, "Le paysage religieux grec traditionnel dans les cités d'Asie mineure occidentale au IVᵉ et au début du Vᵉ siècle," *Revue des ét. grecques*, 117, 2004, pp. 546–77.

25. M. Guarducci, *Epigrafia Greca IV*, Rome: Poligrafico dello Stato, 1978, pp. 401ff.

26. See M. Wallraff, "Geschichte des Novatianismus seit dem vierten Jahrhundert im Osten," *Zeitschr. für ant. Christentum*, 1, 1997, pp. 251–79.

27. C. Luibhéid, "Theodosius II and Heresy," *Journal of Ecclesiastical History*, 16, 1965, pp. 13–38, particularly 14; F. Millar, "Repentant Heretics in Fifth-Century Lydia: Identity and Literacy," *Scripta Class. Israelica*, 23, 2004, pp. 111–30; F. Millar, *A Greek Roman Empire . . .*, pp. 149ff.

28. On the problems arising from the inscription, see G. D. Merola, "Autonomia doganale nella tarda antichità. Intorno a CIL 3, 7151–7152," *Atti accademia romanistica costantiniana*, 13, 2001, pp. 277–92.

29. *PLRE* II, p. 209: "The name is strange, possibly Semitic." Unfortunately, the part of the inscription containing the name *Baralach* has disappeared some time ago, and the reading depends solely on a copy made in the fifteenth century by Ciriaco d'Ancona. I have discussed the origin of the name *Baralach* with René Lebrun, whom I would like to thank.

30. Like Euterius, the Bishop of Nicomedia, Himerius also supported Nestorius at the Council of Ephesus. As punishment, Nicomedia lost its primacy over Bithynia to Nicaea, the city's eternal rival.

31. In the hagiographic version, Hypatius is supposed to have had a premonitory vision of the condemnation of Nestorius at the council of Ephesus (431). On the other hand, the patriarch's supporters argued that he was foretold of his appointment to the episcopal throne of Constantinople, again three years beforehand, through a vision of a very pious woman (John Rufus, bishop of Maiuma, *Plerophories*, 36 [*Patrologia Orientalis*, 8]). The prophetic period of three and a half years in advance can also be found in the Bible (1 Kings, 17, 1; Epistle of James, 5, 17).

IV
The New Rome and Its Prince

1. S. MacCormack, *Art and Ceremony in Late Antiquity*, Berkeley: University of California Press, 1981, pp. 62ff.

2. From 421, the diocese started to exercise a degree of authority over the Churches of the eastern Balkans. This measure provoked a reaction in Rome, which for a short time obtained its repeal, but it cannot have been for long as the law was published in the *Code of Theodosius* (16, 2, 45 = *Code of Justinian*, 1, 2, 6). For current academic opinion and bibliography, see F. Elia, "Sui «privilegia urbis Constantinopolitanae»," in F. Elia (ed.), *Politica retorica e simbolismo*

del primato. Roma e Costantinopoli (secoli IV–VII), Catania: Culc, 2002, pp. 79–105, particularly 97ff.

3. See A. Berger, "Konstantinopel, die erste christliche Metropole?" in G. Brands and H.-G. Severin (eds.), *Die spätantike Stadt und ihre Christianisierung*, Wiesbaden: Reichert, 2003, pp. 63–84.

4. Sources gathered by L. Cracco Ruggini, "Simboli di battaglia ideologica nel tardo ellenismo (Roma, Atene, Costantinopoli; Numa, Empedocle, Cristo)," in *Studi storici in onore di Ottorino Bertolini*, I, Pisa: Pacini, 1972, pp. 177–300, particularly 216, n. 70.

5. C. Mango, *Le développement urbain de Constantinople (IVᵉ–VIIᵉ siècles)*, Paris: de Boccard, 1990², pp. 44ff.

6. See O. J. Maenchen-Helfen, *The World of the Huns. Studies in Their History and Culture*, Berkeley: University of California Press, 1973, p. 76. For Constantinople's city wall and more generally the development of fortifications in the Empire of the East in the fifth century, see J. Crow, "Fortifications and urbanism in late antiquity: Thessaloniki and other eastern cities," in L. Lavan (ed.), *Resent research in late-antique urbanism*, Supplement to *Journal of Roman Archaeology*, 42, 2001, pp. 89–105.

7. Mango, *Le développement . . .* , pp. 40ff.

8. M. M. Mango, "The Commercial Map of Constantinople," *Dumbarton Oaks Papers*, 54, 2000, pp. 189–207.

9. A law of 416 laid down that the wheat in public warehouses should be delivered solely to bakers (*Code of Theodosius* 14, 16, 2). See J.-M. Carrié, "L'institution annonaire de la première à la deuxième Rome: continuité et innovation," in B. Marin and C. Virlouvet (eds.), *Nourrir les cités de Méditerranée. Antiquité–Temps modernes*, Paris: Maisonneuve et Larose, 2003, pp. 153–212.

10. Sources in H. Grégoire and M.-A. Kugener, "Quand est né l'empereur Théodose II?" *Byzantion*, 4, 1927/8, pp. 337–48.

11. See G. Dagron, "Nés dans la pourpre," *Travaux et mémoires*, 12, 1994, pp. 105–42; A. Carile, "Le insegne del potere a Bisanzio," in *La corona e i simboli del potere*, Rimini: Il Cerchio, 2000, pp. 65–124, particularly 84ff.

12. The epithet *porphyrogenite* was particularly exclusive and charismatic: for a long time, Theodosius II remained the only emperor who qualified for this title (John of Ephesus, *Ecclesiastical History*, 5, 14). From 424, only the emperor had the privilege of wearing purple (*Code of Justinian*, 11, 9, 4).

13. On Theodosius's constitution (6, 2, 26 of his codex), see Kelly, *Ruling the Later Roman Empire . . .* , p. 219.

14. For more general information, see K. G. Holum, *Theodosian Empresses: Women and Imperial Dominion in Late Antiquity*, Berkeley: University of California Press, 1982, pp. 79–146; for Eudocia, see J. Burman, "The Athenian

Empress Eudocia," in P. Castrén (ed.), *Post-Herulian Athens*, Helsinki: Suomen Ateenan-instituutin säätiö, 1994, pp. 63–87. On Pulcheria, see C. Angelidi, *Pulcheria. La castità al potere*, Milan: Jaca Book, 1998. On Eudocia's father, Leontius, see below, p. 46.

15. Pulcheria was particularly active in promoting the building of churches, monasteries, and almshouses. It would appear that in 428 she had the Chapel of Saint Stephen fitted out within the palace, so that it could house a precious relic, the hand of the first martyr, which had been discovered in Palestine a few years earlier (Theophanes, *Chronographia*, Year 5920). Given the well-known problems with Theophanes's chronology, this date is by no means certain, and the information is treated with skepticism by C. Mango, "A fake inscription of the empress Eudocia and Pulcheria's relic of Saint Stephen," *Nea Rōmē*, 1, 2004, pp. 23–34.

16. P. Brown, *The Body and Society: Men, Women and Sexual Renunciation in Early Christianity*, New York: Columbia University Press, 1988, p. 238.

17. E. Gibbon, *The Decline and Fall of the Roman Empire*, London: Chatto and Windus, 1978, p. 470.

18. G. Dagron, *Costantinopoli. Nascita di una capitale (330–451)*, Turin: Einaudi, 1991, p. 102 (original title: *Naissance d'une Capitale: Constantinople et ses Institutions de 330 à 451*, Paris: Presses Universitaires de France, 1984).

19. J. Harries, "'Pius princeps': Theodosius II and fifth-century Constantinople," in P. Magdalino (ed.), *New Constantines*, Aldershot: Variorum, 1994, pp. 35–44.

20. See G. Zecchini, "L'immagine di Teodosio II nella storiografia ecclesiastica," *Mediterraneo antico*, 5, 2002, pp. 529–46. For the ideological aspects of ecclesiastical historiography, see P. Van Nuffelen, *Un héritage de paix et de piété. Étude sur les Histoires ecclésiastiques de Socrate et de Sozomène*, Louvain: Peeters, 2004; P. Van Nuffelen, "Sozomenos und Olympiodoros von Theben, oder wie man Profangeschichte lesen soll," *Jahrb. für Antike und Christentum*, 47, 2004, pp. 81–97.

21. See C. Mango, *Le développement urbain. . . .*

22. At the same time, Theodosius did not want to eliminate entirely the last vestiges of the traditional cult of the emperor, at least in the provinces. See A. Al-Azmeh, "Monotheistic Kingship," in A. Al-Azmeh and J. M. Bák (eds.), *Monotheistic Kingship. The Medieval Variants*, Budapest: Ceu, 2004, pp. 9–29, particularly 18.

23. See M. McCormick, *Eternal victory. Triumphal rulership in late antiquity, Byzantium, and the early medieval West*, Cambridge-Paris: Cambridge University Press-Maison des Sciences de l'Homme, 1986, pp. 60, 111, 119.

24. Dagron, *Constantinople*..., pp. 34 and 112ff.

25. See J. Jarry, *Hérésies et factions dans l'empire byzantin du IVᵉ au VIIᵉ siècle*, Le Caire: Institut français d'archéologie orientale, 1968, pp. 102, 557–59; for more general information, see A. Cameron, *Circus Factions. Blues and Greens at Rome and Byzantium*, Oxford: Clarendon Press, 1976; C. Heucke, *Circus und Hippodrom als politischer Raum*, Hildesheim: Olms-Weidmann, 1994.

26. The history of Theodosius's wedding has been handed down like a fairy tale (Malalas 14, 3–5; *Easter Chronicle*, pp. 577ff; see also Socrates, *Ecclesiastical History* 7, 21). For similar cases in Byzantium, see L.-M. Hans, "Der Kaiser als Märchenprinz. Brautschau und Heiratspolitik in Konstantinopel 395–882," *Jahrb. Österr. Byzantinistik*, 38, 1988, pp. 33–53.

27. See P. Lemerle, *Byzantine Humanism*, Canberra: The Faculty of Arts, 1986, pp. 65–68.

28. The latter received further tax exemptions from a law of 13 July 428 (*Code of Theodosius*, 13, 3, 18).

29. A. Cameron, "The Empress and the Poet: Paganism and Politics at the Court of Theodosius II" (first published 1983), in *Literature and Society in the Early Byzantine World*, London: Variorum Reprints, 1985, pp. 217–89, particularly 287.

30. Summary and main references in B. Santalucia, "L'amministrazione della giustizia penale," in *Storia di Roma*, III. *L'età tardoantica*, 2. *I luoghi e le culture*, Turin: Einaudi, 1993, pp. 1035–51.

31. See J. Beaucamp, *Le statut de la femme à Byzance (4ᵉ–7ᵉ siècle)*, II. *Les pratiques sociales*, Paris: Publ. de la Sorbonne, 1992, I, p. 125.

32. V. Neri, *I marginali nell'Occidente tardoantico. Poveri, «infames» e criminali nella nascente società cristiana*, Bari: Edipuglia, 1998, p. 217. Within a few years, procurement was considered a crime. Its suppression was effective, given that the emperor, years later, reminded his new prefect, Cyrus, that Florentius, his predecessor who had since died, had freed the empire of its ignominious reputation caused by "unpleasant depravities" (Theodosius II, *Novella* 18).

33. For the theological situation between Nestorius's election and the Council of Ephesus, see J. A. McGuckin, *St. Cyril of Alexandria. The Christological Controversy. Its History, Theology, and Texts*, Leiden: Brill, 1994, pp. 20–53.

34. K. Schäferdiek, "L'arianisme germanique et ses consequences," in M. Rouche (ed.), *Clovis. Histoire et mémoire*, I, Paris: CNRS, 1997, pp. 185–96. For the definition of "catholic" in Christian literature of Late Antiquity, see the as yet unpublished dissertation by M.-Y. Perrin, *«Civitas confusionis». Recherches sur la participation des fidèles aux controverses doctrinales dans l'antiquité tardive (IIIᵉ s.–430)*, Unpublished dissertation: Université de Paris X, 2004.

35. G. Dagron, *Empereur et prêtre. Étude sur le «césaropapisme» byzantin*, Paris: Gallimard, 1995.

36. Luibhéid, *Theodosius II and Heresy....* Essential outlines of the different heresies can be found in G. Nocera, "Cuius regio eius religio," *Atti Accad. romanistica costantiniana*, 6, 1986, pp. 303–39, and a brief summary in Millar, *Repentant Heretics* . . . , pp. 113–15. For the Marcionites, see above, p. 12; for the Donatists, below, p. 85.

37. For more general information, see M. G. Morony, "Population Transfers between Sasanian Iran and the Byzantine Empire," in *La Persia e Bisanzio* . . . , pp. 161–79.

38. G. Gnoli, "Introduzione generale," in G. Gnoli (ed.), *Il Manicheismo. Vol. I. Mani e il Manicheismo*, Milan: Fond. Lorenzo Valla/Mondadori, 2003, pp. xii–lxvii. See also M. Tardieu, *Manichaeism*, trans. by Malcolm De Bevoise, Champaign: University of Illinois Press, 2008.

39. P. Brown, *Power and Persuasion* . . . , p. 128.

40. According to L. De Giovanni, the actual application of the death penalty was in fact "exceptional" in the numerous cases in which there was a provision for the death penalty; see *Chiesa e Stato nel Codice Teodosiano. Saggio sul libro XVI*, Naples: d'Auria, 1980. But we are in an uncertain area, partly because of the poor condition of the *Theodosian Code*. See R. Delmaire et al. (eds.), *Code Théodosien XVI* [Sources chrétiennes 497], Paris: Éd. du Cerf, 2005.

41. F. De Marini Avonzo, *Pagani e cristiani nella cultura giuridica del V secolo*, 1972 = *Dall'impero cristiano al Medioevo. Studi sul diritto tardoantico*, Goldbach: Keip, 2001, pp. 3–40. The apparent contradiction between the main provisions and their implementation in the wider society was considered a kind of "self-model"—a term used in semiotics—developed to provide "a tolerant image of power, in order to win the trust of religious minorities and gain their collaboration": F. De Marini Avonzo, "I libri di diritto a Costantinopoli nell'età di Teodosio II" (first published 1991/2), in *Dall'impero cristiano* . . . , pp. 53–113, particularly 81ff. Using a more empirical approach, Giorgio Barone Adesi explained the new attitude toward heretics as the application of a healthy political realism; see "Eresie sociali ed inquisizione teodosiana," *Atti Accad. romanistica costantiniana*, 6, 1986, pp. 119–66. On the other hand, the consolidation of the *ecclesia catholica* and its effective hegemony made less radical provisions possible.

42. The *Ecclesiastical History* by the Nestorian Barhhadbeshabba Arbaia (7th c.) [*Patrologia Orientalis*, 9, 5, pp. 522ff.] describes the situation in considerable detail and with a few exaggerations: by way of reprisal, the dancers driven out of the city are supposed to have stolen some children and thrown them into the sea.

43. See V. Grumel, *Les regestes des actes du Patriarcat de Constantinople* (I, 1, 1932), facsimile reprint, Paris: Institut Français d'Études byzantines, 1972, pp. 42ff.

44. See Holum, *Theodosian Empresses* . . . , pp. 152–54.

45. Translation of the Syriac text in F. Nau, *Nestorius. Le livre d'Héraclide de Damas*, Paris: Letouzey et Ané, 1910, pp. 361–66.

46. G. Dagron, "Les moines et la ville: le monachisme à Constantinople jusqu'au concile de Chalcédoine (451)" (first published 1970), in *La romanité chrétienne* . . . , VIII, pp. 229–76, particularly 236.

47. See N. P. Constas, "Weaving the Body of God: Proclus of Constantinople, the Theotokos, and the Loom of the Flesh," *Journal of Early Christian Studies*, 3, 1995, pp. 169–94.

48. According to E. Wypszycka, the fury directed against Nestorius was "exceptional even in such an intolerant world. . . . Nestorius could be easily offended by this extremism, and he lacked the indispensable flexibility needed to lead an important church such as the one in Constantinople. He possessed all the defects of an intellectual who is unable to see anything beyond his doctrinal arguments." See *Storia della chiesa nella tarda antichità*, Milan: Bruno Mondadori, 2000, p. 192.

49. The dating of these texts to 428 is likely to be correct, but has not been completely proven. For the various possibilities, see C. Pietri, *Roma Christiana. Recherches sur l'Église de Rome, son organisation, sa politique, son idéologie de Miltiade à Sixte III (311–440)*, Rome: École Française de Rome, 1976, pp. 1348–53. See also McGuckin, *St. Cyril* . . . , pp. 28–32.

50. Wypszycka, *Storia della chiesa* . . . , pp. 192–94.

V
The Anatomy of an Empire

1. L. Cracco Ruggini, "Pubblicistica e storiografia bizantine di fronte alla crisi dell'impero romano (a proposito di un libro recente)," *Athenaeum*, n.s., 51, 1973, pp. 146–83, particularly 151ff. and 154.

2. F. Millar, "De la frontière au centre: la monarchie centralisée de Théodose II (408–450 ap. J.-C.)," in Moatti, *La mobilité* . . . , pp. 567–77; F. Millar, *A Greek Roman Empire* . . . , pp. 45ff.

3. This information, which is based on Symmachus's history, has often been challenged. For a reassessment with good arguments, see G. Zecchini, *Aezio. L'ultima difesa dell'Occidente romano*, Rome: "L'Erma" di Bretschneider, 1983, pp. 145ff.

4. I. Bóna, *Les Huns. Le grand empire barbare d'Europe, IVᵉ–Vᵉ siècles*, Paris: Errance, 2002, pp. 35ff.

5. For general information, see A. Solignac, under the entry for "Prosper d'Aquitaine" in *Dictionnaire de spiritualité*, 12.2, Paris: Beauchesne, 1986, columns 2446–56. On Prosper's interpretation of Saint Augustine, see M. Vessey, "«Opus imperfectum». Augustine and his readers, 426–435 A.D.," *Vigiliae Christianae*, 52, 1998, pp. 264–85, particularly 271–77.

6. A. Gillett, "The Date and Circumstances of Olympiodorus of Thebes," *Traditio*, 48, 1993, pp. 1–29, particularly 20. The year 425 was also the dividing line between volumes XIII and XIV of the second edition of the *Cambridge Ancient History*. On Olympiodorus, see A. Baldini, *Ricerche di tarda storiografia romana (da Olimpiodoro di Tebe)*, Bologna: Pàtron, 2004.

7. On the *Theodosian Code*, the essential reading is G. G. Archi, *Teodosio II e la sua codificazione*, Naples: Edizioni Scientifiche Italiane, 1976; T. Honoré, *Law in the Crisis of Empire 379–455 AD*, Oxford: Clarendon Press, 1998; and J. F. Matthews, *Laying Down the Law: A Study of the Theodosian Code*, New Haven: Yale University Press, 2000.

8. The expression *magisterium vitae* is rendered in this manner by M. Bretone, *Storia del diritto romano*, Rome-Bari: Laterza, 1995⁹, p. 374.

9. Bretone, *Storia del diritto* . . . , pp. 374ff.

10. S. Mazzarino, *L'impero romano*, Rome-Bari: Laterza, 1986³, p. 772. The concept of the "Balkans" is a relatively modern invention, reflecting a wholly Western mindset: M. Todorova, *Imagining the Balkans*, New York: Oxford Univ. Press USA, 1997). See also L. Wolff, *Inventing Eastern Europe: The Map of Civilization on the Mind of the Enlightenment*, Palo Alto: Stanford Univ. Press, 1994.

11. Constantinople had profited from the region's isolation from Italy during the barbarian occupation of the other provinces in the Balkans. The prefect at the Illyrian *praetorium* had a particularly delicate task: in 428, he was probably still Antiochus, who had been in charge as late as October 427 (*Code of Justinian*, 1, 50, 2a), and would later be recalled to Constantinople to work on drafting the *Code of Theodosius*.

12. An example of this was the diocese of Thessalonica, which obtained this privilege in 424 (*Code of Theodosius*, 11, 1, 33). It has recently been suggested that this kind of measure was part of a more general process aimed at enriching and bolstering Church assets: see F. Marazzi, *I «patrimonia Sanctae romanae Ecclesiae» nel Lazio (secoli IV–X). Struttura amministrativa e prassi gestionali*, Rome: Istituto storico per il Medio Evo, 1998, pp. 62–64.

13. See B. Bavant, "L'Illyricum," in Morrisson, *Le monde byzantin* . . . , pp. 303–46, particularly 310ff.

14. W. E. Kaegi Jr., *Byzantium and the Decline of Rome* . . . , pp. 64–66.

15. A. Karivieri, "The So-Called Library of Hadrian and the Tetraconch Church in Athens," in Castrén, *Post-Herulian Athens* . . . , pp. 89–113. See also M. Di Branco, *La città dei filosofi. Storia di Atene da Marco Aurelio a Giustiniano*, Florence: Leo Olschki Editore, 2006.

16. A. Frantz, *The Athenian Agora*, XXIV. *Late Antiquity, A.D. 267–700*, Princeton: The Amer. School of Class. St. at Athens, 1988, pp. 57–74, and the review of G. Fowden's "The Athenian Agora and the Progress of Christianity," *Journal of Roman Archaeology*, 2, 1990, pp. 494–501. See also Castrén, *Post-Herulian Athens* . . . .

17. A statue of the empress was erected in the middle of the Athens *agorá* close to the Palace of the Giants, probably the seat of the imperial administration. The remains of its pedestal have been found, including a verse inscription in honor of Eudocia: E. Sironen, "Life and Administration of Late Roman Attica in the Light of Public Inscriptions," in Castrén, *Post-Herulian Athens* . . . , pp. 15–62, particularly 51–54. The historical context would appear to suggest that Eudocia promoted the construction of the church close to Hadrian's Library which in turn was close to the *agorá*: see Karivieri, "The So-Called Library of Hadrian . . . ," pp. 111–13.

18. Leontius was not necessarily an Athenian with a perfect pedigree, as has been believed. Some time ago, Holum suggested that Eudocia may have had her origins in Antioch, and his evidence is fairly convincing: see *Theodosian Empresses* . . . , pp. 117ff. For the whole question, see Burman, *The Athenian Empress Eudocia* . . . , pp. 81–83.

19. See the author's introduction to D. P. Taormina (ed.), *Plutarco di Atene. L'Uno, l'Anima, le Forme*, Catania: Università di Catania 1989, pp. 15–93.

20. See A. Frantz, "Pagan Philosophers in Christian Athens," *Proc. of the American Philosophical Soc.*, 119, 1975, pp. 29–38. For the debate on the archeological evidence, see A. Karivieri, "The 'House of Proclus' on the Southern Slope of the Acropolis: a Contribution," in Castrén, *Post-Herulian Athens* . . . , pp. 115–39. See also M. Di Branco, *La città dei filosofi*. . . .

21. See Taormina, *Plutarco di Atene* . . . , p. 16.

22. At one time it was believed that the temple of Apollo in Delphi was destroyed in the fourth century. It has now been shown that the pagan sanctuaries in Greece fell into a slow decline: V. Déroche, "La dernière réparation païenne du temple d'Apollon à Delphes," *Travaux et Mémoires*, 15 (Mélanges J.-P. Sodini), 2005, pp. 231–44.

23. G. Fowden, "The Pagan Holy Man in Late Antique Society," *Journal of Hellenic Studies*, 102, 1982, pp. 33–59, particularly 44ff.

24. Archeologists have discovered the remains of brutal sacrifices and other rites attributable to a Neoplatonist context in the "*Chi* building" to the south

of the Acropolis, which has been identified as the probable site of the school: see Karivieri, "The 'House of Proclus'. . . ."

25. R. M. Rothaus, *Corinth: The First City of Greece. An Urban History of Late Antique Cult and Religion*, Leiden: Brill, 2000.

26. Bavant, "L'Illyricum" . . . , p. 319.

27. Rothaus, *Corinth. The First City* . . . , pp. 47ff. and pp. 126ff.

VI
From Ravenna to Nola: Italy in Transition

1. Valentinian's tutor was Petronius Maximus, a young but powerful aristocratic who had embarked on a distinguished career. For the identity of the tutor documented by the fragment of an inscription from the Aventine, see S. Panciera, "Il precettore di Valentiniano III," in A. Valvo and C. Stella (eds.), *Studi in onore di Albino Garzetti*, Brescia: Ateneo di Brescia, 1996, pp. 277–97. On the *topos* of *principes pueri*, see C. Molé Ventura, *Principi fanciulli. Legittimismo costituzionale e storiografia cristiana nella tarda antichità*, Catania: Ed. del Prisma, 1992.

2. For Galla Placidia, see V. A. Sirago, *Galla Placidia e la trasformazione politica dell'Occidente*, Louvain: Université de Louvain 1961, with the criticisms of L. Cracco Ruggini, "Fonti, problemi e studi sull'età di Galla Placidia," *Athenaeum*, 40, 1962, pp. 373–91; S. I. Oost, *Galla Placidia Augusta. A Biographical Essay*, Chicago: University of Chicago Press, 1968.

3. O. Seeck, *Geschichte des Untergangs der alten Welt*, Stuttgart: Metzler, 1920[2], VI, pp. 67ff. The German historian's view could easily be turned on its head, and Santo Mazzarino has shown how, in troubled times, a new and distinct consideration for women emerged at least in the upper echelons, which differed from the classical values that relegated women to a restricted sphere: see S. Mazzarino, *La fine del mondo antico*, Milan: Rizzoli, 1988, pp. 125ff., and, for greater detail, L. Cracco Ruggini, "Juridical Status and Historical Role of Women in Roman Patriarchal Society," *Klio*, 71, 1989, pp. 604–19.

4. C. Olovsdotter, *The Consular Image. An Iconological Study of the Consular Diptychs*, Oxford: British Arch. Series, 2005, pp. 23ff. The identity of Felix is evidenced by the inscription on the diptych, "Fl(avi) Felicis v(iri) cl(arissimi) com(itis) ac mag(istri)."

5. See A. Pellizzari, *Servio. Storia, cultura e istituzioni nell'opera di un grammatico tardoantico*, Florence: Leo S. Olschki, 2003, pp. 35ff.

6. S. Gelichi, "Le città in Emilia-Romagna tra tardo-antico ed alto medioevo," in R. Francovich and G. Noyé (eds.), *La storia dell'alto medioevo italiano (VI–X secolo) alla luce dell'archeologia*, Florence: All'insegna del Giglio, 1994,

pp. 567–600, particularly 576; for more general information, see G. P. Brogiolo, *La città nell'alto medioevo italiano. Archeologia e storia*, Rome-Bari: Laterza, 1999, p. 103, and G. P. Brogiolo, "Ideas of the town in Italy during the transition from Antiquity to the Middle Ages," in G. P. Brogiolo and B. Ward-Perkins (eds.), *The Idea and Ideal of the Town between Late Antiquity and the Early Middle Ages*, Leiden: Brill, 1999, pp. 99–126.

7. The new direction in military architecture in northern Italy of Late Antiquity, where warfare had caused considerable changes to the urban landscape, is still a disputed question. While the literary sources appear to refer to a climate of desolation and destruction in the second half of the fourth century, the early decades of the fifth century appear to demonstrate intense activity in rebuilding city walls at the very least. In some cases it is possible, with the necessary provisos, to date these new building works—for instance the "selenite walls" of Bologna. See Gelichi, *Le città in Emilia-Romagna . . .* , p. 574.

8. In reality, many texts of Late Antiquity demonstrate an increasing interest in landscapes hitherto considered marginal or indeed barbaric: G. Traina, *Paludi e bonifiche del mondo antico*, Rome: "L'Erma" di Bretschneider, 1988.

9. There have always been cities built on marshland or lagoons in the Mediterranean area; however, they were not one of the models for cities handed down by the ancient world. See L. Cracco Ruggini, "Acque e lagune da periferia del mondo a fulcro di una nuova «civilitas»," in *Storia di Venezia*, I, Rome: Istituto Enciclopedia Italiana, 1992, pp. 11–102.

10. The expression *semirutarum cadavera urbium*, with reference to fourth-century Emilia, was used by Saint Ambrose, *Epistle* 8, 3 Faller. For the various interpretations of this passage, see E. Lo Cascio, the introduction to Mazzarino, *Aspetti sociali . . .* , p. xxiii, n. 54, with the preceding bibliography.

11. The bishop of Ravenna was thus considered the western equivalent of the Greek John Chrysostom. For a complete profile, see A. Olivar, under the entry for Peter Chrysologus, *Bibliotheca Sanctorum*, X, Rome: Città Nuova, 1968, columns 685–91. The succession of bishops of Ravenna in this period is disputed: see R. Benericetti, *Il pontificale di Ravenna. Studio critico*, Faenza: Sem. vescovile Pio XII, 1994.

12. The authority of the bishop of Milan remained a model for both the western and eastern Church Fathers, who admired its independence: see G. Zecchini, "Ambrogio nella tradizione storiografica tardoantica," in L. F. Pizzolato and M. Rizzi (eds.), *«Nec timeo mori». Atti del Congresso internazionale di studi ambrosiani nel XVI centenario della morte di sant'Ambrogio*, Milan: Vita e Pensiero, 1998, pp. 93–106.

13. C. Wickham, "L'Italia e l'alto Medioevo," *Archeologia Medievale*, 15, 1988, pp. 105–24.

14. V. Zangara, "Una predicazione alla presenza dei principi: la Chiesa di Ravenna nella prima metà del sec. V," *Antiquité tardive*, 8, 2000, pp. 265–304, particularly 275ff.

15. G. A. Cecconi, "Vescovi e maggiorenti cristiani nell'Italia centrale fra IV e V secolo," in *Vescovi e pastori in epoca teodosiana*, Rome: Institutum Patristicum Augustinianum, 1997, pp. 205–24.

16. See Mazzarino, *Aspetti sociali . . .* , pp. 180ff.; there is an updated summary in E. Lo Cascio, "La popolazione," in Lo Cascio (ed.), *Roma imperiale. Una metropoli antica*, Rome: Carocci, 2000, pp. 17–69, particularly 59–61. For an important recent work, see B. D. Shaw, "Challenging Braudel: a new vision of the Mediterranean," *Journal of Roman Archaeology*, 14, 2001, pp. 419–53, particularly 446: "Rome's position as a megalopolis depended not on its ability to produce economic goods, but rather on its political position at the center of a militarily sustainable Mediterranean empire. In the 5th c. A.D., when huge forces began to reconfigure the Mediterranean nexuses of which Rome was the center . . . , the city of Rome suddenly collapsed to a fraction of its former size and economic importance; and with it, all of its consumptive demand (with dramatic effects on the producers)."

17. Interpretation of the sources is the subject of some dispute. As W. Liebeschuetz has pointed out, it is more appropriate in some cases to talk of population movements rather than depopulation (*The Decline and Fall of the Roman City*, Oxford: Oxford University Press, 2001, p. 373).

18. L. Pani Ermini, "Roma da Alarico a Teoderico," in W. V. Harris (ed.), *The Transformations of Urbs Roma in Late Antiquity*, supplement to *Journal of Roman Archaeology*, no. 33, 1999, pp. 35–52, particularly 40ff. with bibliography. For the Christianization of the *suburbium*, see L. Spera, "The Christianization of Space along the Via Appia: Changing Landscape in the Suburbs of Rome," *American Journal of Archaeology*, Vol. 107, 1, Jan 2003, pp. 23–43.

19. B. Brenk, "L'anno 410 e il suo effetto sull'arte chiesastica a Roma," in *Ecclesiae Urbis*, Vatican City: Pontificio Istituto di Architettura cristiana, 2002, pp. 1001–16, particularly 1013ff.

20. This line is the only surviving fragment of Olympiodorus's poetic works. See Baldini, *Ricerche di tarda storiografia . . .* , passim.

21. For the development of papal wealth, see Marazzi, *I «patrimonia Sanctae Ecclesiae». . . .*

22. It was only at the end of the Middle Ages that popes adopted the title of *Pontifex Maximus*, which was associated with the traditional Roman religion and became a prerogative of imperial power from Augustus until the fourth century. However, various Christian Latin authors adapted the classical epithet *pontifex* to indicate the power of the more influential bishops. Bibliography in

F. Van Haeperen, "Des pontifes païens aux pontifes chrétiens. Transformations d'un titre: entre pouvoirs et représentations," *Revue belge de philologie et d'histoire*, 81, 2003, pp. 137–59.

23. See Pietri, *Roma Christiana. Recherches* . . . , pp. 1609ff. For an excellent summary of the early centuries of the papacy, see M.-Y. Perrin, "La papauté héritière de saint Pierre et de la romanité (des origines à 604 ap. J.-C.)," in Y.-M. Hilaire (ed.), *Histoire de la papauté*, Paris: Tallandier, 2003², pp. 21–117 and 532–39.

24. P. Brown, *The Rise of Western Christendom*, Oxford: Blackwell, 1996, p. 68.

25. Nestorius's epistle, which has come down us in the *Collectio Veronensis* (3), was entrusted to the "totally loyal" cubicular Valerius, whom we know to be a tireless correspondent of Nilus of Ancyra.

26. Pietri, *Roma Christiana. Recherches* . . . , pp. 1357–60.

27. *PLRE* II, p. 886; B. Bischoff and W. Koehler, "Un' edizione illustrata degli Annali ravennati del Basso impero" (first published in German, 1939), in *Studi romagnoli*, 3, 1952, pp. 1–17. On the other hand, G. Zecchini believes that the violent death of Pyrrhus related to religious problems: *Aezio: l'ultima difesa* . . . , p. 143.

28. In Bischoff and Koehler, "Un' edizione illustrata . . . ," p. 9; Bischoff (p. 3) argues that Pyrrhus, who died this violent death, was a "tyrant."

29. See A. Fraschetti, *La conversione. Da Roma pagana a Roma cristiana*, Rome-Bari: Laterza, 1999, pp. 179ff.

30. S. Roda, "Nobiltà burocratica, aristocrazia senatoria, nobiltà provinciali," in *Storia di Roma*, III. 1 . . . , pp. 643–74, particularly 671.

31. Pellizzari, *Servio. Storia, cultura e istituzioni* . . . , pp. 81ff.

32. Towards the end of 408, at the time of Alaric's first siege, permission was given for the celebration of propitiatory rites by Etruscan haruspices (Sozomen, *Ecclesiastical History*, 9, 6, 1–7; Zosimus, 5, 40–41). See Pellizzari, *Servio. Storia, cultura e istituzioni* . . . , pp. 195ff.

33. S. Mazzarino, "La conversione del senato," in *Antico, tardoantico ed èra costantiniana*, I . . . , pp. 378–97; A. Cameron, "The last pagans of Rome," in Harris (ed.), *The transformation* . . . , pp. 109–23.

34. P. Brown, "Aspetti della cristianizzazione dell'aristocrazia romana" (1961), in *Religion and Society in the Age of Saint Augustine*, Eugene (Ore.): Wipf and Stock, 2007, pp. 151–71, particularly 160ff; C. W. Hedrick Jr., *History and silence. Purge and rehabilitation of memory in late antiquity*, Austin: University of Texas Press, 2000, p. 57.

35. A. Chastagnol, "Le sénateur Volusien et la conversion d'une famille de l'aristocratie romaine au Bas-Empire" (1956), in *L'Italie et l'Afrique au Bas-Empire. Études administratives et prosopographiques. Scripta varia*, Lille: Presses

Universitaires de Lille, 1987, pp. 235–47. In all probability, Volusianus was the person to whom a short poem was written by a recent convert, and which has survived in a collection of poems by Paulinus of Nola (Paulinus, *Carmen* 32). For Melania, see below, pp. 110ff.

36. Zecchini, *Aezio. L'ultima difesa* . . . , p. 144.

37. P. Stewart, "The destruction of statues in late antiquity," in R. Miles (ed.), *Constructing Identities in Late Antiquity*, London: Routledge, 1999, pp. 159–89.

38. B. Caseau, "ΠΟΛΕΜΕΙΝ ΛΙΘΟΙΣ. La désacralisation des espaces et des objets religieux païens durant l'antiquité tardive," in M. Kaplan (ed.), *Le sacré et son inscription dans l'espace à Byzance et en Occident. Études comparées*, Paris: Publ. de la Sorbonne, 2001, pp. 61–123, particularly 71.

39. A. Cameron, "The Date and Identity of Macrobius," *Journal of Roman Studies*, 56, 1966, pp. 25–38.

40. A. Giardina, "Le due Italie nella forma tarda dell'impero" (1986), in *L'Italia romana. Storie di un'identità incompiuta*, Rome-Bari: Laterza, 1997, pp. 265–321. The new system must have been greeted favorably by the senatorial aristocracy, which in this way increased its chances of career advancements through the proliferation of posts in individual provinces.

41. A. Giardina, "Carità eversiva: le donazioni di Melania la Giovane e gli equilibri della società tardoromana," *Studi storici*, 29, 1988, pp. 127–42, particularly 139ff.

42. See A. Giardina, "Uomini e spazi aperti" (first published 1989), in *L'Italia romana* . . . , pp. 192–232, particularly 207ff.

43. G. Noyé, "Villes, économie et société dans la province de Bruttium-Lucanie du IVᵉ au VIIᵉ siècle," in Francovich and Noyé (eds.), *La storia dell'alto medioevo italiano* . . . , pp. 693–733. See the clarification in D. Vera, "I paesaggi rurali del Meridione tardoantico: bilancio consuntivo e preventivo," in G. Volpe and M. Turchiano (eds.), *Paesaggi e insediamenti rurali in Italia meridionale fra Tardoantico e Altomedioevo*, Bari: Edipuglia, 2005, pp. 23–38.

44. Giardina, *L'Italia romana* . . . , pp. 300–306; D. Vera, "I silenzi di Palladio e l'Italia: osservazioni sull'ultimo agronomo romano," *Antiquité tardive*, 7, 1999, pp. 283–97.

45. F. Grelle, "Ordinamento provinciale e organizzazione locale nell'Italia meridionale," in *L'Italia meridionale in età tardoantica* (Atti 38° Conv. Studi Magna Grecia), Naples: Arte tipografica, 2000, pp. 115–39.

46. T. Lehmann, "Lo sviluppo del complesso archeologico a Cimitile/Nola," *Boreas*, 13, 1990, pp. 75–93; S. Mratschek-Halfmann, "«Multis enim notissima est sanctitas loci»: Paulinus and the Gradual Rise of Nola as a Center of Christian Hospitality," in *Journal of Early Christian Studies*, 9, 2001, pp. 511–53; T. Lehmann, *Paulinus Nolanus und die Basilica Nova in Cimitile*, Wiesbaden: Reichert, 2005.

47. Paulinus's works do not record his final years; the last epistle, number 51, has been dated to the period between 423 and 426. For a critical assessment, see C. and L. Pietri (eds.), *Prosopographie chrétienne du Bas-Empire*. 2. *Prosopographie de l'Italie chrétienne (313–604)*, Rome: École Française de Rome, 2000, pp. 1630–54. On Saint Paulinus's epistolary, see S. H. Mratschek, *Der Briefwechsel des Paulinus von Nola. Kommunikation und soziale Kontakte zwischen christlichen Intellektuellen*, Göttingen: Vandenhoeck & Ruprecht, 2002. For a general introduction, see D. E. Trout, *Paulinus of Nola. Life, Letters, and Poems*, Berkeley: University of California Press, 1999.

48. A. Fo, "Percorsi e sogni geografici tardolatini," in *Annali Ist. Orientale Napoli* (Sez. linguistica), 13, 1991, pp. 51–71, particularly 71.

49. P. Brown, *The Cult of Saints. Its Rise and Function in Latin Christianity*, London: SCM Press, 1981, p. 43.

VII
TRIAL RUNS FOR THE MIDDLE AGES

1. Zecchini, *Aezio. L'ultima difesa.* . . . See also the recent biography by T. Stickler, *Aëtius. Gestaltungsspielräume eines Heermeisters im ausgehenden Weströmischen Reich*, Munich: Beck, 2002.

2. For current positions on the question and the bibliography, see G. Wirth, "Rome and its Germanic partners in the fourth century," in *The Transformation of the Roman World* (hereafter referred to as *TRW*) 1, 1997, pp. 13–55.

3. P. J. Heather, "Disappearing and reappearing tribes," in *TRW* 2, 1998, pp. 95–111. The differences between the individual communities are demonstrated by the ambiguity in the way Roman juridical sources perceived ethnic groups, which were loosely referred to as *gentiles*: see W. Liebeschuetz, "Citizen status and law in the Roman empire and the Visigothic kingdom," in *TRW* 2, 1998, pp. 131–52, particularly 139ff. The *Arborychoi*, who were mentioned by Procopius, are an interesting case (*Wars*, 5, 12ff): they were probably Armoricans, a Celtic people who had been in Gaul for a long time and took the side of the empire in the face of the Visigothic advance. They were integrated into the legions (Procopius, *Gothic War*, 1, 12).

4. See P. J. Geary, *The Myth of Nations: The Medieval Origins of Europe*, Princeton: Princeton University Press, 2003, and I. Wood, "Barbarians, Historians and the Construction of National Identities," *Journal of Late Antiquity*, Vol. 1, 1, Spring 2008, p. 61–81.

5. This is one of the interesting theories of the linguist G. Schramm in his ambitious monograph *Ein Damm bricht: die römische Donaugrenze und die*

Invasionen des 5.–7. Jahrhunderts im Lichte von Namen und Wörtern, Munich: Oldenbourg, 1997.

6. As is well known, the German tradition developed a mirror view encapsulated in the concept of *Völkerwanderung*, the "migration of peoples," which is supposed to have opened the way to such peoples as the Goths, Vandals, and Huns, seen as the founders of a new world.

7. B. Beaujard, *Le culte des saints en Gaule. Les premiers temps. D'Hilaire de Poitiers à la fin du VIᵉ siècle*, Paris: Éd. du Cerf, 2000, pp. 133ff.

8. W. Liebeschuetz, "The refugees and evacuees in the age of migrations," in *TRW* 12, 2003, pp. 65–79, particularly 68.

9. B. S. Bachrach, "Fifth Century Metz: Late Roman Christian Urbs or Ghost Town?" *Antiquité tardive*, 10, 2002, pp. 363–81.

10. See A. Giardina, "Banditi e santi: un aspetto del folklore gallico tra tarda antichità e alto medioevo," *Athenaeum*, 61, 1983, pp. 374–89.

11. J. Drinkwater, "The «Bacaudae» of fifth-century Gaul," in J. Drinkwater and H. Elton (eds.), *Fifth-century Gaul: a crisis of identity?* Cambridge: Cambridge University Press, 1992, pp. 208–17.

12. A. Chauvot, "Remarques sur l'emploi de «semibarbarus»," in A. Rousselle (ed.), *Frontières terrestres, frontières célestes dans l'Antiquité*, Paris: Presses universitaires de Perpignan, 1995, pp. 255–71.

13. Stickler, *Aëtius. Gestaltungsspielräume eines Herrmeisters . . .*, pp. 181ff. We know that in 428 Childeric was already on their throne, but the written sources provide almost no other information. See I. Wood, "Ethnicity and the Ethnogenesis of the Burgundians," in H. Wolfram and W. Pohl (eds.), *Typen der Ethnogenese unter besonderer Berücksichtigung in Bayern*, I, Vienna: Österreich. Akad. d. Wissenschaften, 1990, pp. 53–69; I. Wood, "«Gentes», kings and kingdoms, the emergence of states. The kingdom of the Gibichungs," in *TRW* 13, 2003, pp. 243–69.

14. This is shown in A. Schwarcz, "Relations between Ostrogoths and Visigoths in the fifth and sixth centuries and the question of Visigothic settlement in Aquitaine and Spain," in W. Pohl and M. Diesenberger (eds.), *Integration und Herrschaft. Ethnische Identität und soziale Organization im Frühmittelalter*, Vienna: Österreich Akad. d. Wissenschaften, 2002, pp. 217–26, particularly 217–20. See also A. Schwarcz, "The Visigothic Settlement in Aquitania: Chronology and Archaeology," in R. W. Mathisen and D. Shanzer (eds.), *Society and Culture in Late Antique Gaul. Revisiting the Sources*, Aldershot: Ashgate, 2001, pp. 5–25.

15. P. C. Díaz, "Visigothic political institutions," in P. Heather (ed.), *The Visigoths from the Migration Period to the Seventh Century. An Ethnographic Perspective*, Woodbridge: Boydell Press, 1999, pp. 321–72.

16. See Schwarcz, "Relations between Ostrogoths . . . ," pp. 221ff.

17. It appears that the encounter with other peoples stimulated a desire for

ethnic identity among many of the tribes. The ancient traditional legends were thus mixed with much more recent events, giving rise to new foundation myths. In particular, the clash with the Huns was retold in the epic songs of the Germanic peoples. Bibliography in L. Hedeager, "Europe in the Migration Period. The formation of a political mentality," in *TRW* 8, 2000, pp. 15–57, particularly 49ff.

18. Zecchini, *Aezio. L'ultima difesa . . .* , pp. 140ff.

19. The barbarian *foederati* were supposed to be stationed on the frontiers and used in the defense of a frontier that was increasingly exposed, but they tended to be kept away from the internal seas. Indeed, the Goths had already demonstrated the magnitude of the threat by their actions in the Black Sea during the third century. Later, a Gothic "Atlantic fleet" put together by Alaric II would fight against Saxon pirates, but in general the imperial policy appears to have neutralized the Gothic naval strategy: see H. Wolfram, *History of the Goths*, Berkeley: University of California Press, 1992.

20. For a recent summary, see A. Barbero, *Barbari. Immigrati, profughi, deportati nell'impero romano*, Rome-Bari: Laterza, 2006.

21. A decree in the *Code of Theodosius* (3, 14, 1), which prohibited mixed marriages between provincials and "ethnics" (*gentiles*), had been issued in 373 for other contingent reasons; however, at the time of its inclusion in the *Code of Theodosius* (438), events must have provided it with a particular topicality. After that it was interpreted in a restricted manner. A modified version can still be found in the Visigothic compilation, Alaric II's *Breviary* (506), in which there is no longer talk of *gentiles* but of barbarians, a term that probably referred to the Franks. Significantly it was not included in the *Code of Justinian*. See Liebeschuetz, "Citizen status and law . . . ," p. 140.

22. See D. Claude, "Remarks about relations between Visigoths and Romans in the seventh century," in *TRW* 2, 1998, pp. 117–30, particularly 123.

23. For Arles in Late Antiquity, see M. Heijmans, *Arles durant l'Antiquité tardive. De la «duplex Arelas» à l'«Urbs Genesii»*, Rome: École Française de Rome, 2004.

24. Sources in S. Pricoco, *L'isola dei santi. Il cenobio di Lerino e le origini del monachesimo gallico*, Rome: Ed. dell'Ateneo e Bizzarri, 1978, pp. 26ff.

25. Unlike other monasteries, in which the renouncement of all worldly goods was optional, in Lérins this was obligatory. On the "Lérins faction," see R. W. Mathisen, *Ecclesiastical factionalism and religious controversy in fifth-century Gaul*, Washington (D.C.): Catholic Univ. America Press, 1989, pp. 69ff.

26. See J. Gaudemet, "De la liberté constantinienne à une Église d'État" (1973), in *Église et société en Occident au Moyen Âge*, London: Variorum Reprints, 1984, I, pp. 59–76, particularly 71.

27. F. Cordero, *Fiabe di entropia. L'uomo, Dio, il diavolo*, Milan: Garzanti, 2005, p. 263.

28. D. Woods, "The origin of Honoratus of Lérins," *Mnemosyne*, 46, 1993, pp. 78–85. A. Coşkun, *Die «gens Ausoniana» an der Macht. Untersuchungen zu Decimius Magnus Ausonius und seiner Familie*, Oxford: Linacre College, 2002. During this period, the aristocracy was adopting a less hostile attitude to monks: see J. Fontaine, "L'aristocratie occidentale devant le monachisme aux IVeme et Veme siècles," *Riv. di storia e lett. religiosa*, 15, 1979, pp. 28–53.

29. For general information, see M. Heinzelmann, *Bischofsherrschaft in Gallien*, Zurich: Artemis, 1976; see also M. Heinzelmann, "The 'affair' of Hilary of Arles (445) and Gallo-Roman identity in the fifth century," in Drinkwater and Elton (eds.), *Fifth-century Gaul . . .* , pp. 239–51.

30. This vitality is confirmed by the archeological sources. In the second quarter of the fifth century, amphoras demonstrate imports from Spain, Italy, and Africa: see T. S. Loseby, "Marseille and the Pirenne thesis, I: Gregory of Tours, the Merovingian kings, and «un grand port»," in *TRW* 3, 1998, pp. 203–29.

31. Mathisen, *Ecclesiastical factionalism and religious controversy . . .* , p. 74.

32. On Saint John Cassian's thought, see the collected essays in *De saint Pachôme à Jean Cassien. Études littéraires et doctrinales sur le monachisme égyptien à ses débuts*, Rome: Pont. Ateneo S. Anselmo, 1996, pp. 271ff.; see also C. Badilita and A. Jakab (eds.), *Jean Cassien entre l'Orient et l'Occident*, Paris: Beauchesne, 2006. On the Abbey of Saint-Victor, see M. Fixot and J.-P. Pelletier (eds.), *Saint-Victor de Marseille: Etudes archéologiques et historiques*, Brepols, Turnhout, 2009.

33. In spite of its heretical overtones, Cassian's *Conferences* was very well received by his contemporaries, and indeed continued to be a success in the West throughout the Middle Ages. Saint Benedict recommended it to his brethren and Thomas Aquinas read it every day: De Vogüé, *De saint Pachôme . . .* , pp. 345–57 and on its more recent success, pp. 507–22.

34. W. Liebeschuetz, "The refugees and evacuees in the age of migrations," in *TRW* 12, 2003, pp. 65–79.

35. There are some examples in R. W. Mathisen, "Emigrants, Exiles, and Survivors: Aristocratic Options in Visigothic Aquitania," *Phoenix*, 38, 1984, pp. 159–70.

36. D. Woods, "The origins of Honoratus. . . ."

37. See Wickham, *Framing the Early Middle Ages*, pp. 62–64; Wickham expresses doubts on Salvian's reliability as a source on taxation in Late Antiquity.

38. See most recently M. Maas, "Ethnicity, orthodoxy and community in Salvian of Marseilles," in Drinkwater and Elton (eds.), *Fifth-century Gaul . . .* , pp. 275–84.

39. J. Guyon, "Toulouse, la première capitale du royaume wisigoth," in G. Ripoll and J. M. Gurt (eds.), *Sedes regiae (400–800)*, Barcelona: Reial Acadèmia de Bones Lletres, 2000, pp. 219–40.

40. The sources for the victories are not very clear. Sidonius's poem, written in 458, would appear to refer to another of Aetius's victories over the Franks, which occurred about twenty years later and in which the future emperor Majorian also fought. For this reason, many prefer to use the poem as a source for the second battle, including A. Loyen, *Recherches historiques sur les panégyriques de Sidoine Apollinaire*, Paris: Honoré Champion, 1942, p. 65. The debate on dating this episode is covered by Zecchini, *Aezio. L'ultima difesa . . .* , pp. 151 and 227ff.

41. The Franks' wedding customs can be determined by later Merovingian traditions. See R. Le Jan, *Famille et pouvoir dans le monde franc (VIIe–Xe siècle). Essai d'anthropologie sociale*, Paris: Publ. de la Sorbonne, 1995, pp. 263ff. and 298ff.

42. Most Franks were by then living in various regions of Gaul, where the imperial authorities had deported them to remedy the problem of depopulation: see A. H. Bredero, "Les Francs (Saliens ou non-Saliens) aux IIIe et IVe siècles sur la rive droite du Rhin: guerriers et paysans," in Rouche (ed.), *Clovis. Histoire et . . .* , pp. 43–58; H.-W. Goetz, "«Gens», kings and kingdoms: the Franks," in *TRW* 13, 2003, pp. 307–44. For the ambiguity of the name of the most important Frankish tribes, see M. Springer, "Gab es ein Volk der Salier?" in D. Geuenich, W. Haubrichs, and J. Jarnut (eds.), *Nomen et gens*, Berlin: de Gruyter, 1997, pp. 58–83; M. Springer, "«Riparii»-Ribuarier-Rheinfranken nebst einigen Bemerkungen zum Geographen von Ravenna," in D. Geuenich (ed.), *Die Franken und die Alemannen bis zur "Schlacht bei Zülpich" (496/97)*, Berlin: de Gruyter, 1998, pp. 201–69.

43. F. Beisel, *Studien zu den fränkisch-römischen Beziehungen*, Idstein: Schulz-Kirchner, 1987, pp. 39ff.

44. This is argued by F. Staab, "Les royaumes francs au Ve siècle," in Rouche (ed.), *Clovis. Histoire et . . .* , pp. 539–66, particularly 546. Staab dates the occupation of Cologne to earlier than 428, on the basis of Pseudo-Fredegarius, *Chronicle*, 3, 2, while others put it at a much later date (459 or 461); for information about the whole context, see É. Demougeot, *La formation de l'Europe et les invasions barbares*, 2. *De l'avènement de Dioclétien (284) à l'occupation germanique de l'Empire romain d'Occident (début du VIe siècle)*, Paris: Aubier, 1979, pp. 485–87.

45. Zecchini, *Aezio. L'ultima difesa . . .* , pp. 143ff. For Aetius's policy of trying to reconcile the interests of the senators with the requirements of the *foederati*, see S. Mazzarino, "Aezio, la «Notitia Dignitatum» e i Burgundi di Worms"

(first published 1975), in *Antico, tardoantico ed èra costantiniana*, II, Bari: Dedalo, 1980, pp. 132–60.

46. For general information, see H. Elton, "Defence in fifth-century Gaul," in Drinkwater and Elton (eds.), *Fifth-century Gaul . . .* , pp. 167–83.

47. On the Alans, see V. Kouznetsov and I. Lebedynsky (eds.), *Les Alains. Cavaliers des steppes, seigneurs du Caucase Ier–XVe siècles apr. J.-C.*, Paris: Errance, 2005.

48. E. Chrysos, "Conclusions: «de foederatis iterum»," in *TRW* 1, 1997, pp. 185–206. See the lucid summary by Wickham, *Framing the Early Middle Ages . . .* , pp. 84–87, and the more recent further clarification by G. Zecchini, "La formazione degli stati federali romano-barbarici," in G. Zecchini (ed.), *Il federalismo nel mondo antico*, Milan: Vita e Pensiero, 2005, pp. 129–48.

49. E. Chrysos, "Legal Concepts and Patterns for the Barbarians' Settlement on Roman Soil," in E. Chrysos and A. Schwarcz (eds.), *Das Reich und die Barbaren*, Vienna: Böhlau, 1989, pp. 13–23.

50. Brown, *The Rise of Western . . .* , p. 85.

51. See A. Alemany, *Sources on the Alans. A Critical Compilation*, Leiden: Brill, 2000, p. 112.

52. It cannot be excluded that Constantinople took some part in the murder of Ataulf, which took place in 415; in any case, the Eastern capital celebrated the official news of his death with festivities and games (Olympiodorus, fr. 26).

53. During the Merovingian age, chroniclers spread peculiar myths about the foundation of the Frankish people, such as the one about their "Trojan" origins. Once again it was Fredegarius's *Chronicle* that told the remarkable and heroic story of the Trojan diaspora, which is supposed to have divided into three branches: the Macedonians, the Franks, and the Turks. The legend underwent further developments. Although there are no sources from before Fredegarius, it is not improbable that this tradition was developed at the time of the Frankish settlement in Gaul, in order "to preserve the identity of the dominant people and to propitiate an extraordinary policy of integration" (from A. Giardina, "Le origini troiane dall'impero alla nazione," *Settimane di Spoleto Alto Medioevo*, 45, 1998, pp. 177–209).

54. For a review of the various concepts of the Mediterranean, see D. Abulafia, "Mediterraneans," in W. V. Harris (ed.), *Rethinking the Mediterranean*, Oxford: Oxford University Press, 2004, pp. 64–93.

55. R. Van Dam, "The Pirenne thesis and fifth-century Gaul," in Drinkwater and Elton (eds.), *Fifth-century Gaul . . .* , pp. 321–33.

56. A. Rousselle, *Croire et guérir. La foi en Gaule dans l'Antiquité tardive*, Paris: Fayard, 1990.

57. K. Dark, "The Late Antique Landscape of Britain, AD 300–700," in N. Christie (ed.), *Landscapes of Change. Rural Evolutions in Late Antiquity and the Early Middle Ages*, Aldershot: Ashgate, 2004, pp. 279–99, particularly 288ff.

58. The sources on "sub-Roman" Britain are particularly problematic. See D. N. Dumville, "Sub-roman Britain: history and legend" (first published 1977), in *Histories and pseudo-Histories of the Insular Middle Ages*, Aldershot: Variorum, 1990, I, pp. 173–92. The form *Vortigern*, which was introduced later by chroniclers, is now the most widely used one.

59. In spite of the differences from the other traditions, the dates appear to be relatively reliable. See Martindale, *PLRE* II, pp. 538 and 1185, and Dumville's collected essays in *Histories and pseudo-Histories . . .* , and *Britons and Anglo-Saxons in the Early Middle Ages*, Aldershot: Variorum, 1993.

60. I. Wood, "The end of Roman Britain: Continental evidence and parallels," in M. Lapidge and D. N. Dumville (eds.), *Gildas: new approaches*, Woodbridge: Boydell & Brewer, 1984, pp. 1–25.

61. B. S. Bachrach, "«Gildas», Vortigern and Constitutionality in Sub-Roman Britain" (first published 1988), in *Armies and Politics in the Early Medieval West*, Aldershot: Variorum, 1993, I, pp. 126–40.

62. Bibliography in S. T. Loseby, Power and Towns in Late Roman Britain and Early Anglo-Saxon England," in Ripoll and Gurt (eds.), *Sedes regiae . . .* , pp. 319–70, particularly 344ff. An example of continuity can also be found in Cologne: see S. Schütte, "Continuity problems and authority structures in Cologne," in G. Ausenda (ed.), *After Empire. Towards an Ethnology of Europe's Barbarians*, San Marino: Boydell Press, 1995, pp. 163–69 and 170–75 (debate).

63. See the summary by Dark, "The Late Antique Landscape. . . ."

64. See J. D. Richards, "An Archaeology of Anglo-Saxon England," in Ausenda (ed.), *After Empire . . .* , pp. 51–66, and 66–74 (debate); J. Hines, "Cultural Change and Social Organisation in Early Anglo-Saxon England," in Ausenda (ed.), *After Empire . . .* , pp. 75–88 and 88–93 (debate).

65. Sources in P. C. Bartrum, *Early Welsh Genealogical Tracts*, Cardiff: Wales University Press, 1966.

66. These are two written works known as *The Gallic Chronicle of 452* and *The Gallic Chronicle of 511*, which were interpreted by M. E. Jones and P. J. Casey, "The Gallic Chronicle Restored: A Chronology for the Anglo-Saxon Invasions and the End of Roman Britain," *Britannia*, 19, 1988, pp. 367–98. In spite of their rather crude analysis (see R. W. Burgess, "The Dark Ages Return to Fifth-Century Britain: The 'Restored' Gallic Chronicle Exploded," *Britannia*, 21, 1990, pp. 185–95), the underlying historical intuition is essentially correct;

see E. Chrysos, "Die Römerherrschaft in Britannien und ihr Ende," *Bonner Jahrb.*, 191, 1991, pp. 247–76.

67. I. Wood, "The Fall of the Western Empire and the End of Roman Britain," *Britannia*, 18, 1987, pp. 251–62.

68. We owe the comparison between Germanus and Rabbula to P. Brown, *La nascita dell'Europa cristiana*, Rome-Bari: Laterza, 1995, p. 82.

69. Constantius claims that Germanus was trained in rhetoric in Gaul, which was followed by legal studies in Rome (*Life*, 1), but his information is sketchy. See R. Borius's introduction in Constance de Lyon, *Vie de Saint Germain d'Auxerre* [Sources chrétiennes 112], Paris: Éd. du Cerf, 1965, pp. 7–108, particularly 34ff.

70. Zecchini, *Aezio. L'ultima difesa* . . . , p. 153; Wood, "The Fall of the Western Empire. . . . "

71. We therefore have to redress Momigliano's suggestive judgement, "La caduta senza rumore di un impero . . . ," p. 167: "There is no mention in the book of Attila or a precise description of the situation in Gaul as it began to break up (a process that was complete by the time Constantius was writing). The various miracles and his personal piety prevail against the political and social situation. Saint Germanus is presented, unexpectedly for us, as a saint of normal, Roman life. The only exception is the episode in Britain at the battle against the Picts and the Scots, which by then was outside the empire. Constantius does not look back and does not want to look back. The real enemies are the devils, the possessed and the specters."

72. See Pietri, *Roma Christiana. Recherches* . . . , pp. 1039ff, in particular 1041: "After all, Prosper says more within a few lines than Constance in the lengthy account of his *Life*. Even the narration of the whole hagiographic saga of Saint Patrick, the founder of Irish Christianity, hints at the existence of Palladius whereas Constance makes no mention of him."

VIII
WAITING FOR THE VANDALS

1. R. W. Burgess, *The Chronicle of Hydatius and the «Consularia Constantinopolitana». Two Contemporary Accounts of the Final Years of the Roman Empire*, Oxford: Clarendon Press, 1993. Gallaecia in Late Antiquity included the Basque Country, present-day Galicia, and Minho in present-day Portugal.

2. Bibliography in the introduction to K. Bowes and M. Kulikowski (eds.), *Hispania in Late Antiquity. Current Perspectives*, Leiden: Brill, 2005, pp. 1–26,

particularly 16–18. See also M. Kulikowski, *Late Roman Spain and Its Cities*, Baltimore: Johns Hopkins U.P., 2004, and the review by P. Le Roux, *Mediterranean Historical Review*, 20, 2005, pp. 247–51.

3. The rather obscure text is visibly corrupt.

4. For the ethnogenesis of the Vandals, see W. Liebeschuetz, "The Vandals," in *TRW* 13, 2003, pp. 55–83. See J. Arce, "Los Vándalos en Hispania (409–429 a.D.)," *Antiquité tardive*, 10, 2002, pp. 75–85; N. Francovich Onesti, *I Vandali. Lingua e storia*, Rome: Carocci, 2002, pp. 17–28. On the Alans in Spain, see Kouznetsov and Lebedynsky, *Les Alains. Cavaliers . . .* , pp. 118–20.

5. See J. Arce, "The fifth century in Hispania," in *TRW* 13, 2003, pp. 135–59. This does not appear to add anything to the archeological study by K. E. Carr, *Vandals to Visigoths. Rural Settlement Patterns in Early Medieval Spain*, Ann Arbor: University of Michigan Press, 2002.

6. A. Chavarría Arnau, *El final de las villae en Hispania (siglos IV–VII d.C.)*, Turnhour: Brepols, 2007.

7. As is well known, they are indebted for their fame to Abbot Grégoire, who in 1794 coined the word *vandalisme* when referring to the destruction of France's cultural heritage by the sans-culottes: the neologism spread and quickly became common usage in all European languages. See C. Courtois, *Les Vandales et l'Afrique*, Paris: Arts et métiers graphiques, 1955, pp. 58–64. A new monograph edited by Y. Modéran is being prepared.

8. Other scholars have interpreted the epigram as an allusion to the Vandals' heretical rites: bibliography in Francovich Onesti, *I Vandali . . .* , pp. 139–44.

9. See *PLRE* II, pp. 496–99. Procopius, *Wars*, 5, 3, 33 (followed by Theophanes, *Chronicle*, Year 5931) claims that Gunderic was killed by his brother, while he is supposed to have been killed by the Germans in Spain according to a Vandalic tradition recorded by Procopius (*PLRE* II, p. 522).

10. Germanists call this custom "tanistry," a term that derived from Old Irish. See Francovich Onesti, *I Vandali . . .* , p. 27.

11. The Maurians were beginning to form as an ethnicity during this period, and the first historical references start from around the mid-fifth century: see Y. Modéran, "Les Maures de l'Afrique romaine dans l'Antiquité tardive, *Revue des études latines*, 82, 2004, pp. 249–69.

12. Arce, "Los Vandalos . . . ," pp. 82ff.

13. According to Hydatius (77), the Vandals are supposed to have invaded Mauritania around 425, following a raid on Baetica and the Balearics; Prosper's *Chronicle* dates these operations to 427. See N. Villaverde Vega, *Tingitana en la antigüedad tardía*, Madrid: R.A.H., 2001, p. 348.

14. *PLRE* II, p. 546.

15. In 423, when Galla Placidia had fled to Constantinople, Bonifacius avoided compromising himself with the usurper Joannes, and preferred the support of Theodosius II. After Placidia's return, Bonifacius obtained a promotion to high dignitary of the court, but remained in Africa to control the increasingly threatening movements of the indigenous tribes. For Bonifacius, see *PLRE*, pp. 237–40; and the important work, J.L.M. de Lepper, *De rebus gestis Bonifatii comitis Africae et magistri militum*, Tilburg-Breda: Diss., 1941, and the review by W. Ensslin, *Gnomon*, 18, 1943, pp. 139–42; see also Sirago, *Galla Placidia e la trasformazione* . . . , passim; P. Calabria, "La monetazione non imperiale: Bonifacio," in *L'Africa romana*, 15, Atti del convegno, Rome: Carocci, 2004, pp. 1723–28.

16. Honorius's law of 422 informs us that the *res privata* stood at about 18 percent of cultivable land in the province of Proconsular Africa (Zeugitania), and about 15 percent in Byzacena (*Code of Theodosius*, 11, 28, 13): see C. Lepelley, "Déclin ou stabilité de l'agriculture africaine au Bas-Empire? À propos d'une loi de l'empereur Honorius" (first published 1967), in *Aspects de l'Afrique romaine. Les cités, la vie rurale, le christianisme*, Bari: Edipuglia, 2001, pp. 217–32.

17. D. Vera, "«Conductores domus nostrae, conductores privatorum». Concentrazione fondiaria e redistribuzione della ricchezza nell'Africa tardoantica," in *Institutions, société et vie politique dans l'empire romain au IVᵉ siècle ap. J.-C*, Rome: École Française de Rome, 1992, pp. 465–90, particularly 471.

18. According to the Byzantine tradition (in particular Procopius, *Wars* 5, 1, 3), Aetius was also involved in court intrigues against Bonifacius. However, the rivalry between the two generals developed a few years later: probably the news was spread by senatorial propaganda. Zecchini, *Aezio. L'ultima difesa* . . . , pp. 34ff., 60, 146.

19. For a brief introduction to the problem, see P. Brown, "Christianity and Local Culture in Late Roman Africa" (1968), in *Religion and Society* . . . , pp. 265–85.

20. Bonifacius's policy can be inferred partly from the letter by the "Catholic" Augustine and partly from the chronicles that reflected the official position. These accounts should therefore be interpreted with caution. The rivalry between Aetius and Bonifacius was also reported by John of Antioch, fr. 290 Roberto, who possibly took his information from Priscus of Panion: U. Roberto, *Ioannis Antiocheni Fragmenta ex Historia chronica*, Berlin: De Gruyter, 2005, pp. cxliv–clvi.

21. See O. Schmitt, "Die «Buccellarii»," *Tyche*, 9, 1994, pp. 147–74. It is not entirely impossible that Bonifacius also recruited some Vandal mercenaries, as suggested by Y. Modéran, "L'effondrement militaire de l'Afrique romaine face

aux Vandales (429–431)," in J. Lopez Quiroga (ed.), *Galia e Hispania en el contexto de la presencia «Germanica» (ss. V–VII)*, Oxford: BAR International Series, 2006, pp. 61–77. See also R. W. Mathisen, "Sigisvult the Patrician, Maximus the Arian and political stratagems in the Western Roman Empire (*c.* 425–440)," *Early Medieval Europe*, 8 (2), 1999, pp. 173–96.

22. De Lepper, *De rebus gestis Bonifatii* . . . , pp. 57–63, dates the event to 426; but see *PLRE* II, p. 492.

23 F. M. Clover, "The Pseudo-Boniface and the «Historia Augusta»" (first published 1990), in *The Late Roman West and the Vandals*, Aldershot: Variorum, 1993, XII, pp. 73–95. According to epistles 10 and 11 of the correspondence, the magnanimous Bonifacius greeted his former rival, Castinus, in Africa.

24. This question is examined in Modéran, "L'effondrement . . ."

25. Zecchini, *Aezio. L'ultima difesa* . . . , p. 150, attributes the Procopius tradition to a source close to the Caeionii-Decii.

26. See *PLRE* II, pp. 347ff., 1155.

27. See P. Brown, *Augustine of Hippo. A Biography* (2nd, revised and corrected edition, London: Faber & Faber, 2000).

28. On this community, whose presence has been substantiated by an inscription on a rock face, see H.-I. Marrou, "Un lieu dit «Cité de Dieu»," in *Augustinus Magister 1*, Paris: Études augustiniennes, 1955, pp. 101–110. For the influence of Saint Augustine in Gaul, see Vessey, "«Opus imperfectum». Augustine and . . ." See also G. Zecchini, "Il IV libro del «De civitate Dei»," in *Lettura del «De civitate Dei libri I–X»*, Rome: Inst. Patristicum Augustinianum, 2003, pp. 91–107, particularly 96–97.

29. See *Les lettres de Saint Augustin découvertes par Johannes Divjak*, Paris: Études augustiniennes, 1983.

30. C. Wolff, "À propos des voleurs d'enfants: saint Augustin, Lettre 10*," in *L'Africa romana* . . . , pp. 1711–22. See C. Lepelley, "Quelques aspects de l'administration des provinces romaines d'Afrique avant la conquête vandale," *Antiquité tardive*, 10, 2002, pp. 61–72.

31. For the polemical implications of this passage and the debate on the frontier in Late Antiquity, see Traina, "La frontiera armena . . . ," pp. 359ff.

32. P. Brown, "Saint Augustine" (1963), in *Religion and Society* . . . , pp. 25–45, particularly 34.

33. For general information, see J. Straub, "Augustins Sorge um die «Regeneratio Imperii»" (first published 1954), in *Regeneratio Imperii*, Darmstadt: Wissenschaftliche Buchgesellschaft, 1972, pp. 271–95.

34. For the complex relations between Saint Augustine and southern Gaul, and the religious tensions in Marseilles during this period, see Cordero, *Fiabe di entropia* . . . , pp. 336–48.

35. M. Falcioni (ed.), *Sant'Agostino, Opere antieretiche*, Rome: Città Nuova, 2003, pp. 7–9. Against the traditional theory, A. Kappelmacher (*Wiener Stud.*, 49, 1931, pp. 89–102) has argued that the deacon and bishop Quodvultdeus were in fact two different persons.

36. J. de Menasce, "Augustin manichéen" (1956), in *Études iraniennes*, Paris: Association pour l'avancement des Études iraniennes, 1985, pp. 19–33. See J. Van Oort, O. Wermelinger, and G. Wurst (eds.), *Augustine and Manichaeism in the Latin West*, Leiden: Brill, 2001. In his writings against the Manichaeans, Saint Augustine revealed the complicated and esoteric symbolic mythology of Manichaeism, and contributed to the perception of it as a separate religion rather than a clearly defined Christian heresy. This attitude was understandable, given that in this period Mani's doctrine was the only one that could have realistically rivaled the orthodox Christian one, because of its universality and the organization of its Church.

37. See Perrin, *«Civitas confusionis». Recherches* . . . .

38. See also *De Vera Religione*, 6, 10 (dated to 389/90), and *De Agone Christiano*, 12, 13 (396/7).

39. For general information, see C. Ando, "Pagan Apologetics and Christian Intolerance in the Ages of Themistius and Augustine," *Journal of Early Christian Studies*, 4, 1996, pp. 171–207, particularly 197.

40. A. Trapè, "Un libro sulla nozione di eresia mai scritto da sant'Agostino" 1985, in Falcioni, *Opere antieretiche* . . . , pp. 22–26.

41. Since 415, Theodosius II identified the imperial army more firmly with the Christian empire by banning non-Christians from military service (*Code of Theodosius*, 16, 10, 21). For a brief reflection on the legal aspects, see L. Loreto, *Il «bellum iustum» e i suoi equivoci*, Naples: Jovene, 2001, pp. 101–5; see A. A. Cassi, "Dalla santità alla criminalità della guerra. Morfologie storico-giuridiche del «bellum iustum»," in A. Calore (ed.), *«Guerra giusta»? Le metamorfosi di un concetto antico*, Milan: Giuffrè, 2003, pp. 101–58.

IX

PAGANS AND CHRISTIANS ON THE NILE

1. G. Geraci, "Alessandria, l'Egitto e il rifornimento frumentario di Roma in età repubblicana e imperiale," in Marin and Virlouvet (eds.), *Nourrir les cites* . . . , pp. 625–90.

2. See J.-M. Carrié, "Séparation ou cumul? Pouvoir civil et autorité militaire dans les provinces d'Egypte," *Antiquité tardive*, 6, 1998, pp. 105–21.

3. Documentation in F. De Romanis, "Τραιανὸς Ποταμός. Mediterraneo

e Mar Rosso da Traïanos a Maometto," in R. Villari (ed.), *Controllo degli stretti e insediamenti militari nel Mediterraneo*, Rome-Bari: Laterza, 2002, pp. 21–70, particularly 32ff. and notes.

4. J. Desanges, "D'Axoum à l'Assam, aux portes de la Chine. Le voyage du «Scholasticus de Thèbes» (entre 360 et 500 ap. J.-C.)," *Historia*, 18, 1969, pp. 627–39.

5. J. Hahn, "Gewalt und religiöser Konflikt. Studien zu den Auseinandersetzungen zwischen Christen, Heiden und Juden im Osten des Römischen Reiches (von Konstantin bis Theodosius II)," *Klio*, Beih. 8, Berlin: Akademie Verlag, 2004, pp. 106ff. A papyrus of 417 shows that there was a Jewish community in Antinoöpolis: see F. Millar, "Christian Emperors, Christian Church and the Jews of the Diaspora in the Greek East, CE 379–450," *Journal of Jewish Studies*, 55, 2004, pp. 1–24, particularly 12ff.

6. For the textual problems of the *Coptic History of the Church of Alexandria*, see A. Grillmeier and T. Hainthaler, *Christ in Christian Tradition*, IV, *From the Apostolic Age to Chalcedon (451)*, London: Mowbray, 1996. Other stories (summarized in McGuckin, *St. Cyril of Alexandria*..., pp. 16–20) have turned out to be prior hagiographical legends, such as that of the medical-oracular cult of the saints Cyrus and John, which was introduced by Cyril in 427 to the great pagan shrine in Menouthis. See J. Gascou, *Les origines du culte des saints Cyr et Jean*, http://halshs.archives-ouvertes.fr/halshs-00009140 (accessed November 12, 2008). On the problems associated with sources on Alexandria, see J. Gascou's review of C. Haas, *Alexandria in Late Antiquity. Topography and Social Conflict* (Baltimore: Johns Hopkins U.P., 1997), *Topoi*, 8.1, 1998, pp. 389–95.

7. See S. Ronchey, "Hypatia the Intellectual," in A. Fraschetti (ed.), *Roman Women*, trans. by Linda Lappin, Chicago: University of Chicago Press, 2001, pp. 160–89.

8. See R. Lizzi, "«Discordia in urbe»: pagani e cristiani in rivolta," in F. E. Consolino (ed.), *Pagani e cristiani da Giuliano l'Apostata al sacco di Roma*, Soveria Mannelli: Rubbettino, 1995, pp. 115–40 (with examples for the fourth and fifth centuries).

9. A. B. Bowman, *Egypt after the Pharaohs*, London: British Museum Press, 1992, p. 88.

10. Bowman, *Egypt after the Pharaohs*, pp. 157–58.

11. For the recent bibliography and current positions in the debate, see S. Emmel, *Shenoute's Literary Corpus*, Louvain: Peeters, 2004.

12. E. Amélineau, *Monuments pour servir à l'histoire de l'Egypte chrétienne au IVᵉ et au Vᵉ siècles*, Paris: Ernest Leroux, 1888, pp. 30–37.

13. Brown, *Power and persuasion*..., pp. 140ff.

14. Besa records the name of the local landowner, Gesios, which was never

used by Shenute (who only refers to him with insulting epithets). The similarity with Flavius Aelius Gessius, governor of the Thebais around 376–378 has been pointed out, but this is exactly the detail that suggests that this person was at least partly fictional. See S. Emmel, "From the Other Side of the Nile: Shenute and Panopolis," in A. Egberts, B. P. Muhs, and J. van der Vliet (eds.), *Perspectives on Panopolis: an Egyptian town from Alexander the Great to the Arab conquest*, Leiden: Brill, 2002, pp. 95–113; Emmel goes so far as to portray Gessius as a "crypto-pagan" figure.

15. The contrast between a "cultured" urban world and an "uncultured" monastic one, which was boosted by such famous events as the martyrdom of Hypatia, has been amplified by historians in the specific case of Egypt: see E. Wipszycka, "Le monachisme égyptien et les villes," in *Travaux et Mémoires*, 12, 1994, pp. 1–43.

16. D. Frankfurter, *Religion in Roman Egypt. Assimilation and Resistance*, Princeton: Princeton University Press, 1998, pp. 265ff.

17. Frankfurter, *Religion in Roman Egypt . . .*, pp. 75ff.

18. The important shrine to Amun in Luxor, which by this time had been abandoned, had been partially occupied by the Roman garrison under Diocletian. But as Frankfurter has observed (*Religion in Roman Egypt . . .*, p. 36), the decision to organize imperial hearings on this site demonstrated a desire to stress the emperor's divinity.

19. Caseau, "ΠΟΛΕΜΕΙΝ ΛΙΘΟΙΣ. La désacralisation . . .," pp. 119ff.

20. Frankfurter, *Religion in Roman Egypt . . .*, p. 265.

21. G. Lecuyot, "Le Ramesseum à l'époque copte. A propos des traces chrétiennes au Ramesseum," *Études coptes*, VI, Louvain: Peeters, 2000, pp. 121–29.

22. B. Ward-Perkins, "Re-using the architectural legacy of the past, entre idéologie et pragmatisme," in *TRW* 4, 1999, pp. 225–44. There is, however, no systematic study even at regional level.

23. Frankfurter, *Religion in Roman Egypt . . .*, p. 193.

24. Maraval, *Lieux saints et pèlerinages . . .*, pp. 319–22. Bibliography in A. Papaconstantinou, *Le culte des saints en Égypte des Byzantins aux Abbassides*, Paris: CNRS, 2001, pp. 146–54. See S. Bangert, «The archaeology of pilgrimage: Abu Mena and beyond», in D. M. Gwynn and S. Bangert (eds.), *Religious Diversity in Late Antiquity*, Brill, Leiden, 2010, pp. 293–327.

25. U. Wilcken, "Heidnisches und Christliches aus Ägypten," *Archiv für Papyrusforschung*, 1, 1901, pp. 396–436, particularly 408–11.

26. B. Caseau, "The fate of rural temples in Late Antiquity and the christianisation of the countryside," in W. Bowden, L. Lavan, and C. Machado (eds.), *Recent Research on the Late Antique Countryside*, Leiden: Brill, 2004, pp. 105–44, particularly 116.

27. D. F. Graf, "Rome and the Saracens . . . ," pp. 349–51; Modéran, "Les Maures de l'Afrique . . . ," passim.

28. The inscriptions, as with the other texts mentioned here, have been edited and commented upon in «*Fontes Historiae Nubiorum*». *Textual Sources for the History of the Middle Nile Region between the Eighth Century BC and the Sixth Century AD*, III, Bergen: Bergen University Press, 1998, nos. 300 and 311.

29. Amélineau, *Monuments pour servir . . .* , p. 49.

30. See the new edition of D. Feissel and K. A. Worp, "La requête d'Appion, évêque de Syène, à Théodose II: P. Leid. Z révisé," *Oudheidkundige Mededelingen*, 68, 1988, pp. 97–111; see also *Fontes Historiae Nubiorum*, III . . . , no. 314. See Brown, *Power and Persuasion . . .* , p. 142.

31. The term *legeōn* ("legione") has been considered a mistake for linguistic reasons (<Lat. *legio*)/*regeōn*? (<Lat. *regio*). For the bibliography, see Feissel and Worp, "La requête d'Appion . . . ," pp. 101–3. In reality, terms such as *legio* and *numerus* (cavalry units) were used as place-names during this period.

32. M. Speidel, "Nubia's Roman Garrison," in *Aufstieg und Niedergang der röm. Welt*, II.10.1, Berlin: De Gruyter, 1988, pp. 767–98, particularly 773.

33. Wilcken, "Heidnisches und Christliches . . . ," p. 403.

34. Amélineau, *Monuments pour server . . .* , pp. 45ff. and 66ff.; Frankfurter, *Religion in Roman Egypt . . .* , pp. 68ff. For the opposing arguments, see M. Smith, "Aspects of the preservation and transmission of indigenous religious traditions in Akhmim and its environs during the Graeco-Roman period," in Egberts, Muhs, and Van der Vliet (eds.), *Perspectives on Panopolis . . .* , pp. 233–47, particularly 245–47.

35. Sound arguments have been used to demonstrate that there was a continuum between Upper Egypt and Lower Nubia: see Frankfurter, *Religion in Roman Egypt . . .* , p. 105.

X

EASTER IN JERUSALEM

1. The suggestion of any other date was clearly considered a serious attack on orthodoxy: see Millar, "Repentant Heretics in Fifth-Century Lydia. . . . "

2. E. Bermejo Cabrera, *La proclamación de la Escritura en la liturgia de Jerusalén*, Jerusalem: Studium Biblicum Franciscanum, 1993.

3. The text has survived in a collection of hymns in Georgian, as in Georgia the liturgy used in fourth- and fifth-century Jerusalem is still observed: see C. Renoux, "La Pâques du dimanche à Jérusalem au IVe siècle," *Connaissance des Pères de l'Église*, 81, March 2001, pp. 52–58.

4. The most famous description is the one by the pilgrim Egeria, who visited the Holy Places in 383/4; see Cabrera, *La proclamación de la Escritura . . .*, pp. 193ff.

5. For this figure, see E. Honigmann, "Juvenal of Jerusalem," *Dumbarton Oaks Papers*, 5, 1950, pp. 211–79.

6. As early as the first half of the fourth century, Eusebius of Caesarea put forward the idea of a celestial Jerusalem, as opposed to the terrestrial one of the Jews. See J. Binns, *Ascetics and Ambassadors of Christ. The Monasteries of Palestine, 314–631*, Oxford: Clarendon Press, 1994, pp. 82ff.

7. E. D. Hunt, *Holy Land Pilgrimage in the Later Roman Empire AD 312–460*, Oxford: Clarendon Press, 1982. See H.J.W. Drijvers, "Promoting Jerusalem: Cyril and the True Cross," in Drijvers and Watt (eds.), *Portraits of Spiritual Authority . . .*, pp. 79–95.

8. See H. Sivan, *Palestine in Late Antiquity*, Oxford: Oxford University Press, 2008, pp. 213ff.

9. *Iuvenalis* is, for example, the name of the bishop of Narni, who was active in the second half of the fourth century.

10. Bishop Juvenal refers to these documents (not however conserved in the *Code of Theodosius*) in the *Acts of the Council of Chalcedon* of 451 (VIII, 17).

11. Maraval, *Lieux saints et pèlerinages. . . .* For the chronological problems, see above, p. 148, n. 15.

12. Similarly, in 415, on the occasion of the rebuilding of Santa Sophia, the bishop of Palestine had offered the relics of Zechariah, a minor prophet of the Old Testament. The monument built around Zechariah's relics in the form of a theater is depicted on the distinctive map of the Holy Places produced in the sixth century on the floor mosaic in a church in Madaba (Jordan). See Y. Tsafrir, "The «Loca Sancta» and the invention of relics in Palestine from the fourth to seventh centuries: their impact on the ecclesiastical architecture of the Holy Land," in A. M. Lidov (ed.), *Vostochnohristianskie relikvii*, Moscow: Progress-Tradicija, 2003, pp. 56–76, particularly 60.

13. Bibliography in Honigmann, "Juvenal of Jerusalem . . . ," p. 219.

14. See Y. Hirschfeld, *The Judean Desert Monasteries in the Byzantine Period*, New Haven: Yale University Press, 1992; for the problems of rediscovering the structure of a *láura* on the basis of comparisons between hagiographical and archeological sources, see M. Joly, "Les fondations d'Euthyme et de Sabas. Texte et archéologie," in *Les saints et leur sanctuaire . . .*, pp. 49–64.

15. Hirschfeld, *The Judean Desert Monasteries . . .*, pp. 18ff.

16. For a description of the site, see Y. Hirschfeld, "Euthymius and his monastery in the Judean desert," *Liber annuus*, 43, 1993, pp. 339–71.

17. The date, provided by Cyril of Scythopolis, *Life of Euthymius*, 16, is disputed. The source provides two dates: the indiction XI, which corresponds

to 428, and the fifty-second year of Euthymius's life, which would correspond to 429.

18. Binns, *Ascetics and Ambassadors* . . . , pp. 97–102.

19. Binns, Ascetics and Ambassadors . . . , p. 81.

20. For the production and consumption of alcoholic drinks in the Middle East, see "Alcohol" (Acts of the XIX Aram Conference), *Aram*, 17, 2005.

21. See A. Lewin, "Il Negev dall'età nabatea all'epoca tardoantica," *Mediterraneo Antico*, 5, 2002, pp. 319–75.

22. The *Life of Euthymius* provides his name before conversion, *Aspebetos*, which is actually a Persian title (*aspapet*, "cavalry leader").

23. Cyril of Scythopolis, *Life of Euthymius*, 51. According to Cyril (10, 18, 19ff.), the phylarch of the Saracens, Aspebetos had helped many Christians to flee during Yazdegerd's persecution, and then ended up having to flee as well. According to Cyril, he was greeted by Anatolius, the *magister utriusque militum per Orientem*, who appointed him phylarch of the Saracens on the Roman side. Aspebetos was a pagan and therefore a "just one"; his son Terebon was miraculously cured by Saint Euthymius. The "just" Aspebetos was then baptized and took the name of Peter. Given that Anatolius was not yet *magister utriusque militum per Orientem* in the period around 420 (he actually fulfilled the role from 443 to 446), the story is in all probability anachronistic. *PLRE* resolves the problem by attributing the appointment as phylarch to Terebon, on the supposition that Cyril confused the appointment of the father with that of the son. On the other hand, Moses Khorenats'i (*History of the Armenians*, 3, 57–58) reports on Anatolius's involvement in the war of 421/2.

24. Binns, *Ascetics and Ambassadors* . . . , p. 112.

25. Hirschfeld, *The Judean Desert Monasteries* . . . , p. 83.

26. Hirschfeld, *The Judean Desert Monasteries* . . . , pp. 88–91.

27. For the methods transferring assets, see Giardina, "Carità eversiva. . . ."

28. The story of Melania the Younger exemplifies the evolution of the feminine element in the Christian world: F. E. Consolino, "Modelli di comportamento e modi di santificazione per l'aristocrazia femminile d'Occidente," in A. Giardina (ed.), *Società romana e impero tardoantico*, I, Rome-Bari: Laterza, 1986, pp. 273–306, 684–99.

29. A. Giardina, "Melania the Saint," in Fraschetti, *Roman Women* . . . , pp. 190–208 (quote on p. 201); Sivan, *Palestine* . . . , pp. 298ff.

30. See B. Ward-Perkins, "Re-using the architectural legacy . . . ," pp. 225–44, particularly 233ff.; B. Caseau, "ΠΟΛΕΜΕΙΝ ΛΙΘΟΙΣ. La désacralisation . . . ," pp. 96ff.

31. Y. Hirschfeld, "The importance of bread in the diet of monks in the Judean desert," *Byzantion*, 66, 1996, pp. 143–55.

32. A. M. Rabello, "The Attitude of Rome towards Conversions to Judaism (Atheism, Circumcision, Proselytism)" (first published 1999), in *The Jews in the Roman Empire: Legal Problems, from Herod to Justinian*, Aldershot: Ashgate, 2000, XIV, pp. 37–68, particularly 65ff.; Millar, "Christian Emperors, Christian Church . . . ,"; Millar, *A Greek Roman Empire . . .* , pp. 126ff.

33. Exhilarated by the parable in the Gospels, like all the marginalized social groups around the fourth century, many Samaritans in the countryside took part in bloody acts of brigandage, together with Christians and Jews: see John Moschus, *Pratum spirituale*, p. 165. See K. G. Holum, "Caesarea and the Samaritans," in R. L. Hohlfelder (ed.), *City, Town and Countryside in the Early Byzantine Era*, New York: Columbia University Press, 1982, pp. 65–73, particularly p. 67. For general information, see A. D. Crown, "The Byzantine and Moslem Periods," in A. D. Crown (ed.), *The Samaritans*, Tübingen: Mohr, 1989, pp. 55–81. Their heterodox religious beliefs are supposed to have led to their extermination by Islam, which did not consider them a People of the Book like the Jews and Christians, but there was already considerable friction at the time of the Christian empire, which led to three bloody revolts: in 484, 529/30, and 556. L. Di Segni, "Mutual Relations between Samaritans, Jews and Christians in Byzantine Palestine, as Revealed through the Epigraphic Finds," in A. D. Crown and L. Davey (eds.), *New Samaritan Studies*, Sydney: Mandelbaum, 1995, pp. 185–94; Sivan, *Palestine . . .* , pp. 107ff.

34. Z. Safrai, *The Missing Century. Palestine in the Fifth Century: growth and decline*, Louvain: Peeters, 1998, particularly p. 54. In Modern Hebrew, the *nāsī'* is the president of Israel.

35. A. Linder, *The Jews in the Legal Sources of the Early Middle Ages*, Detroit: Wayne State University Press, 1987, pp. 71ff.

36. Linder, *The Jews in the Legal Sources . . .* , pp. 320–23.

37. Safrai, *The Missing Century . . .* , pp. 78–82.

38. Apart from all other factors, the great scholars of Judea moved to Galilee after the suppression of the Jewish revolt under Hadrian, and contributed to the formation of its religious landscape. For the problems of periodization in Israeli archaeology, see E. M. Meyers, "Byzantine Towns of the Galilee," in Hohlfelder (ed.), *City, Town and Countryside . . .* , pp. 115–31, particularly 117.

39. N. Janowitz, "Rethinking Jewish identity in Late Antiquity," in S. Mitchell and G. Greatrex (eds.), *Ethnicity and Culture in Late Antiquity*, London: Duckworth, 2000, pp. 205–19. Fabrizio Lelli has informed me of a recent study that suggests the *minim* were Manichaeans: see M. Ryzhik, "*Manim* who are *minim* and *miminim* who are *manim*," in *Mehqarim ha-lashon* [Linguistic Studies], 9, 2003, pp. 217–50 (in Hebrew).

40. J. Neusner, "Judaic uses of history in Talmudic Times," in A. Rapoport-Albert (ed.), *Essays in Jewish Historiography*, Middletown (Conn.): Wesleyan University, 1988, pp. 12–39 (quotation on p. 14). For the development of these strategies, see L. Valensi, "From Sacred History to Historical Memory and Back: the Jewish Past," *History and Anthropology*, 2, 1986, pp. 283–305; M. Fishbane (ed.), *The Midrashic Imagination. Jewish Exegesis, Thought, and History*, Albany: SUNY Press, 1993.

41. M. Fishbane (ed.), *The Midrashic Imagination* . . . , pp. 32ff. See also Hescher, Catherine and Schaefer, *The Talmud Yerushalmi and Graeco-Roman culture*, I–III, Tübingen: Mohr Siebeck, 1998–2002.

XI
THE GREAT KING AND THE SEVEN PRINCESSES

1. For an examination of this passage, see A. Panaino, "Astral Characters of Kingship in the Sassanian and Byzantine Worlds," in *La Persia e Bisanzio* . . . , particularly pp. 571ff.; see also, "I Magi e la stella nei Sermoni di san Pier Crisologo," in *Ravenna da capitale imperiale* . . . , pp. 559–92.

2. This work, which was completed in 1197 and dedicated to the prince Ala'uddin Qizil Arslan of Maragheh, was one of a cycle of five poems which would enjoy great fame. For an exhaustive analysis of the poem, see M. Barry, *Le Pavillon des Sept Princesses par Nezâmî de Gandjeh*, Paris: Gallimard, 2000. For an English version, usually referred to as *The Seven Beauties* or by its original name, *Haft Paikar*, see Ganja Nizami of Ganga, *Haft Paikar*, 2 vols. (1924), trans. by C. E. Wilson, Whitefish: Kessinger Publications, 2003.

3. In pursuit of his poetic and symbolic system, Nezāmī distorted the geography of the region and placed Hīra in Yemen, the land of the legendary Belqīs, the Queen of Sheba (Saba). Around the fourth century, when Yemen was under Sassanian dominion and Hīra had sunk back into the sands, the architecture of *Arabia Felix* was more suited to its legend.

4. Bibliography in G. Traina, "Le «gentes» d'Oriente fra identità e integrazione," *Antiquité tardive*, 9, 2001, pp. 71–80, particularly 74ff.

5. Fowden, *The Barbarian Plain* . . . , pp. 65ff. See above, p. 12.

6. Past experiences had shown the weakness of tactics based on the use of elephants, but they had also shown that the use of a very large number of elephants could be decisive in battle. In medieval India, wars could be fought for the sole purpose of capturing enemy elephants, and this method of warfare continued until the introduction of firearms. See G. Busquet and J.-M. Javorin,

Tombeau de l'éléphant d'Asie, Paris: Chandeigne, 2002, pp. 144ff. For the military use of elephants in Late Antiquity, see P. Rance, "Elephants in Warfare in Late Antiquity," *Acta antiqua Hungariae*, 43, 2003, pp. 355–84.

7. Malchus of Philadelphia (fr. 1) speaks of Saracen *foederati* (*toùs hypospóndous Sarakēnoús*) in both the Roman Empire and the Persian Empire. To avoid defections, the treaty of 422 prohibited both sides from taking in rebel Saracens.

8. The expert on Iranic studies, Michael Barry, draws attention to the Turkish epithet *gūr-khan* or *görkhan*, which referred to the princes of the Qara Khitai dynasty, and the further association with *gōr* in Persian meaning "tomb": *Le Pavillon des Sept Princesses* . . . , p. 735. The epithet used with reference to Bahrām already appears in the Pahlavi treatise (8th–9th centuries) on *The Provincial Capitals of the Land of Iran*, which also refers to a city of *Vahrām-Gōr* founded by the eponymous king in the land of Media. On this work, see C. Cereti, *La letteratura pahlavi. Introduzione ai testi con riferimenti alla storia degli studi e alla tradizione manoscritta*, Milan: Mimesis, 2001, pp. 202ff.

9. Nezāmī tells us that his historical sources for his poem were the chronicle in Arabic by al-Tabarī (838–923), its adaptation in Persian by Bal'amī, the vizier of Bukhara (died 973), and the *Book of Kings* by Ferdowsī (*c.*940–*c.*1025). For *Khoday-namak*, see Cereti, *La letteratura pahlavi* . . . , p. 191. Other Sassanid traditions appear to have been handed down in other works, known from the medieval *Āyin-nāme*, which deals with the organization of the empire, the class division, and the court's complex etiquette: see A. Tafazzoli under the entry *Āʾīn nāma*, in *Encyclopaedia Iranica* 6, London: Boston and Henley 1985, p. 692. One of the treatises was used by the Arab author al-Jahiz, who in the ninth century wrote a *Book of Peoples and Kingdoms*, with a series of ethical and didactic concepts taken from model rulers of the past, commencing with the Sassanids. Thus the courtiers of Baghdad and Samarra learned the Iranic etiquette with its complex rules and hierarchy of privileges. Al-Jahiz depicts Bahrām as a monarch particularly given to luxuries and pleasure seeking.

10. Barry, *Le Pavillon des Sept Princesses* . . . , p. 537.

11. The western equivalents are Ares and especially Heracles. See G. Scarcia, "Heracles-Verethragna and the Miʾrāj of Rustam," *Acta Orientalia Hungariae*, 37, 1983, pp. 85–109.

12. S. H. Rapp, "Images of Royal Authority in Early Christian Georgia," in Al-Azmeh, *Monotheistic Kingship* . . . , pp. 155–72, particularly 160.

13. Even though the nature of the text does not allow us to place it in a specific historical context, various clues provided by other Pahlavi texts suggest that this *Wahrām* could have been Bahrām V: see C. Cereti, "Again on Wahrām ī Warzāwand," in *La Persia e l'Asia centrale da Alessandro al X secolo*, Rome:

Accademia dei Lincei, 1996, pp. 629–39. For *Bundahishn*, see Cereti, *La letteratura pahlavi* . . . , pp. 87–105.

14. After 491, a similar procedure was also introduced in Constantinople, with the coronation of the emperor by the patriarch. The two empires, apparently so different, displayed clear signs of interrelationship, particularly when it came to parading their power through dress and ceremonial.

15. B. Croke, "Evidence for the Hun Invasion of Thrace in A.D. 422," *Greek, Roman and Byzantine Studies*, 18, 1977, pp. 347–67.

16. See H. W. Bailey, "Hārahūna," in *Asiatica. Festschrift Friedrich Weller*, Leipzig: Harrassowitz, 1954, pp. 12–21.

17. The expression is modern and was introduced in the nineteenth century by geographers.

18. See J. Diethart and E. Kislinger, "«Hunnisches» auf einem Wiener Papyrus," *Tyche*, 2, 1987, pp. 5–10.

19. N. Sims-Williams, *Bactrian Documents from Northern Afghanistan. I: Legal and Economic Documents*, Oxford: Oxford University Press, 2000, pp. 42ff.

20. É. de La Vaissière, *Sogdian Traders: a History*, trans. by J. Ward, Leiden: Brill, 2005 (original title: *Histoire des marchands sogdiens*, 2nd edition, Paris: Collège de France, 2004, pp. 94–96).

21. The Buddhist pilgrims continued to move around fairly freely: see É. de La Vaissière, *Sogdian Traders* . . . , p. 66.

22. É. de La Vaissière, *Sogdian Traders* . . . , p. 103.

23. S. D. Loginov and A. B. Nikitin, "O nachal'nom etape chekanki bukarskih podrazhanik drahmam Varahrana V," in *Obshchestvennye Nauki v Uzbekistane*, 6, 1985, pp. 49–53.

24. De La Vaissière, *Sogdian Traders* . . . , pp. 96–98.

25. R. A. Stein, *The World in Miniature: Container Gardens and Dwelling in Far Eastern Religious Thought*, trans. by P. Brooks, Palo Alto: Stanford U.P., 1990, p. 278 (original title: *Le monde en petit. Jardins en miniature et habitations dans la pensée religieuse d'Extrême-Orient*, Paris: Flammarion, 1987).

26. G. Orofino, "The Tibetan Myth of the Hidden Valley in the Visionary Geography of Nepal," *East and West*, 41, 1991, pp. 239–71.

27. In *Sikender-nāme*, the poem on Alexander the Great, Nezāmī speaks of his conception as of a royal pearl inseminated by the spring rain.

28. R. N. Frye, "The political history of Iran under the Sassanians," in E. Yarshater (ed.), *The Cambridge History of Iran*, III.1, Cambridge: Cambridge University Press, 1983, pp. 116–80, particularly 145.

29. Al-Tha'alibī, *Ghurar Mulūk al-Fārs: Histoire des Rois des Perses*, ed. and trans. by H. Zotenberg, Paris: Impr. Nationale, 1900, pp. 560–64. See also V. Fiorani Piacentini, "International Indian Ocean Routes and Gwadar Kūh

Batil Settlement in Makrān (2nd–6th centuries AD)," *Nuova Rivista Storica*, 72, 1988, pp. 307–39, particularly 327ff. In a recent review of studies into the economy of Late Antiquity, M. G. Morony follows the parallels between the Mediterranean world and the Sassanian Empire, and notes the latter's supremacy over trade in the Indian Ocean: M. G. Morony, "Economic Boundaries? Late Antiquity and Early Islam," *Journal of the Economic and Social History of the Orient*, 47, 2004, pp. 166–94.

30. At the beginning of his term of office, which lasted until 456, the new leader of the Church did not have an easy time. His rivals managed to have him imprisoned, but he survived these difficulties with the help of Theodosius II's diplomacy and resolved them entirely in 424, with a New Council of Seleucia/Ctesiphon: see above, p. 8.

31. J. Labourt, *Le christianisme dans l'empire perse sous la dynastie sassanide (224–632)*, Paris: Librairie V. Lecoffre, 1904², pp. 119–25.

32. Labourt, *Le christianisme . . .*, p. 125. See also J.H.E. Dijkstra, *Philae and the End of Ancient Roman Religion. A Regional Study on Religious Transformation (298–642 CE)*, Leuven: Peeters, 2008.

33. However, this anecdote appears with a very different date in Socrates, *Ecclesiastical History*, 7, 8; see C. Mango and R. Scott, *The Chronicle of Theophanes Confessor. Byzantine and Near Eastern History AD 284–813*, Oxford: Oxford University Press, 1997, p. 133.

34. See De La Vaissière, *Sogdian Traders . . .*, p. 92 (he claims anachronistically that it was a Nestorian see).

Epilogue

1. This calculation of the date based on the foundation of Rome was mainly observed by the official bureaucracy, particularly in the Western Roman Empire, where the Roman tradition was more closely adhered to. At the beginning of 449 Polemius Silvius, a former imperial official resident in Gaul, went so far as to write a breviary that attempted to integrate the traditional calendar of Roman feast days with the new Christian ones: see Fraschetti, *La conversione . . .*, pp. 300–306. Polemius Silvius, a friend of important prelates in Gaul, was considered to be "mentally disturbed" (*Gallic Chronicle of 452*, Year 438).

2. G. Traina, "La forteresse de l'Oubli" (with an appendix by C.A. Ciancaglini), *Le Muséon*, 115, 2002, pp. 399–422.

3. A Greek poem, called *Blemmyomachia*, was composed around this time: see E. Livrea (ed.), *Anonymi fortasse Olympiodori Thebani Blemmyomachia* (P. Berol. 5003), Meisenheim am Glan: Hain, 1978.

4. For a critical examination of the sources, see W. Goffart, *Barbarians and Romans A.D. 418–584. The Techniques of Accommodation*, Princeton: Princeton University Press, 1980, pp. 231–34. See also W. Goffart, *Barbarian Tides. The Migration Age and the Later Roman Empire*, Philadelphia: University of Pennsylvania Press, 2006.

5. Zecchini, *Aezio. L'ultima difesa* . . . , pp. 150ff.; Stickler, *Aëtius. Gestaltungsspielräume eines Herrmeister* . . . , pp. 46ff.

6. On this tradition, see Zecchini, *Aezio. L'ultima difesa* . . . , pp. 95ff. For a different interpretation, see Modéran, "L'effondrement militaire de l'Afrique. . . . "

7. For an overview of this question, see M. Mazza, "Bisanzio e Persia nella tarda antichità. Guerra e diplomazia da Arcadio a Zenone," in *La Persia e Bisanzio* . . . , pp. 39–76.

8. G. Morgan, "Hagen and Aetius," *Classica et Mediaevalia*, 30, 1969, pp. 440–50.

9. For the measurements of the various columns of Simeon Stylites in the hagiographical tradition, see H. Delehaye, *Les saints stylites*, Brussels: Société des Bollandistes, 1923, pp. xxvii ff.

· INDEX ·

heresy); interior land urbanization and, 20; just war and, 91; Kingdom of Armenia and, 7–8; land donations to, 60; martyrs and, 14–15; medieval transition and, 63–79; monasticism and, 10–14 (*see also* monasticism); Nestorius and, 7–9, 13; pagan influence and, 21–22; Pelagians and, 56–57; Persians and, 8; politics and, 7–9, 13; Pontifex Maximus title and, 156n22; Popes and, 56–57, 69–71, 79, 94, 129, 156n22; power shoring of, 7–8, 56–57; Ravenna and, 54; saint worship and, 11–12; slavery and, 87; Temple of Augustus and, 21; *Theotókos* controversy and, 38–39, 57, 91; travel dangers and, 19–20; Virgin Mary and, 38–39, 91

Roman Empire, xii, 132, 156n22; African estates of, 84; Bahrām V and, 118–27; barbarians and, 64 (*see also* barbarians); Brittania and, ix, xi, 56, 77–79, 130; circus games and, 76–77; Eastern, xvi, 7 (*see also* Constantinople); Egypt and, 93–103; fall of, ix–x, xix, xv–xvii, 55–56, 58, 71, 130; fall of Kingdom of Armenia and, 1–6; imperial unity and, xvi; Jerusalem and, 106–7; medieval transition of, 51–79; "new Rome" and, 27–39; *partes* (border sections) and, 44–45, 54, 134n6; Platonists and, 131; Pontifex Maximus and, 156n22; public baths and, 76–77; regionalized areas and, 59; religious power shoring by, 7–15; reunification and, 41–45; Simeon Stylites and, 11; social banditry and, 66; taxes and, 45, 66, 73, 84; unification of public law and, 43–45; use of Christianity's strength by, 10; utopianism and, 10

Rom civilization, 125

Rome, 132, 180n1; Alaric and, 55; assassination of Pyrhhus and, 57; bishop (pope) of, 56; Christian consolidation of, 55–56; divine founding of, 114; as Eternal City, 55; Holy Places of, 55, 57; identity and, 117; Lakhmids and, 118; as megalopolis, 156n16; monasticism and, 70; prestige of, 55; rebuilding of, 55; sacking of, xv, 55–56, 58, 71, 130; semi-Pelagianism and, 69; Senate and, 57–58; Valentinian III and, 55; Visigoths and, 55–56

Romulus Augustus, xv, 133n3

Rouphinianai, 24

Rouran, 123

Ruga, King of Huns, 129

Rutilius Namatianus, 69

Sabbatians, 35

sacred sites. *See* Holy Places

sacrum cubiculum (imperial rooms), 29–30

Safrai, Zeev, 113

Sahak, 3–4, 129

Saidas (Sa'id) of Phaeno, 109

saint worship, 11–12, 18, 33, 98

Salamis, 90

Salian Franks, 74–75

Salvian of Marseilles, 73, 76, 130

Samaritans, 111–12, 176n33

Samarkand, 123–24

Sanliurfa, 12–13

Sanskrit, 120

Santa Sophia, 174n12

Santo Mazzarino, xvi, 44

Saracens, 143n31; Bahrām V and, 118–27; conversion of, xi–xii, 109; *foederati* and, 178n7; al-Mundhir and, xviii, 118–19; phylarch of, 175n23; stereotype of, 14–15; Treaty of 422 and, 178n7; water and, 109

Sardinia, 60

Sarpedon, 22

Sassanian Empire, 1, 117; Bahrām V and, 118–27; Christians and, 126–27, 129,